LAWN CARE & GARDENING

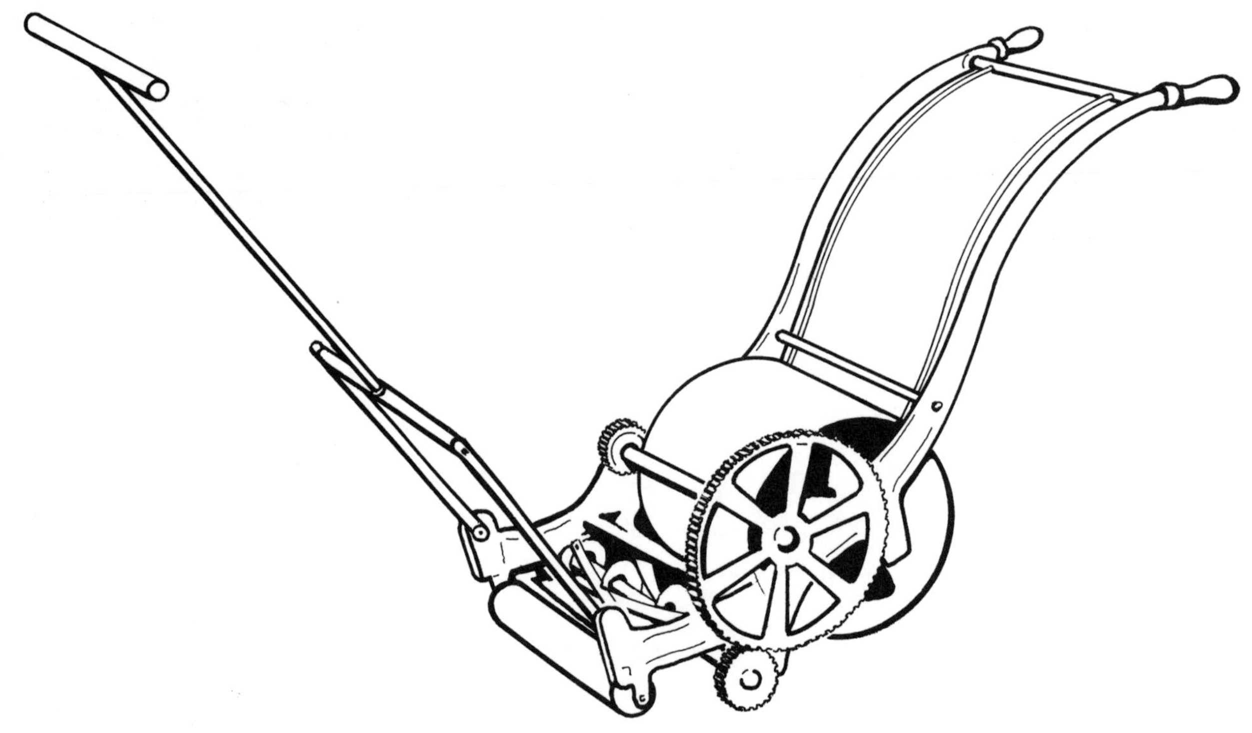

LAWN CARE & GARDENING

A Down-to-Earth Guide to the Business

Second Edition

Mickey Willis

Revised and expanded from the
First Edition by Kevin Rossi

Acton Circle
Ukiah, California

Lawn Care & Gardening: A Down-to Earth Guide to the Business, Second Edition

Published by: Acton Circle Publishing Company
P.O. Box 1564
Ukiah, CA 95482

Cover by Jeanne Koelle, Koelle & Gillette. Illustrations of Edwin Budding's lawn mower (including frontispiece) and "parts of a tree" by Irene Stein. Grass Species illustrations: USDA Miscellaneous Pub. No. 200, *Manual of the Grasses of the United States*, by A.S. Hitchcock; 2d rev. ed., Agnes Chase; Washington, D.C., U.S. Government Printing Office, 1950.

Published March 2001
10 9 8 7 6 5 4 3 2 1

Library of Congress Cataloging in Publication

Willis, Mickey, 1962-
Lawn care & gardening: a down-to-earth guide to the business/Mickey Willis.—2nd ed.
p. cm.
Rev ed. of: Lawn care & gardening/by Kevin Rossi. 1994.
Includes bibliographical references (p.).
ISBN:0-9639371-5-4
1. Lawn care industry. 2. Landscaping industry. 3. Small Business. 4. New business enterprises. 5. Self-employed. I. Title: Lawn care and gardening. II. Rossi, Kevin. Lawn care & gardening. III. Title.

SB433.27 .R66 2000
635.9′647′0681—dc21

00-064305

PART IV: ESTIMATING AND BIDDING

Part I

Introduction

What It Takes and Has to Offer

The Advantages

The Residential Market

The Non-Residential Market

A Local Industry

Branching Out

Building Up an Asset

The Downside

A Few Words about Gender

Chapter 1

LAWNS AND LANDSCAPING – A CAREER IN THE OPEN

LANDSCAPE MAINTENANCE—basically mowing lawns and gardening—can open a way to financial success through self employment that most people overlook. It can also be a welcome escape from the big-business or institutional cage that many of us seem to be caught in. Some years ago, soon after I received my teaching credential, I put in my first day as a substitute teacher for a class of 7th graders. By day's end I had just about been tied up and burned at the stake. I made a lightning career choice right then and there to get out of "education." I had always loved the out-of-doors and worked at a retail nursery during high school. Through college I mowed lawns for landlords and spent one summer as a gardener for the university housing department. While I continued to substitute, I began to build up our present landscape maintenance business until I was able to flee the torture of dealing with 7th to 12th graders.

If you're considering a change like this, make sure your family and friends support your decision before you do it, because it isn't like getting a paycheck twice a month. I also recommend trying to hang on to your old job, painful as it might be, until you can afford to make the switch. On the other hand, you don't have to commit much money to start small or part-time. You can do it essentially with a power mower, some hand tools, a truck, and your own drive and determination.

Where the demand exists and you acquire the training to do the job well, you are on your way. If you are willing to invest your earnings to build up the business, then eventually, if you don't mind hard work and long hours, you can equal or better your current salary and build a successful career and life.

This book is intended to introduce you to both. You won't learn everything about the business in this or any other single book. Our intent here is to survey it and make the technical stuff easier to learn later on.

To run your business well you have to learn some gardening techniques and basic management skills. You'll have to take risks, but you'll never be bored, and you ought to have a fine time doing it. Best of all, you will be your own boss. If you're like me, an added bonus is that you are always working outdoors and usually in pleasant green surroundings. The work can be heavy at times, but I find the results tangible and satisfying.

What It Takes and Has to Offer

This is an industry with hugely diverse features. There are nationwide chains and franchises, and local part-timers working out of a pickup truck. It is pursued by men and women with degrees in horticulture, and by youngsters and retirees who merely have (or think they have) a knack for keeping plants green. Nobody knows how many ply the trade in the United States. It could be between 15,000 and 50,000. People move easily in and out of (as well as up and down in) the business. The numbers depend not only on how and when you count, but what you include as "the business." Is it only mowing lawns and perhaps gardening, or a widening circle of services that includes leaf and snow removal, tree care, a nursery—a backhoe? What exactly is full-time when the weather may shut you down every year? Drawing lines and defining the business is very risky, indeed.

This book will discuss what we consider the core of landscape maintenance, while noting related work; and it will only mention and contrast landscape *contracting*, which is in large part a construction trade. However you define the business, we hope to stress the importance of offering quality work in all you do to gain a competitive edge and to help you know the satisfaction of a job well done.

What a landscape maintenance service does is horticultural work. My Webster's defines horticulture as the "cultivation of a garden or orchard; [the] art of growing fruits, vegetables, [and] ornamental plants." The work is simple and complex at the same time. On a basic level you can push a power mower or spreader around on a lawn or you can coax a marginal plant into a showpiece and anchor the whole corner of a yard. Both the practice and the art can give you the satisfaction of accomplishment and secure you a steady, paying clientele. But working the power mower can be enough to start with.

As noted, this business does not require a large capital outlay or specialized skills to start with. You can develop what you know into a quality service of any size. That's up to you. Like many, you can start small and learn as you build up the business. All you need is determination, enthusiasm, a willingness to work, common sense, a good attitude, and good health. If you like to learn, there is no end to learning the trade. And your expertise can be an asset that good customers will pay you well for.

The Advantages

If you like working outdoors and cultivating plants, landscape maintenance may be your ticket. First, as your own boss, you can work at your own pace, as hard or easy as you want. We don't endorse becoming a slave to your business, but as your own boss you can schedule as many jobs as you want and compensate yourself accordingly.

You don't need a big financial investment. You will be selling your knowledge and labor supplemented by the use of a few basic tools. The supplies necessary to amend soils, encourage plant growth, and control disease can be acquired as needed from local or national suppliers. The knowledge you need can be acquired free or very inexpensively through your agricultural extension service, the public library, or a local community college or vocational school.

You can work out of your home. All you need is a place to store your truck, supplies, tools, and equipment, and a corner of the house in which to set up your office. This should not be the kind of work that needs approval of the local zoning or community planning department; but you may have to inform the neighbors of your plans. In any case, all the work you do will be away from home and no bother to anyone living nearby.

The hours are reasonably flexible. True, you can only work during daylight, but at the height of the growing season you can get in plenty of business.

Unless you become involved in landscape construction, which requires a contractor's license, there is no red tape or regulation. Because landscape construction contractors are a building trade that uses heavier equipment and more complex means to construct landscape systems and facilities, they are usually regulated by their state's contractor's license board and must qualify for the work by passing an examination. The customer is the only examiner for landscape maintenance. While some states may require a contractor's license when you bill over a certain amount for gardening, those laws are more often ignored than observed. You should know about them, however, to avoid the risk of a nasty surprise from the license board later on. All states are federally mandated also to regulate spraying pesticides, but we'll deal with that in Chapter 18.

In short, there is easy entry to the trade and room to grow, and if you offer top quality service you will get plenty of work because your best recommendations will be in plain view all over town.

The Residential Market

If you live where population and home ownership are increasing, your market is growing. Owners of new housing especially need landscape services to get things growing in their yards. Owners of older homes need their lawns and gardens maintained, and often freshened and renovated. Even in areas with a stable population there are many people who don't know the advantages of professional yard care. Also, people in an area of stable population usually are aging. Their incomes tend to be higher and often they want to do other things than tend to their lawns or gardens themselves. When you set out to build a customer base, remember that this high-income, older population can be your best market.

Sometimes a one-time job can land you a steady customer if you do a good job and explain where a little work can make big improvements. With the increase of two-income families, many lack the time to care for their lawns and gardens. Even if they like gardening, there may be too much for weekend work, and they may shift the heavy or skilled tasks to a landscape maintenance service.

Also, whether you are in a stable or growing area, others are retiring from the business when you are starting. It may be possible to acquire their accounts. It is also possible to ask suppliers if they know of a landscape service that may want to sell its accounts, or even the entire business.

The Non-Residential Market

Many people think of landscape maintenance as residential work. There is plenty of opportunity, however, in maintaining commercial and light industrial grounds, common areas in condominium complexes, and property that real estate companies manage or want to spruce up for sale. Although local governments maintain most public grounds with their own employees, public spending cuts sometimes put these jobs up for bid. If you want the work, there is no reason not to bid on a commercial or public job.

A Local Industry

Bidding on commercial jobs often will put you in direct competition with national chains. One of the largest is LandCare USA, which has been growing in recent years through a chain of mergers with firms in large to middle-sized population centers. Companies like LandCare USA enjoy the advantage of national advertising and access to low-cost materials purchased in quantity. Still, no large landscape company is ever better than its individual worker on the turf.

Don't worry that the chains and franchises advertise nationwide. This is one line of work that is still made up of independent small business owners and will probably remain so. Your business will be built on quality results, and a small operator can equal or better the work of any big-name landscape maintenance service.

Branching Out

Others in the business develop sidelines like renting and maintaining interior plant decor, maintaining swimming pools, snow removal, installing Christmas lights, yard clean-up and hauling, heavy-duty lawn aeration, operating nurseries, composting services, greenhouses, sod farms or, though it requires a licensing exam, landscape construction contracting.

Building Up an Asset

Once you have built up the business you will have an earning asset that you could sell when you get ready to retire. An earning asset is valued for the cash it will generate over time, not just its physical elements like land, buildings, equipment, tools, etc.

The Downside

There are drawbacks in every line of work, but we all try to work at jobs in which we can handle the disadvantages. The problems peculiar to landscape maintenance are neither unusual nor overwhelming.

Some landscape maintenance work is heavy — Ill health or injury may force you to quit. I know of more than one gardener whose bad back forced an early retirement. On the other hand, you may do hard physical work already. Staying fit on the job depends on work habits. You lift, carry, and tug sensibly in this line of work, or you don't do it for long. If you're unsure how to do that, consult a physical therapist, physician, or good book on how the body works and learn to labor properly.

Business drops off in the winter months — You may have to develop a sideline until your in-season business carries you through the winter. We will discuss sidelines briefly later in this book. When you build a base of steady customers you may also want to use year-around billing, which is easy to set up.

You have to handle hazardous materials — Unless you want to garden 100-percent organically, which so far doesn't assure 100-percent results, you will have to deal with some poisonous substances. If you read and understand the warning labels, and take reasonable precautions, they pose no more danger than most people already face in the workplace. If you are concerned about the environment, you will want to use such chemicals judiciously. Most states impose licensing or certification requirements to apply horticultural chemicals as even an incidental part of a business.

You will have to work with potentially dangerous machinery — Selecting sturdy, well designed equipment, using and maintaining it properly, and taking precautions against fatigue, will reduce this hazard to a minimum. Most work today is mechanized, and presents the same hazards. Using care in the work place is universal good practice.

You have a "lead thumb" — Even if your present horticultural skills are nil, you can start small on simple jobs. This business can be learned. Some may need more time than others, but if you are dedicated and willing to learn, there is no reason why some day you can't take prizes.

A Few Words About Gender

Except for this paragraph, we will give you a quarter for every "he," "she," "him," or "her" you find in this book when we are not referring to actual people: Edwin Budding, inventor of the lawn mower, or a few professors. This is a gender-neutral business, and so is the book. Scores of women are highly successful professional gardeners. In a city half a day's drive south of us, a high proportion of gardeners are women. They get the most well-to-do customers, they subcontract much of their work at a tidy markup, and they've created some of the best looking landscapes in town. So forget about gender; your sex is your own affair. If you want to do this work, go to it!

Kentucky bluegrass. (USDA)

Getting Customers
Tools and Technique
How to Estimate and Bid
Collecting the Money
Building a Successful Business

Chapter 2

QUICK START – UP AND MOWING WITH THE BASICS

EACH CHAPTER after this will begin with a Quick Start Capsule to brief you on the basic information it contains and let you skim the book's contents. We inserted this chapter in the first edition with the idea that no one wants to wade through a few hundred pages of instructions in order to become an expert before doing. We prefer the capsules to checklists and review questions because this isn't a textbook and there won't be any quizzes.

We think the chapter does provide a brief survey of how the business works—in case you already have your power mower loaded on the pickup, all set to get to work. The beauty of this business, as we said in the introduction, is that you don't need to buy a lot of expensive equipment or be an expert just to go out and do it. We recommend that you do read all the chapters in this book, because there's a clear advantage in knowing how to do the job better than the competition.

Meanwhile, here is how you start.

Getting Customers

The first thing you need is people who will pay you to mow their lawns. You can knock on doors, but we've found it to be the most discouraging way to get customers. These days people are much less receptive than in the past to talking to strangers at their door. Those you get this way are not loyal customers, either. A little door-knocking is all right, but be selective. Pick on houses that look in need of help. Keep track of houses that have sold recently and knock on their doors. While you're at it, check with realtors and property managers. Introduce yourself to other gardeners and ask them to refer work they can't do to you. Go to senior centers and introduce your business. Put flyers on hospital bulletin boards. Go to chamber of commerce meetings. Get a yellow page ad. And get out and talk to potential customers wherever you think you can find them.

Before you start you will need a fistful of business cards. You want them fast. Nothing fancy to start with. You can make them on a computer if you have one or go to a full-service copier business like Kinko's. Or check your yellow pages for printers and see how fast and cheaply you can get 500 cards. That is usually the minimum order. Sometimes discount office supply stores offer special rates on cards. If you try to market your services without a business card, people probably will forget your name, and they certainly will forget your telephone number. Business cards take up so little room that people stick them in picture frames, mirrors, drawers, rolodexes or wherever else they keep them. You can also use flyers from an instant printer or made on your computer. Put a fold-up flap on the bottom to hold your business cards and post it on community bulletin boards.

Whatever you get, be sure it looks as professional as possible. It should give your name, business address and telephone number, and say that you mow lawns and will give a free estimate. Estimates are the only believable freebie left. If you work from home, it's a good idea to omit the address so customers don't drop by the house.

Later you can invest in a better card that conveys a message about you and your services, in advertising that brings in customers, and in flyers and brochures that get you business where you want to work.

Getting commercial accounts is similar to residential jobs. If you think you can handle commercial jobs, make a direct personal contact by walking in. If the account seems to require a formal approach, write to make an appointment. See the sample letter in Chapter 5.

Tools and Technique

We began by saying that you need a truck to haul your tools. If that means buying a truck, it doesn't have to be fancy. But it does have to be reliable. Buy a used one, a pickup or possibly a van, but first have it checked out by a mechanic whose opinion you trust. Nothing will ruin your business like not keeping to your schedule because your transportation keeps dying. Get your business name painted on the truck as soon as possible and park it where people can see it. Be sure to file your business name with the county or state, as local law requires, and to get a business license.

If you already have a power mower for your own lawn, you can use it for awhile, but you will need—and want—a self-propelled industrial/commercial (I/C) model sooner than you think. Get all the power they build them with—a big one but not too big to handle. You won't be able to wait until the grass dries if you mow professionally, and a consumer model bogs down in wet grass. If you cut in wet grass or any grass, be especially careful of your footing. Shoes with lugged or cleated soles help, but your own alertness is the best protection.

Whether you stick with the family power mower or invest in an I/C model, plan to maintain it more than you have so far. Clean the air filter to keep its power up and prevent grit from being drawn into the cylinders. Change the oil and clean the oil filter about every 20 to 25 hours of operation. Frequent oil changes are the cheapest way to extend the life of any engine. Clean the underside of the deck daily to prevent corrosion and improve bagging or mulching. Sharpen the blade daily if you want to leave good looking lawns behind you. Balance the blade each time you sharpen it with a $5 balancing weight. It's a cheap way to reduce wear on the mower and you.

Buy your I/C mower from a shop that specializes in mowers and allied equipment. Be sure they will service it if necessary and can advise you about keeping it sharp and running well. Have a back up machine, your own or one you can borrow, for when the main mower needs repair or service. Learn to fix your own eventually.

Take reasonable safety precautions by wearing heavy, steel-toed shoes, a long-sleeved shirt and long pants as protection against objects thrown out by the mower. Wear a hat against too much sun and ear protection. Comfortable safety glasses you can wear all day are a must. Get polychromatic lenses that adjust to the light level and also block ultraviolet (U-V) rays. Know your machine and the hazards it presents. Don't work when you are too tired to be careful. Don't make adjustments with the engine running. If yours is an old machine without a deadman device, turn off the engine and *disconnect the spark plug wire* before fiddling with moving parts!

If you have a mulching mower that deposits finely chopped clippings back on the lawn for compost, be sure first that there is not too much thatch. Bermuda and similar southern grasses are prone to thatch, and their clippings should be hauled away. The same goes for some bred-up bluegrasses.

You will need a powerful string trimmer and a sharp half-moon hand edger to give the lawn a crisp finish. A mowed lawn always looks better with an edge; it's the frosting on the cake. A small chain saw and gas-powered hedge trimmer are also good investments.

Take along some other tools just in case. A fan rake, broom, pruners, shears, loppers, shovel, fork, possibly a hose, garbage bags, tarps, buckets, a hand spreader, and fertilizer will come in very handy if the customer asks for an additional job while you are there. Don't forget repair tools like a sharp blade, spark plug wrench, crescent wrench, screwdrivers, socket set and pliers. They take up little space and can save valuable time when you need them. Also include a good all-purpose fire extinguisher and a first-aid kit in a waterproof case.

Figure in advance what to charge for your services and tell the customer how much before you do the job. You do not want any misunderstandings. Now you are ready.

Before mowing be sure the lawn is clear of debris. Mow cool season bluegrasses and fescues high, 2" to 2½". Cut warm season St. Augustine Grass high, too, but Bermuda and similar grasses down to 1" or so. Don't take off more than one-third of the blades per cut if you can help it. Mow the perimeter first, then back and forth in straight passes without overlapping. Mow in a different direction or pattern from the last time to avoid making ruts. Don't mow across what you've already done to take a shortcut back to the truck. Clean up the area, leaving it better than you found it. Clean and load your equipment. You'll save time by billing for the job rather than hanging around to get a check, and you can go right on to the next job.

How to Estimate and Bid

In order to make a competitive bid, you need to learn what the competition charges. Read the ads, telephone, or ask in person. Say why you want to know. Ask, "Do you charge by the hour?" "What is your hourly rate?" You won't be taking anybody's customers away, you are out to find your own. Ask how the business estimates a job. You will find a lot of your competition charges a fairly standard fee for the average lawn. Others will charge based on a standard lawn and adjust for variations from that standard. Most people who have been in the business know how long it takes them to do the average lawn and what difference these variations will make.

You estimate jobs to know what they COST *you to do.*

Starting out, you can safely charge the going rate; but don't wait too long to make some calculations. They can be as easy or complex as you need. If you take an easy approach and end up with plenty of money, equipment, and customers at the year's end, you are doing all the figuring you need. If the equipment, customer base, or money shrink, you had better look closer at the numbers. My own feeling is that you should do some hard calculating before losses get too big. We discuss the calculations in Chapter 6 on bookkeeping and Chapter 20 on estimating and bidding.

The easy way is to figure a minimum market-based rate for the smallest jobs which takes rough account of everything—the costs of being in business, the effort of getting to the job, doing it, and set-up, clean-up, and break-down. Then you adjust up from the small job *in steps.* Costs don't rise proportionately with each square foot of turf.

That's a good seat-of-the-pants way to figure jobs. You can work backwards from what you charge to see if you are covering expenses. A lot of beginners forget to allocate a portion to fixed costs, depreciation, and profit in their charges. Don't omit them.

The estimating methods in the last chapters of this book may be more detailed than you will ever need and are certainly more than you need at the outset. They do show how to analyze job costs, however, and you might want to try them to figure a couple of jobs to see how they shake out.

One more thing. Don't forget to charge for any supplies you apply to the lawn. If you buy fertilizer or soil amendments at a discount to apply to lawns, you can charge the customer the retail price or a little less and legitimately keep the difference.

Your hourly rate will depend on what others in the business charge. You will want to be competitive. Chances are slim that you will take any business away from other competent landscape maintenance businesses, but you want to be able to attract new business at a good return. Although you estimate by the hour, bill by the job. If you get more efficient and beat your estimated time, you can decide whether to use your competitive edge to cut prices or to enhance your services.

You can work on an oral contract if the job is quick and easy. If it gets complicated you should put the agreement in writing. Look over the sample contract in Chapter 21. We're not lawyers, and you should have a local attorney draft you a contract if you plan to use one.

Collecting the Money

If you are starting out fast, you probably won't read the chapter on record keeping right away, but you should read it before you are too far along in the business. We've kept it pared down to the basics and encourage computerizing it.

Before you do anything, go outside right now and write down the mileage on your truck. Keep a daily record of beginning and ending mileage for every day you use the truck for business. If you don't, you can't deduct the expense from your income taxes. You would be surprised how many beginning business people forget to do that. The IRS has a special form (number 4562 last we looked) for you to write in the year's total business and personal miles in order to claim the deduction.

Next get a 8½" x 11" spiral-bound notebook to take along, and start keeping records. Even haphazard records are better than none when you first start out. Also take a pad of two-part receipts for when your customers pay you cash. Give them the top copy and keep the carbon for your records. Try not to spend the cash before you deposit it in the bank, but at least keep a record that you got it. Have a rubber stamp with your business name, address, and telephone number to put on the customers' receipts. This will be a very temporary system, but use it so that your very first records are organized and written down.

You will find that this book and every other guide to starting and running businesses emphasizes the importance of keeping good records. Without them you can't tell if you are making money or slowly going broke. You'll want to know before you're in too deep, and that requires keeping your records from the beginning. Also when you finish the year your tax person will need your records to get you the best deal possible; so you had better record everything.

We recommend billing at the end of the month as soon as you set up a system. Chapter 6 will describe a simple hand method of bookkeeping. It will help you understand the flow of income and expenses. To begin with, you may find handwritten books easier to work with. But even the simple method in this book will overwhelm you by the time you have about 30 customers. Sitting down to do the books after a hard day's work is the last thing you'll want to do; but if you put it off it will only get worse. The computer will save you time and an enormous amount of work, and it will give your business a more professional appearance. The outlay of cash and effort to acquire and learn to use a computer is definitely worth it. If the idea intimidates you, find a 14-year-old (no fooling) to work with and help you out until you can do it on your own.

Even with a computer there are things you will continue to do by hand. You must keep a record of all your expenses just as you do your mileage. Open a business checking account and pay for everything by check. (Eventually you may write checks on the computer, but for now we'll discuss handwritten checks.) Write one for petty cash and put the money in an envelope with a sheet of paper to write the date, purpose, and amount of all cash purchases. Put the receipt for each purchase in the envelope. When you get low on petty cash, add up the sheet to see if the purchases and the left over money equal the original amount. A small difference doesn't matter. Keep the sheet and receipts. Then write another check to bring petty cash up the full amount.

For the time being, use the notebook for daily receipts. The business check register will record expenses. You should transfer these daily entries into a permanent monthly record. Daily receipts drop out of the picture when you bill monthly. Chapter 6 explains how to keep books by hand and what to look for in a computerized system. Use another part of the notebook to write down information about your customers. Enter their names, addresses, and telephone numbers, and make notes about their lawns and gardens. You may want to set up a card file until you get a computer; so set aside one page, or a large part of it, for one customer. Write in anything you think is important. It can go onto index cards, but your working life will be much better when it is on a computer disk.

Building a Successful Business

No matter how anyone else may view your business, you should realize that it is nothing more than all your individual customers taken together as a group. Anybody who lacks satisfied, paying customers will not have a business. At least not for long. It is not a matter of the customer is always right. The customer is all there is. Without any, you are out of business.

You have to develop the skills of your craft to attract customers willing to pay you what you ask. Having customers who want you to keep returning to maintain their property and who will recommend you to other customers is the difference between having all the work you want and scrabbling just to get by.

We're not saying too much by advising that your every business thought should be about how your services will please your customers more. Whether you stick with lining up 30 or 40 hours of lawns to mow a week, or build up a major regional landscape business, the principle is the same. It can take you as far as you want to go. If you don't know how to begin to please your customers, read the rest of the book. It's a beginning.

Red fescue. (USDA)

Part II

Business Considerations

Your Truck and Public Image
Equipment, Tools, and Supplies
Business Cards and Stationery
Office Equipment and Supplies
The Telephone
Your Business Address
Get a Computer
You Need a Plan

Chapter 3

EQUIPMENT AND SUPPLIES – A CAPITAL INVESTMENT

Quick Start: *START cheap, be stingy, and buy quality equipment (but cheap tools if you tend to lose them a lot). Put a trailer hitch on your truck and get a trailer, not a bigger truck, to haul more. If you can't buy new, shop the classifieds, flea markets, and garage sales for used tools. Open a business checking account. Get a table or cheap desk and set up your office in a corner of your house. Until you computerize, you'll need a typewriter and a printing calculator. We recommend getting a computer as soon as possible. The computer and printer will be necessities soon enough. Get an answering machine for your business telephone line. A fax machine won't hurt, and a rubber stamp with your business name and address is handy.*

Get business cards and a sign for your truck. Have a T-shirt made with your company name on it and wear it all over town.

HOW MUCH MONEY YOU NEED to start the business depends on how much basic equipment, tools, and supplies you need to buy. The rule is to start small, keep your expenses low, and invest all you can of your earnings and knowledge in the business.Try not to borrow, otherwise you'll be starting out under a double burden. If you must borrow, it's all the more reason to keep start-up expenses low. Acquire equipment as you build the business.

Open a business checking account. It will simplify record keeping and tax preparation. It also looks more businesslike than writing checks out of the family's personal account. You may need your banker for a loan someday, and it helps to have an account for the business. If the account has a sufficient balance, it could earn interest, too.

Your Truck and Public Image

You will need a pickup truck with a trailer hitch. The truck does not have to be right off the showroom floor, but it will reflect the pride you take in your work and it should be clean and polished. The truck should be reliable. Nothing will work against you more than the inability to meet your schedule because your transportation has broken down. A smaller truck will get better mileage. If you need more carrying capacity, get a trailer. Commercial vehicle insurance usually covers the trailer, but you will need a business liability policy for its contents.

You can get either a magnetic sign or a decal for your truck. Look in the telephone book for a sign shop. The shop will discuss design with you. For a while at least, this will be the only advertising you have. Make sure your business name and telephone number are clearly visible on it, and park the truck prominently in front of your jobsites.

Although for tax purposes you can't deduct the cost of the ordinary clothes you work in, the IRS seems to allow deducting the cost of uniforms or outfits that you can only wear for work. So have a shirt or T-shirt made up with your company name and logo. It's good advertising. When you're on the job, or at the supply store or bank, people will see your business name. Depending on your personal style, the company name can be blazoned across your back and chest, or parked neatly over the shirt pocket. Look in the Yellow Pages under T-Shirts or Screen Printing, and under Uniforms-Retail. If you already have that computer, there is software for T-shirt prints.

Equipment, Tools, and Supplies

Our rule is that you are money ahead buying quality. It applies to equipment—and to tools if you don't lose them on a regular basis. It may not matter how long tools last, how much better they work, or how little aggravation they cause long term. When you—or your employees—lose them right and left, there isn't any long term. This book will offer general guidance on buying tools. Some things count even for cheap tools, and you shouldn't have to struggle with a dud just to save a buck. In Chapter 17 we'll tell you how to be a savvy buyer, and you can ask your supplier or others in the trade.

You will probably buy most of your tools and equipment locally, but there are national suppliers listed in the Appendix whose prices are competitive with if not lower than the local market. The same is true of supplies, but less so because they are sold at discount in large retail outlets or discounted to the trade. You can get good deals when you know what to look for. (Local suppliers may also be good sources of trade information and new accounts.)

Business Cards and Stationery

When you start out have a batch of basic business cards run up, nothing fancy, just the essential information. You can buy plain stationery and forms from an office supply store, and get a rubber stamp with your business name, address, and telephone number on it.

Later, when your business becomes successful, you could go to a printer for your cards and letterhead paper. Job printers have produced cards and stationery for hundreds of businesses before yours, and the good ones have some worthwhile ideas on commercial design. Between the printer and you, you can create an over-all business identity that conveys the right message to your potential customers. If you are not satisfied with what a printer suggests, it may be worth finding a graphic artist or designer to create the right image for your business. Sometimes a local school or college can recommend someone who can do good work at a reasonable price.

In this business, however, the visible results of your work provide practically all the identity you may ever need. All your cards and stationery have to do is to connect you with the end product. The ideal card, letterhead, shirt, and truck logo is one that identifies you with the yards you work on; they are your trademark.

Office Equipment and Supplies

The basic office equipment in the first edition included a ten-key printing calculator, a big wall calendar, a typewriter, and a place at home to use them. Computers and the appropriate software have replaced all of them. Today even a start-up business should consider a computer and printer. More on that later. An unused bedroom, an enclosed porch, or just a corner where you can keep things together is enough. Your customers are buying your service, not your office decor.

You will also need two-part billing statements, 3" x 5" or 4" x 6" cards for customer and vendor lists and a box to keep them in, manila file folders for each account, and a giant one-year wall calendar that you can write on. A computer will let you replace much of this, but you will still need a good map of your area, an appointment book, paper clips, a stapler and staples, postage stamps, postcards for follow-up reminders, and a desk, file cabinet, or cardboard cartons to store your records in. You will need a rubber stamp with your business name, address, and telephone number to use on your receipts and stationery.

In the truck you will need a clipboard with lined and graph paper, probably a cheap hand calculator, a two-part cash receipts book and manila envelope for payments on the job, and plenty of pens and pencils in both the office and truck. You'll also want a 100-foot cloth tape measure and a pad for estimates, either with your logo or a place to rubber stamp.

The Telephone

Although you may be working out of your home, be businesslike from the beginning. This means a separate business telephone. It usually doesn't cost much to install a second residential line and use it exclusively for the business. Also, get an answering machine. Customers are not impressed when your five-year-old takes a business call. Make a point always to return your telephone calls within 24 hours. You may not be able to do anything for your caller, but your prompt response shows the right professional attitude.

Always make notes about your telephone calls, whether you take them directly or from the answering machine. Write down the caller's name, address, phone number, the time and date, and the message. Keep the notes where you can find them, preferably in a regular note pad by the telephone. When the note pad is full save it. It doesn't have to be a fancy spiral-bound two-part pad from an office supply store, but you may want to make a duplicate of the message for a customer's file if it is important. Make sure that everyone who answers your telephone for you keeps notes in the pad, too. You should keep these pads and similar records for a few years. Memories are unreliable and you never know when you will need to confirm a conversation.

E-mail hasn't eliminated fax machines yet. Even though your customers probably get next-day mail, a fax machine is useful for dealing with out-of-town suppliers and similar business contacts.

Your Business Address

You will want to get a post office box if you're working from home. If your address is clearly residential, and you want to appear as professional as possible, a post office box may be the answer. Private postal-box businesses give you a street address and a *suite* or *box* number. (Only the U.S. Postal Service gets to call them P.O. Boxes.) An added advantage is that your customers do not come knocking on your door when you want to get away from work. Whichever you choose you will have to defer business cards and stationery until you settle on a permanent address.

Get a Computer

A computer and printer are valuable assets but you don't need them right away for a small landscape maintenance business. On the other hand, new computers are pretty cheap now. They are easier to use and reasonably reliable. Software is available and easy to install and learn for practically every business need. The software I use to run the business cost less than $150. Most of it came with the computer, and if you shop you can buy a new computer for about $800.

When should you buy one? Once you feel you've spent all day working, then come home and have to spend all evening working on the books, you'll want a computer. Then you can get rid of the typewriter and printing calculator. You'll have to how learn to use a word processor an accounting program, perhaps a spreadsheet, and a few other applications, but once you do you'll wonder why you waited so long. If you enjoy playing with the computer, as many people do, you can use graphics and desktop publishing programs in your business.

Get a good brand-name model like a Hewlett-Packard, IBM, Compaq, Dell or Gateway 2000. They are solid machines, their manufacturers provide good service contracts, they'll be around awhile, and you'll be able to find replacement parts. Be wary of ultra-cheap "e-machines." You get exactly the computer you pay for. Cheap computers use corner-cutting hardware that goes out of date fast and is hard to replace. A locally built machine will do fine if the shop is "user-friendly" and looks like it will also be around awhile. Even if not, as long as the shop uses good-quality generic electronics, the pieces that fail can be replaced, even upgraded. Prompt and reliable local technical support will keep your machine—and business—running.

Once you feel you've spent all day working, then come home and have to spend all evening working on the books, you'll want a computer.

You'll need a printer. New ones are cheap, and good used laser printers are just as cheap. Ink in ink-cartridge printers runs when wet, like old fountain-pen ink. Hewlett-Packard pioneered in and dominates laser printers. Others, particularly older models, match H-P to one degree or another. Make sure the one you buy "emulates" the H-P standard enough to work with your software.

The Internet: This can be the greatest time-waster you ever met. It is also the world's greatest vehicle for useful information since moveable type. If your machine has a modem, you can sign up with an Internet provider. Shop for Internet service; our local provider is cheaper than the national providers. Juno (juno.com) and a few other companies provide free web service and are worth looking into. There are hundreds of useful Internet gardening sites. Entering your question or the name of a plant in an Internet "search engine" will get you hundreds of answers. Let your imagination roam; just type in "gardening" and see what you get!

We've discussed IBM-compatible computers (PCs) and operating systems because it's what we're familiar with, but you can find excellent programs on Apple's Macintosh. Macs are usually more expensive but are excellent machines with reliable software. Base your decision on the software programs not the hardware. This is critical because there is much more business software available for PCs than Macs.

You Need a Plan

Ideally, your thoughts about a start-up strategy and expenses should go into a written business plan. Even as a bunch of guesses, a plan in writing is better than rushing ahead and spending money piecemeal. A plan (1) makes you analyze your whole business financially, (2) lets you manage and check results against the plan, and (3) helps tell other people, like lenders and installment sellers, about your business. Finally, the plan can be very useful when you think about expanding or diversifying the business.

Every business plan gives at least basic data: Your name, address, telephone number, and the business's name and location. It explains what the business will do by stating its purpose and summarizing its objective. It tells how the business will work and estimates its share of the proposed market. That means making a rough forecast of income and expenses. Writing down the numbers and information will give you a clearer idea of your plans. For a more complete statement, the best way to approach this "simple" opening summary is to work out all the plan's pieces. Then, based on them, go back and write your statement of purpose and objectives.

The pieces you want to analyze and write out for the big plan are:

The business - Tell if the business will be a sole proprietorship, partnership, or corporation. Tell what equipment it has or will acquire, what products and services it will offer. List who will do what, how they are qualified to do it, and what happens if they leave. Also list who has assisted in the start-up like any lawyers, accountants, or business consultants.

The market - Work down from the greater and intermediate markets to your potential market and how much of it you expect to acquire. Describe your expected market economically, geographically, and socially. Think about population changes and shifting demand.

Competitive analysis - You've probably already compared your projected business with the competition mentally. But put it on paper. Work out and write down how you think your competitors appeal to customers, where they succeed and miss, and what their major problems seem to be. Then tell how, and with what techniques, your business will fit in.

Development plans - Here is where the plan gets serious about growth and requires careful thought about the future. Using your analyses of the market and the competition, lay out a time line and project how you will expand the business. This may be only a few sentences if expansion involves merely increasing your customer base for lawn care and basic gardening. If you have something more complicated in mind, list what services and equipment you will use to expand. Tell what skills you will acquire to provide the services. Make out a timed development budget for reaching your goals.

Operations - This is a set of financial tables that list expenses like labor, equipment costs, and overhead. You'll try to figure out how expansion is tied to acquiring new equipment and staff to do the extra work. This will help keep income and expenses under control and let you manage the expansion better.

Financial projections - If you plan on an elaborate business, you will want professional help to set up projected income statements, cash flow, and balance sheets. This means making income and expense projections for monthly then quarterly intervals for the first few years of planned operation. Even for an ordinary start-up you might do rough financial projections to help see how the business begins to shape up.

As you see, a full-bore business plan can be plenty of work, and most of us probably can't do it alone. We include a good guide to drafting business plans in the Appendix. Also, every state now has a Small Business Development Council (SBDC) that operates through county governments or community colleges. Many will sit down and help you set up a business plan. The federal Small Business Administration (SBA) offers assistance as well. Check the federal and local government pages of your telephone book. Anyone who decides to draft a serious business plan, however, should do as much of it personally as possible, in order to know what to expect the business to do and to show how it actually is doing over time.

If you have a very uncomplicated business in mind, your plan doesn't have to be elaborate. A few sentences and some financial projections may be enough to get you started. But put it in writing. It should be a statement you can build on later if you decide to expand the business. If you do, there are books and software for creating a business plan that are worth consulting. We list a few items in the Appendix.

Once you've gone to the trouble of writing a business plan, don't put it away and forget it. Keep checking your progress against it, and revise the plan as needed. For example, if you seem to be getting plenty of business but are not netting the income you planned on, try to adjust your prices or see what expenses to cut. Remember the best plan is only an elaborate guess. Stay flexible; it's not there to follow to the letter. As Dwight D. Eisenhower said just before D-Day, "Before the battle is joined, planning is everything, but once the bullets start flying, plans are worthless."

What to Name Your Business

Licenses

Legal Structure of the Business

Legal and Other Aid

Chapter 4

LEGAL MATTERS – MAKING IT PROPER

Quick Start: *UNLESS you work under your own name, file and publish a fictitious business or assumed name statement. Go to the county clerk's office, call the commissioner of corporations, and see your local library to be sure your trade name does not infringe on anyone else's. You may have to get a business license. There are many local variations on who needs a license and who issues them. Start by checking with your county clerk. Your business will be a sole proprietorship unless you have a partner. Partnerships that start with a handshake can end with a fistfight; so either have a lawyer write out a partnership agreement or write one and let a lawyer review it. When money starts growing on trees for you, look into forming a corporation. Check with a broker about your business insurance needs.*

THIS CHAPTER doesn't give you legal advice, and you won't find any here. Our intention is to alert you to the leading legal matters new businesses must deal with. These are the business name, lcoal licenses, and the business's structure, or ownership. There will be plenty of other legal things you will have to learn about later on, like it or not, but we think this will get you started.

What to Name Your Business

If you were named Sandy MacDuff and you promoted your landscape maintenance service as "Sandy MacDuff, Gardener," you wouldn't have to do anything more. You are entitled to use your own name without registering with anybody. When the time came to sell the business, however, you would have a hard time selling the goodwill to someone who was not named Sandy MacDuff and had to change the name and lose the business identity. There is also the consideration of picking a name that will be high up in the Yellow Pages, like "Ace Lawn Care." If you are named Zimmerman, you know the problem.

When you pick a business name, you become [Your Name Here], dba (doing business as) "Classic Lawn Care." You will have to file a fictitious business name, assumed name statement, or the like with the county in most states, but occasionally with the state. Your name will then be in the public records so that if anyone has a complaint about the business they can find you to let you know. In California, if you do not file a fictitious business name statement you are not allowed to bring a lawsuit in the business's name. Your bank will probably require a copy of your fictitious or assumed name filing before it will let you open a business checking account.

Before you settle on a business name, you will have to check the fictitious or assumed name filings to be sure you are not infringing on someone else's trade name. Filing also protects your business name so that no one else can use it without infringing on yours. It is probably also worth a telephone call to the office of your state's Secretary of State to be sure that no corporation is using the name. Corporations get an exclusive right to use a name state-wide. As a last check, scan the telephone directories at the libraries, too. If you do infringe on someone's business name, you may get a call from their lawyer.

The laws on assumed or fictitious business names vary from state to state. In California, for example, a fictitious business name also includes one that does not use the owner's last name or suggests additional owners, as in "& Associates," "& Company," or "& Daughters." You must pay a fee of $10 for one fictitious business name and $2 for each additional name. The $10 covers two partners; each additional partner costs $2. You must also publish a legal notice of your business name in a newspaper of general circulation. If your state has a law like this, have the county clerk or state official tell you which these papers are. Then look for the cheapest rate. Laws on business names vary from state to state, and you'll have to check to learn the requirements.

There are no easy answers on what kind of name to pick, except that it should identify and promote the business. You could include a unique or at least an unusual term in the name that no other business is likely to use, such as a local geographical feature. If you plan to expand your services, pick a name the business can grow into. Don't pick a name that is hard to pronounce; potential customers may not call you because they're unsure how to pronounce the name. Be careful about clever puns: *e.g.*, Avalawn, that is, Avalon, which some people may also find a tongue twister. Keep an eye on your state's contractor licensing laws, too. In California a gardener can use ©landscape care" or "landscape maintenance," but not "landscaper" or "landscaping" in a business name.

Fictitious or assumed business name filings are good for a given number of years, five in California, and then they must be renewed to stay active.

Licenses

If you operate your business in a city, you will have to get a business license. In some states the counties issue business licenses. The license is not based on any qualification other than payment of the fee. It is a revenue source for the local government and a way to keep track of commercial activity. In most states, if the business is in an unincorporated area of the county, you probably won't need to get a business license.

Complying with the legal requirements is going to cost you, but evading them will tarnish your business's image from the outset. You want it to be as professional as you can make it; so pay your dues!

Legal Structure of the Business

Before you begin canvassing the neighborhoods to get customers, you need to do a little more initial planning and preparation. One start-up issue is the business's the legal structure.

The Sole Proprietorship - A sole proprietorship is the easiest form of business to set up. If you go out to work right away, you are a sole proprietor. It is as simple as that. Accounting and taxes are easy, although as a self-employed person you will have to file a few more state and federal tax forms. As sole proprietor you have complete freedom in decision-making, with no one else to consult with or please. To wind up the business you just pay your outstanding bills and close the doors. Sole proprietorships are far and away the commonest form of small business ownership, and they make sense for the beginning business with few assets and low start-up income and expenses.

The drawbacks are that you are completely liable for the business's debts or the damages it causes, your access to financing is limited to what you can pull in yourself, it is hard to attract good employees, and there is only one person to do all the bookkeeping, marketing, labor, managing, and legal work.

The Partnership - When two or more people go into business together they usually form a general partnership. The main attraction is that two or more people can pool their knowledge, skills, and resources. They can cover each other's absences and vacations. More funds are available, and the partnership can be formed without state approval. All the partnership earnings are divided and taxed as personal income. A partnership can attract and keep employees with the lure of being made a partner.

On the other hand, partnerships split up faster than marriages. A partner never learns other partners' bad habits until after they go to work together. Also, each partner has unlimited liability for any other partners' business debts and damages. Finally, a partnership can be very difficult to dissolve.

Many partnerships exist on a handshake. That has real disadvantages. All states but one have adopted the Uniform Partnership Act, and informal partnerships are governed by the Act. That won't suit every partnership. It is almost impossible to terminate a partnership without a lawyer. In order to avoid the problems that may arise from things like one partner's death, incapacity or departure, it is worth a few hundred dollars to have a lawyer draft a simple but custom partnership agreement. The agreement will spell out how to cope with problems before they come up.

It is also a good idea to insure each partner's life so that, in case one dies, the surviving partners can use the policy benefits to buy out any interest the heirs have in the partnership. Partners should also decide how to value and buy out a withdrawing partner's interest; sometimes installment payments work best.

Partnership agreements can also deal with whether the partnership or the partners will own the partnership assets, whether the partners can work at other jobs, whether there is a managing partner, which partner or partners will sign the checks, and a lot of things that should be thought out and put into writing.

There are books that can help you draft a partnership agreement. If you use such a book, be sure after reading it that it will not save a small legal fee now but buy a big legal problem later on. If you do draft your own agreement, it should cost very little to have a lawyer review it.

A limited partnership is complex enough to require professional help to set up, but it is cheaper to form and run than a corporation. It's also a good way to raise money. A limited partnership comprises any number of general partners who run the business—as in a regular partnership—and no more than 35 limited partners. Limited partners must be real people, usually residents of your state. Although the general partner or partners will still have unlimited liability for the partnership's obligations, limited partners are liable for only as much as they invest in the partnership. In order to keep their limited liability, they can't take part in running the business.

If a limited partner dislikes the way you run the business, all that partner can do without becoming fully liable for all the risks is to sell the partnership share to someone else whom the general partners approve of and get out. The general partners have complete control. The disadvantage is that usually the 35 people who invest are 35 people you know and who know each other. You have to be careful to set up formal funding agreements and follow them to the letter. Otherwise you will find that money has a way of ruining all sorts of relationships.

The Corporation - The time may come when you want to consider incorporating. Corporations can be expensive to start and maintain. They require a lot of paperwork and professional assistance from time to time to make sure you are running it legally. At the critical point, however, a corporation's benefits outweigh all these burdens. A corporations' main attraction is that owners' liability is limited to whatever they have invested in the corporation. It is possible to raise money and expand a corporation by selling more stock. It's also easier to transfer ownership of a corporation, and hiring expert management is easier.

Regular corporations, or what the tax laws call C corporations, are taxed twice—once on corporate income and again on shareholders' dividend income. A way to avoid double taxation is to set up an S corporation. One person can be the entire corporation, the president, the board of directors, the whole annual meeting. There is strong official encouragement for small businesses to start S corporations. You can set one up through your own or any other state. A good business lawyer should be able to find the best state in which to incorporate.

Legal and Other Aid

When you're looking for a lawyer, bookkeeper, accountant, or insurance broker to help with the problems of running a successful small business, don't rely on newspaper ads or the yellow pages alone. Ask other small-business people for referrals to lawyers, bookkeepers, etc., who specialize in small businesses and have gotten good results for their clients. In the meantime there are a number of easy-to-use guides that you should consult to answer your everyday legal and technical business questions. A short list of them appears in the Appendix.

The "Mass Media"
Flyers and Brochures
Credentials
Personal Contact
Other Approaches
Coordination

Chapter 5

MARKETING – BUILDING YOUR CUSTOMER BASE

Quick Start:

KEEP marketing costs low by doing all you can yourself. Target your market and coordinate marketing. Use flyers with your business cards on bulletin boards. Speak at senior centers. Introduce yourself to other gardeners and offer to handle their excess business; offer a referral fee. Call them for jobs up for bidding. Try a Yellow Page display ad. They're dynamite in some places but don't work in others. Classified ads in the newspaper usually aren't worth the money. Track the results of all advertising.

Personal calls are a hard way to get business but they're a good way to learn how to sell your services. When you call, make a good impression of competence, courtesy, and enthusiasm. Park your truck with its name showing. Relax and be yourself. Know what you're talking about and take an interest in the yard. Answer all the prospects' questions. Be prepared to inspect the property. Don't steal another gardener's customer.

Offer discounts to people in the same neighborhood. Do more for the customers you already have.

MARKETING is only as good as the product behind it. That's as true for a lawn care business as any other. What you're taking to market is the good quality of your work and it's the core of your marketing plan. You must not only maintain the product's quality but have a plan for getting it before the public. Without a marketing plan you can waste time, money, and energy with precious little result. Also, you'll want the most response you can buy for that time, money, etc.; so it's worth learning a few marketing basics.

The best promotion for your business, hands down, is a referral from a satisfied customer. It costs nothing and is the most credible form of publicity. Before you have customers who will give personal endorsements, however, you'll have to take a different approach. And even once established, word-of-mouth alone may not keep your business's name before the public. You'll need to advertise and engage in public relations to some degree at least.

First decide what markets you want and how to reach them. You will probably start with residential customers. Concentrate on neighborhoods that are "easy to service" and mostly owner-occupied. Tenants will devote only minimal efforts, if any, at keeping property up, and many landlords don't want to deduct extra gardening costs from their income from single-family rentals. If you want to maintain rental property grounds, contact apartment house owners and property management companies.

"Easy to service" does not necessarily mean close to home. Look for a neighborhood where most people take pride in their surroundings. It should be easy to drive to. Ideally, your customers will be reasonably close together; or, if there is some distance between two or more likely neighborhoods, try to group all your jobs within each area for a given day.

The "Mass Media"

Advertising through the newspapers or yellow pages may or may not target your chosen markets, but their advantages and disadvantages are worth noting. If you can afford area-wide advertising, it may help you determine where your best markets are. Be sure that the return justifies the cost. Spreading yourself too thin will be expensive and inefficient.

The Yellow Pages - Yellow page ads for landscape maintenance are often located under *Gardening*. Those for lawn mowing are under *Lawn Maintenance*. If you expand from mowing lawns, you will want one under both headings. Your business phone will get you a one-line entry under the proper heading in the yellow pages. We get lots of business from the Yellow Pages. It depends on where you live and on the competition. Everything is local. There are areas where a display ad in the Yellow Pages may be a waste of advertising dollars. When we worked in Redding, California, there were three telephone books, Pacific Bell's and two private publishers. We got very little business from the Pacific Bell directory. In Arcata the telephone rings off the hook from the Pacific Bell ad.

Sometimes a telephone directory publisher offers new businesses half-price deals for display ads. You can take them up on the offer and decide the next year, when you are better established, whether to use the display ad, a boldface line, or something in between. The telephone company often will make up ads for you, but you can shop around if you believe a local advertising firm can create a more productive ad for you.

Classified ads - The cost of classified ads in a daily newspaper is not worth the cost. Ads in free weekly shoppers can be productive. Some people scan every line of them for bargains and don't miss a single item. If the shopper in your area lists local business services, that's all the more reason to advertise in it. If your local newspaper has a special classified section for business and professional services, see if the same businesses keep advertising in it. If they do, it is probably because the ads are paying off.

Also consider non-traditional marketing, such as speaking at a senior citizens center, participating with a local newcomers group (Welcome Wagon or whatever has replaced it), community relations, and business associations. If you or a family member likes to write, consider press releases or articles for business and property management newsletters. Many local newspapers have "how-to" kits for sending in information. If you follow the rules, you get more in print. A release should not be fancy, just send a brief outline of facts, starting with the most important and winding down into the details. You would tell about awards, any new employees, new services or landscaping trends, or observations of something new in local landscapes (perhaps it relates to a national trend or seems important on its own). This is pretty unusual for a lawn care and gardening business, but a little good publicity, if you can get it, never hurts.

Flyers and Brochures

Self-printed notices like flyers can reach just the market you choose. A flyer is a one-page notice that publicizes your business, or possibly a special price or service you may offer for a limited time. In addition to handing out flyers to people you talk to on your rounds and sticking them on doorknobs, you can post them on bulletin boards in shopping malls and community centers.

Flyers need not be expensive to be eye-catching and persuasive. Some small printers and desktop publishing shops offer advice and facilities for designing them. A friend or family member who is handy with a computer word processor could set one up. Then you can produce a colorful product for little more than a black and white one by using colored paper and ink. Stay away from colors that are too garish or make the message hard to read. The design should make as professional a statement as the words. Figure 5.1 illustrates a very basic flyer that gets the message across. If you distribute flyers in a neighborhood, attach a business card that can be pulled off and kept. Two-sided tape or a drop of rubber cement will do the job. The flyer will probably be thrown out, but the card may not be. Finally, don't blanket a neighborhood with flyers unless you want to appear wasteful and a litterbug. Jot a personal note and leave a flyer at houses that look like good prospects. For bulletin boards you can make a "pouch" in the flyer by folding the bottom 1½" up to make a pocket for business cards.

Brochures for small businesses normally are printed on 8½" by 11" paper folded in thirds or on 8½" by 14" paper folded in quarters. The text is printed down each panel of the folded paper. Unless you are offering a special service when you start off, you probably won't want a brochure until you have been in business awhile. Unless you are very skilled at using a computer, setting it up will require the services of a local desktop publishing service. It won't be cheap, but at that point, a brochure with photos and text on your company's abilities and accomplishments can be very persuasive and tell much more than your card.

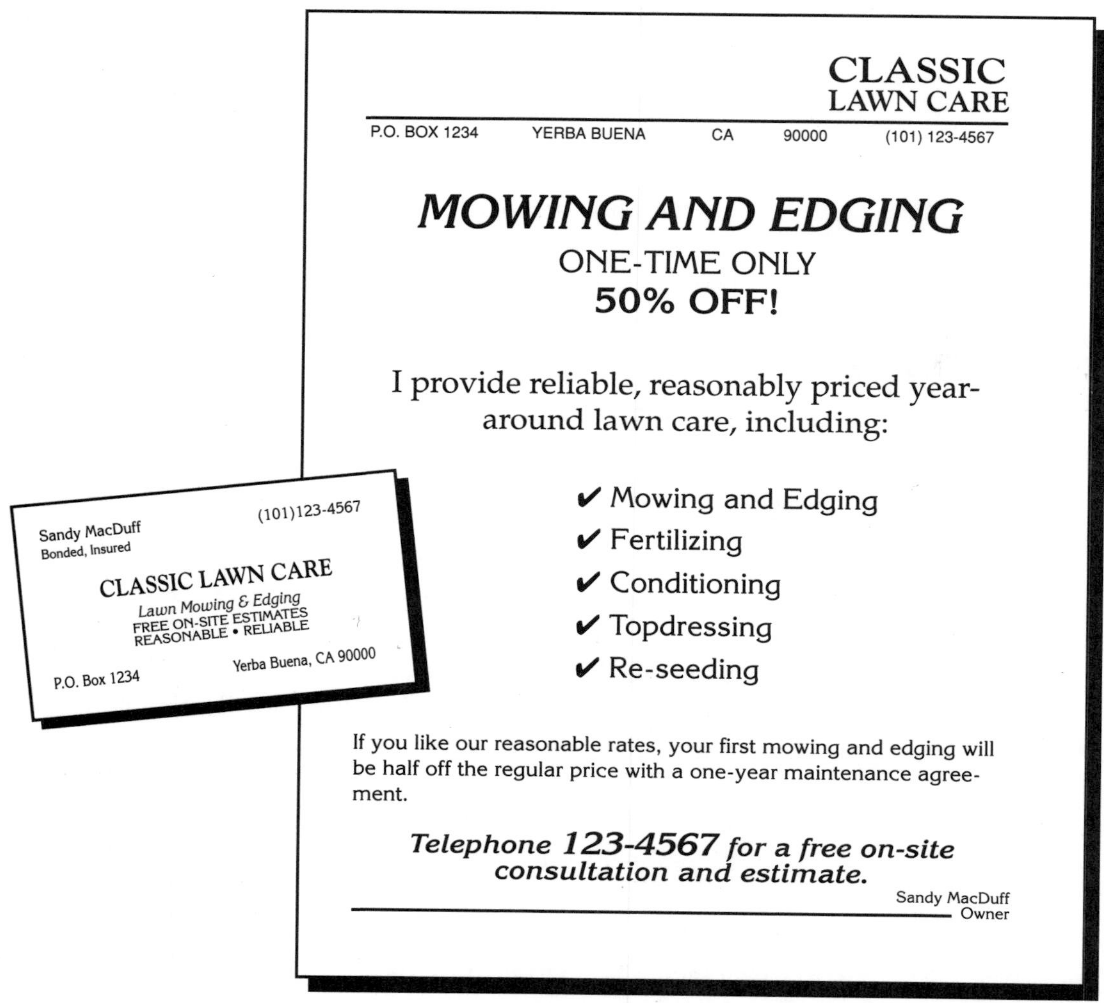

Figure 5.1. A sample card and advertising flyer.

Credentials

Bonds - Many homeowners have been told their landscape service firm should be bonded. The recommendation comes from licensed contractors' associations because state laws require contractors to be bonded. The laws are for consumer protection but only indirectly. A state will revoke the licenses of contractors who lose their bonds to customers' claims. The bonds themselves don't provide much real consumer protection. The bond amount is usually low—$5,000 in California—and very hard to collect. Liability insurance, which you definitely should carry, protects the consumer better because it comes in more realistic amounts and is easier to collect.

Noting on your business cards and stationery that you are bonded as well as insured does carry weight with some people, and the annual cost is small, around $100. See also if other gardeners in your area claim to be bonded. If few are, it may not be worth the expense or effort. If you think a bond will pay for itself as *advertising*, then get one. Any bonding company will cheerfully oblige. But being insured is better.

Professional Associations - It is worth spending a few hundred dollars as soon as you can to join a professional association. You can also put that on your cards and stationery to show that you take the quality of your work seriously. The association publications will in fact help inform you about new developments. Membership benefits often include group plans for business liability and casualty insurance, group health insurance, employee benefit packages, and credit unions. Most associations support valuable horticultural research and publish useful books which are discounted to members. State and regional landscape associations, even out-of-state associations, may publish just the horticultural or business information you need. We list a few associations in the Appendix. You can also try the Internet. One place to begin might be the Associated Landscape Contractors of America (ALCA) website at http://www.alca.org. It's a good source of books on horticulture, pest control, trees, management and marketing. Books are sold discounted to members. Annual dues are currently $375 for sole proprietors. The American Nursery and Landscape Association (ANLA) is at www.anla.org.

Some professional associations will provide members and nonmembers with attractive, informative, reasonably priced brochures to send to customers. You can use them to introduce your services to potential customers or to keep in touch with your current customers. It's a good idea to get a sample of the brochure first to make sure you agree with what it says. We list more professional associations in the Appendix.

Personal Contact

A personal meeting with potential customers, when you encounter them, can be a good, cost effective way to promote your services. I don't recommend canvassing whole neighborhoods. It's hard work, discouraging, and unproductive. There are houses in every neighborhood, however, where the yards may be run down because, although the owners care, they lack the skills or time to do a good job of gardening. If you spot one of these, it can be worth a visit. After a while, you might even develop a nose for promising sites like these. Then you can use the opportunity to show that good quality landscape maintenance need not be expensive.

Rather than dropping a flyer on the front step, or even writing a letter, it's worth visiting such properties personally; but even that is easier said than done. Sad to say, it's unlikely that strangers can make friendly house calls in most places in this country any more. Even if you think it's all right where you live, make sure people can see your truck with your business name on it. Point it out to them to help them feel more at ease.

Knocking on doors is hard work, and you will get a lot of rejection. If you decide to pursue it, make it as easy on yourself as you can. The best time to call depends on the neighborhood. For working families, early evenings or mid-day Saturdays are probably best. If there are a lot of retired people in the neighborhood, you can call during weekdays. Later, once you begin to work in a neighborhood, you will meet the neighbors while you're on the job and you can use the opportunity to promote your services in an easy, relaxed way. Finally, don't forget that the company shirt you may be wearing around town can be a conversation starter.

Whenever you have the opportunity to speak to a homeowner directly it's an opportunity to sell your services. Every yard has problem areas. When making calls you will have seen the properties already and know what their problems are. Think how they can be corrected. Make notes about what you will discuss at each property. Don't write out long speeches, keep the notes brief, a word or two as reminders, so that the conversation turns naturally to each point.

Every yard has problem areas. When making calls you will have seen the properties already and know what their problems are. Think how they can be corrected. Make notes about what you will discuss at each property. Don't write out long speeches, keep the notes brief, a word or two as reminders, so that the conversation turns naturally to each point.

Be neat and clean, when you call to introduce your service. Be sure your truck and the tools in it make a good impression. Don't be discouraged if it takes a few such calls to hit your stride. If you get used to personal calls, you can get customers this way.

You will be doing a selling job with these personal calls. Don't think you aren't up to it. It amounts only to chatting easily about something that interests you. You are not only offering to mow the lawn. You will edge and trim around trees, shrubs, fences and foundations. You will also set up a program of maintenance. It is something you enjoy and excel at. It won't cost the customers much, and it will give them time to enjoy their leisure. You are there to improve appearances and make life easier at a fair price. Point out the property's good points and how you can improve them. Try to anticipate questions. This is how you learn to sell.

You must know your business and you must put yourself in your customer's shoes. Think about the businesses you patronize and why you prefer them. It is probably because of their competent, courteous people who give you good service. That is what your customers want and what you will give them. You can inspire their confidence by your understanding of the job and a sincere concern about the appearance and vitality of their landscaping.

Your product. You are selling *TIME* and a way for your customers to enjoy it by:

1. Making their landscaping expand their leisure and not be a set of chores that consume it;
2. Arriving on a regular schedule, so they can plan their leisure better;
3. Billing monthly, so that they need not be home to pay you on the job;
4. Providing a written bid that lists what tasks they won't have to do anymore; and
5. Cleaning up and hauling away clippings so they will not have to.

You'll have to learn to sell if you want customers, that is, if you want a business at all. Selling comes naturally to some people; the rest of us have to learn it. If you haven't tried selling anything before, make it a game and try it out on friends or relatives. Try to persuade them to *hire* you to maintain their yard. Eventually, you will find that the most important thing in selling is to listen. Pay attention to what people ask. These are objections to overcome. The job will be yours only when you have answered all the objections the customer raises. Not until then should you ask for the job.

I am not a high-pressure salesperson. I try not to say too much because sometimes I end up with my foot in my mouth. But I do make sure I understand what the customer wants done. I let the customer know I do quality work, that I have other accounts in the neighborhood (if I do), how much I charge, my terms, and how I bill. I have all of this on a pre-printed handout with my name and telephone number, which I give to the customer along with my card.

For example, you may find yourself suggesting to an elderly couple that you could prune back the overgrown shrubbery in their yard. They may respond that they like the privacy it provides. You may agree that while it gave them plenty of privacy, it might also be an invitation to burglars. Then you could show them how to open it up for security without giving up their privacy.

Figure 5.2. The author's promotional calendar.

Recently I consulted with a woman who was preparing her house for sale. She had large, unwanted crop of wild onions under her redwood tree. I suggested that, rather than put a lot of money into landscaping a small area where little would grow and needles would fall, we mow the wild onions, and edge and blow the paths for a clean tidy back yard (which smelled like fresh salad!). As she wasn't going to be a long-term customer, I gave a high estimate for the work, and she called the next day to okay it.

The important part of selling is never to disagree with the customer. Agree and offer your professional opinion and suggestions. This should tell them something they had not considered and that they are hiring the right gardener.

It's a good idea to walk around the premises with the owners and discuss problem areas, plans for improvement, or maintenance schedules. During your walk, keep asking questions about how much time the owners spend on gardening, what jobs they like, what jobs they would prefer to pay to have done. Give compliments and stress the positive. Keep selling in this low key manner as you tour the property.

If the prospect becomes a customer, be prepared from the beginning. In case the job needs an elaborate estimate, you should have in your car or truck some estimate forms, a clipboard with note or graph paper, a tape measure (preferably 100-foot), and a pocket calculator. If there is not enough time to do it then, make an appointment to come back later. You can even inspect on your own and meet the customer later to discuss what you saw.

Closing the sale: When you have answered all the objections, ask for the job. This may be as simple as asking whether they prefer you to come on Tuesday morning or Thursday afternoon, or by beginning to write an estimate, if you can, of what work there is to be done and how much it will cost. When you get to this point you will offer several choices, depending on how much the homeowners want to do themselves. You can always start by doing a little for a customer and gradually take on more duties as the customer gains confidence in your skills and ability.

If your prospects are not interested in your service, thank them for their time. Be courteous and friendly. Someday, when they want landscape maintenance services, you want them to think of you. Keep records of when you visited your likeliest prospects in a special file folder. Then, follow up with a letter thanking them for letting you visit and tell them again briefly about your service. Write your follow-up letters from the customers' point of view. Compliment them on their attractive home (here you will use your notes again) and refer to the work that you do at this season of the year. A few months later do another follow-up. The idea is to indicate that you know your business, that you take an interest in people's property, and that you would consider it a privilege to help them maintain it. Ideally, you should send individual letters. You can send form letters but you should sign them individually. The University of Missouri has a calendar of lawn care tasks at an Internet site, www.muextension.missouri.edu. You or a family member could use something like that for the subject of a note or as a guide for building a newsletter.

Everyone lives by selling something.
—ROBERT LOUIS STEVENSON

You can also buy or make small calendars for the first of the year that will fit in an envelope to send to customers and potential customers. The calendar would display your name, logo, and business information prominently so customers can find you fast. At the bottom you can briefly list quarterly gardening tasks and a list of your company's services. Figure 5.2 displays the calendar we send out.

It is worth your time and effort to sell to customers who do their own gardening. First, they are interested in landscape maintenance and they know about the burdensome or specialized jobs, like aerating, dethatching, and heavy pruning, that are best left to a professional service. Do *not* try to acquire another gardener's customers. Your introductory remark, in fact, should bring out whether a prospect already employs professional landscape services. It is not only bad practice to go after other gardener's customers, it also gets you disloyal customers, who eventually will also drop you for someone else.

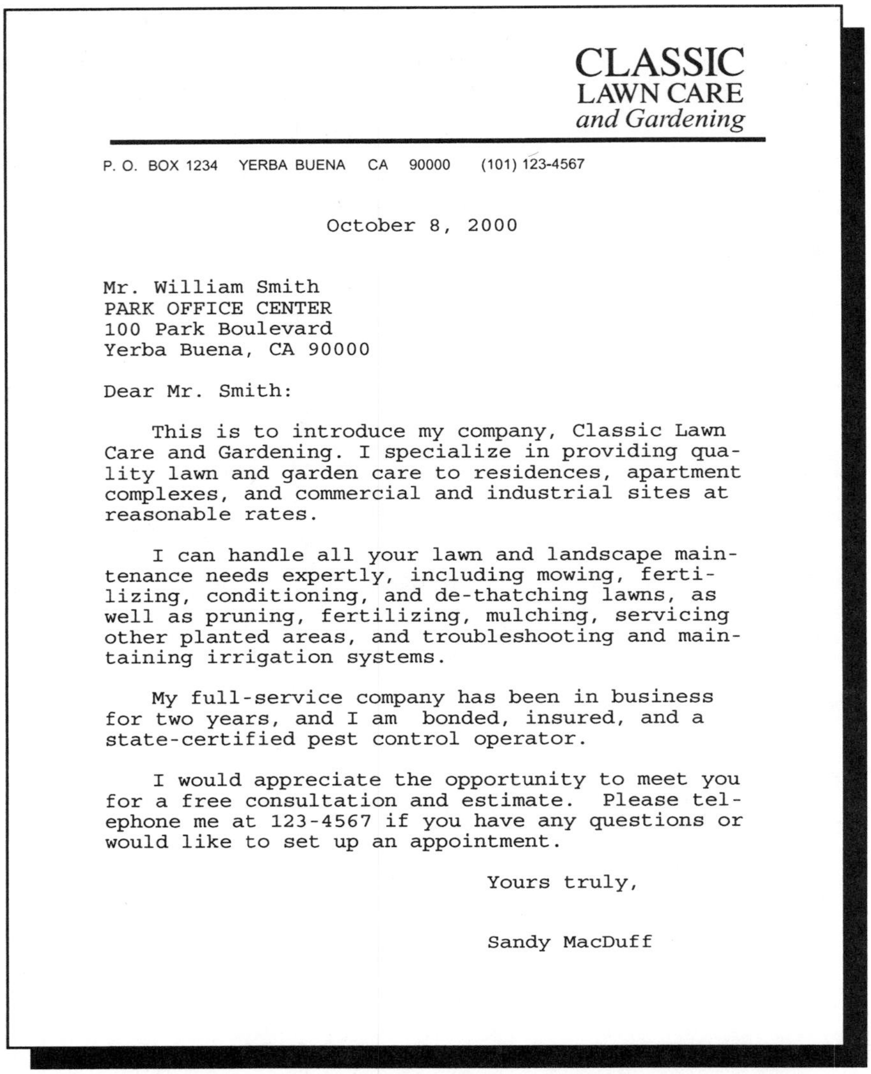

CLASSIC
LAWN CARE
and Gardening

P. O. BOX 1234 YERBA BUENA CA 90000 (101) 123-4567

October 8, 2000

Mr. William Smith
PARK OFFICE CENTER
100 Park Boulevard
Yerba Buena, CA 90000

Dear Mr. Smith:

This is to introduce my company, Classic Lawn Care and Gardening. I specialize in providing quality lawn and garden care to residences, apartment complexes, and commercial and industrial sites at reasonable rates.

I can handle all your lawn and landscape maintenance needs expertly, including mowing, fertilizing, conditioning, and de-thatching lawns, as well as pruning, fertilizing, mulching, servicing other planted areas, and troubleshooting and maintaining irrigation systems.

My full-service company has been in business for two years, and I am bonded, insured, and a state-certified pest control operator.

I would appreciate the opportunity to meet you for a free consultation and estimate. Please telephone me at 123-4567 if you have any questions or would like to set up an appointment.

Yours truly,

Sandy MacDuff

Figure 5.3. Sample letter for commercial account.

When you work on a property, and it starts to show improvement, others in the neighborhood will notice the change. Then the next time you swing through the area you can introduce yourself as the gardener who works on that yard.

If a prospect asks for a discount because they are close to your other accounts in the neighborhood, agree to it and say you will discount to them even further for every new customer they can get you. It's a good way to get customers (if you need them). Remember that having customers in one neighborhood cuts driving time that you don't get paid for. Also, let people in a neighborhood know that you will discount your services if a certain number or percentage of them hire you.

Commercial/Industrial Accounts - The same method of acquiring new customers can be applied as you continue to expand the scope of your services. Working commercial jobs shifts your work from landscape "maintenance" to landscape "management." That is, you take over all the gardening and often the entire responsibility of managing the grounds. If you want to take on commercial or industrial accounts, a personal visit is still the best way to get the account. You will make an appointment first by writing a letter or calling to inquire whether the account comes up for bid and asking to be notified when it does. Do not hesitate to make bids. If the work is within your capability, you should make the effort. If you want to maintain rental properties operated by a property management company, write to the company for a personal visit. Figure 5.3 illustrates a sample letter.

Other Approaches

Introduce yourself to other reputable gardeners. Tell them you are starting out and would appreciate any business they may throw your way. Offer them a percentage as a finder's fee if you want. Stay in touch with them by calling them regularly to see if they have any jobs you can bid on.

Look for move-ins. New owners usually have ideas about improving their new surroundings and will often want to renovate the garden. In addition, if they are from out of state or from a different area, they will not have your knowledge of local conditions and plants. You could send them a list of your services and your best looking sites.

Immediately after you finish a one-time job, write a reminder card and file it in a special calendar for mailing on the date for a follow-up call.

Become familiar with local garden suppliers and nurseries that are in or near the areas where you plan to work. If they do not operate their own gardening service, tell them what you do and leave your business cards. The suppliers may have ideas about what neighborhoods may provide prospects for your work. Keep in touch with these suppliers. If you buy your supplies from them, they will have an incentive to see you are kept busy. As you increase the scope of your services, you will want them to know it. Let your customers know, too.

Coordination

Your sales methods should be coordinated. Have a plan for following up each kind of customer contact. Telephone or visit them personally. Keep lists of likely customers that you sent letters to. Your lists should indicate the date and kind of contact, and the result. Don't forget the customers you already have. Always ask about other things they might like you to do. Ask whether they know other people who would like your services.

The strategy underlying your house calls and follow-up letters is to create a base of potential customers in the neighborhood. All this coordination and strategy involves "marketing." Unless you've run a small business before, it's something to which you probably haven't given much thought. It also draws on a lot of unfamiliar skills, and probably the best and most entertaining place to begin learning about them is in Jay Conrad Levinson's *Guerrilla Marketing* series. Don't let the paramilitary titles fool you. Levinson was a vice president of a big Madison Avenue firm and now consults with *Fortune* 500 firms and small businesses. Most public libraries carry the books, and we list the first title in our Appendix.

At the same time keep working on the quality of your services. Study and apply what you learn. Read books and trade periodicals. Get on the Internet and take a look at www.grounds-mag.com, www.turfpro. com, and www.lawnandlandscape.com. Take community college courses. Get an associate degree in horticulture if you are so inclined. Ask your suppliers about the characteristics of their products and how to get the best results from them. You will become more skilled and will enjoy doing a better job. Keep following up on prospects to be in the right place at the right time. Become the landscape service for each neighborhood you select.

Your business should reflect an image of enthusiasm and positiveness. You want to develop trust and inspire confidence in your ability and integrity. The customer can always hire the kid down the street if they only want their lawn mowed. You have to provide a better service and do a better job. If you strive for quality from the outset, your jobs will show it and you won't lose customers to the kid down the street.

Bermuda grass. (USDA)

The Income Journal
Receivables and Collections
The Expense Journal
Petty Cash
The Annual Summary
The Depreciation Record
Other Records
The Most Important Part
Further Reading

Chapter 6

Keeping the Books – A Stethoscope on the Business

Quick Start: *KEEPING good books for the business lets you know if the patient is well or dying. You must do it, but it's easy.*

It's simple to keep the books by hand: If you have a business checking account, your expense records fall right into place. Divide your expenses into categories on ten- to twelve-column accounting paper. You use a new sheet for each month. At the year's end add up the monthly totals for each column, setting aside accounts payable for the year. There are minor records like petty cash and equipment depreciation, but they are even easier.

Even this simple system will overwhelm you, however, once you get busy. Computerize your books or find an affordable bookkeeper as soon as you can. This chapter refers to some free IRS bulletins and a first rate small-business accounting guide that will get you over every hurdle. With a computer it's even easier and much faster. The important thing is to keep your books right from the beginning and not to fall behind; otherwise you will detest bookkeeping. And . . .

Record your truck mileage now!

MOST START-UP ENTREPRENEURS hate to hear about this subject, but it's one of the most important. *Before* you load up the truck and make your first call, you must have a set of books, or at least their beginning, to record your first expenses and receipts.

Your books are the business. You won't keep books just because the IRS and state income tax agency require information about your earnings (although they do and you must). You will keep books because *you* need the information.

Unless you keep good records, you won't have any idea of how well or poorly your business is doing. It could be bleeding money steadily until, inevitably, you go broke. You won't lose just the business, you could lose everything that you and your family own. You will look back and probably never know what hit you. With a complete set of books, however, you can adjust your prices and expenses, anticipate trouble, improve profitability, and make plans for future growth.

Although the bad news is that you have to keep a set of books at all, the good news is that keeping books for a lawn care or landscape maintenance company is very simple.

All you need for doing them by hand is a business checking account, five sets of simple records, and a 10-key printing calculator. These are "single entry" books, so you won't have to learn double-entry bookkeeping which takes a one-semester college course to learn. You could also keep your books on a cash, rather than accrual basis, except for minor adjustments at the end of the year. The process is diagramed in figure 6.1.

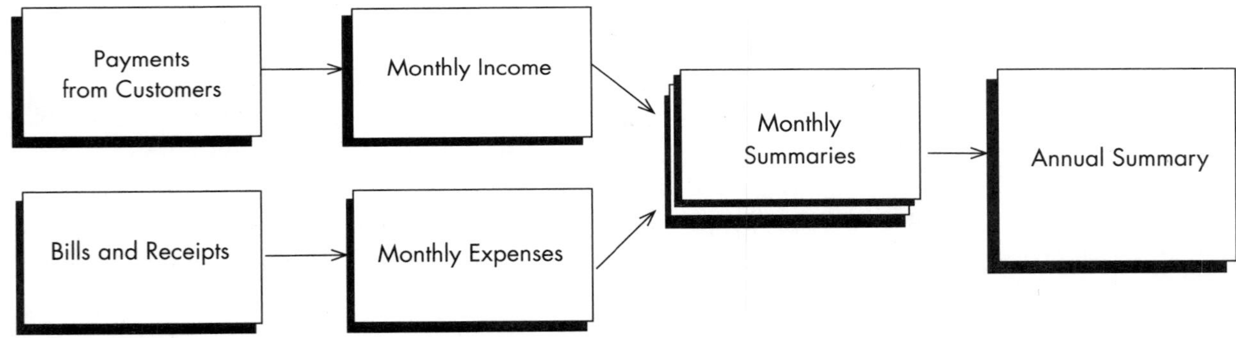

Figure 6.1. The accounting process.

Knowing the process is essential. Once you have about 30 customers, doing the books will be an overwhelming task. Buy a computer and learn to use a simple bookkeeping program, such as *QuickBooks®*, *M.Y.O.B.®*, or the like. I use *QuickBooks*. If you don't think you're ready for a computer or nobody among your friends or family is available to run one for you, look for a good affordable, bookkeeper. "Affordable" is the key. Bookkeepers charge a fair sum for their services. You may find you can't afford one. You can still do your own books to get started. Scan the system below. It will run the business, and it's a fair introduction to what computerized books do. Once you've spent a few evenings after a hard day's work at the books, you'll be eager to computerize. Meanwhile, here's the old fashioned way.

1. The Income Journal

Let's get basic. When customers pay you on the job, you will need to take a receipt book with you in the truck. You'd use a spring clip to fasten a manila envelope of the same size to the receipt book. If the receipts were not pre-numbered, you'd number them consecutively. Every time you were paid for a job, you'd write a receipt on one of those two-part receipts from the office supply store and rubber-stamped with your business name and address. You'd only stamp the customer copy, keeping the carbon or NCR copy in the receipt book. The cash or check from each job would go into the manila envelope, which you'd clip to the receipt book, and lock the book and envelope

INCOME JOURNAL

DATE		RECEIVED FROM	AMOUNT	
MAY	3	H. WILSON	25 -	
		L. JENSEN	18 50	
		MRS. BROWNING	42 50	
		L. + B. HARDWARE — REFUND	6 22	
		JOHNSON PROPERTY MANAGEMENT	136 -	
	5	SOUTH MAIN OFFICE PARK	200 -	
		R. BARTON	53 25	
		W. WALTERS	32 -	
	7	WARWICK PLAZA APARTMENTS	150 -	
		HARTLEY + SONS	74 75	
		A. BENSON	32 -	
		J. + A. PROPERTY MANAGEMENT	247 43	
		G. PETERSON	100 -	
		CAMPBELL / ANDREWS	42 50	
		TOTAL FOR WEEK		1160 15

Figure 6.2. The income journal.

in a safe place in the truck. At the end of the day you'd run a tape of your receipts (you still have the 10-key printing calculator) and compare it with the cash in the manila envelope.

Your income journal is a record of all your income every day. Figure 6.2 illustrates an income journal. There are columns for the date, customer name, and amount of payment. The amount of each receipt goes in the income journal. Mark each receipt as you enter it, so you don't count it twice.

You deposit the cash and checks in your business checking account the next day, or at least every few days. Never leave any money laying around so it gets mislaid, lost, or "raided." Do not tap into any form of income casually as it comes in. If you need money from the business, write yourself a check as a salary draw from the business account so that you'll have a record of the payment.

At the end of the month you add up all the daily receipts in the income journal for your gross monthly income. Then you start a new income page for the next month. And that does it. Collecting on the job does provide cash, but that's not reason enough to do it much beyond start-up.

1(A). Receivables and Collections

Simple as the above cash system seems, I prefer and recommend billing at the end of the month. Most people *do not* want to be bothered with paying cash on the spot. They dislike the interruption. It's one more reason why they don't hire the kid down the street. Many who pay cash will want to chat with you. Others will spend time searching for their checkbook then writing the check. I bill at the end of the month with the dates and monthly costs. I enclose an address envelope to speed up payment. On the bill I include "Payment due in full by the 10th of the month." It's easy and painless. My customers like it.

This chapter will illustrate monthly billing by hand. Computers are made for it, believe me. For customers that you bill monthly you will have "accounts receivable." An account receivable is money a customer owes you. A few days before the end of the month send out your billing statements. As customers pay their bills, enter the money in the income journal. Until you actually receive the money as income, you will need a secondary accounts receivable file. Keep it in a manila file folder. Keep a ledger sheet inside the file folder with the name of the "charge" customers and how much each one owes you. The accounts receivable ledger sheet has columns for "Customer Name," "Month," "Amount Due," and "Date Paid." As your customers pay you, line out the information, writing when they do under "Date Paid," and transfer the amount to the income journal. See figure 6.3. (I do this with Microsoft *Works*.)

You will also keep copies of the monthly bills you sent to each customer in the accounts receivable file folder. The bill should include the customer's name and address, the billing date, the kind of service performed and materials supplied, your charges for them, any overdue payments owed, and a brief statement of your billing policy. Transfer the paid bills to a storage file. If a customer hasn't paid last month's bill you will have to staple it to the current bill or the previous bill or bills.

ACCOUNTS RECEIVABLE

DATE	CUSTOMER NAME	AMOUNT DUE	DATE PAID
APRIL 5	JOHNSON PROPERTY MANAGEMENT	~~136 –~~	5/3
6	WARWICK PLAZA APARTMENTS	~~75 –~~	5/7
7	SOUTH MAIN OFFICE PARK	~~100 –~~	5/5
	CAMPBELL / ANDREWS	~~42 50~~	5/7
8	CRAIN COMPANY	75 –	
	R. DOUGLAS	42 50	
13	WARWICK PLAZA APARTMENTS	~~75 –~~	5/7
	J + A PROPERTY MANAGEMENT	~~100 –~~	5/7

Figure 6.3 The accounts receivable ledger.

Keep 'em moving - Don't let your customers fall behind in their payments. It makes your bookkeeping harder and can be a source of bad feeling between you and the customer. You might want to encourage prompt payment by offering a discount for payment within a certain time and a late charge for failing to pay by some time after that. Some invoices that state "2/10, net 30," which means a two-percent discount for payments received in ten days, with full payment due in 30 days.

30-DAY LETTER

Dear :

Our records show that your outstanding balance with our company is $_____ for lawn care services that we provided to you in July and August 2000.

If you have a problem with our bill, please telephone so that we can settle it. Otherwise, please pay the stated amount now to bring your account current. I have enclosed a stamped reply envelope for your convenience.

Until your account is current we will provide you further services for cash only.

Yours truly,

60-DAY LETTER

Dear :

Your bill for $_____ is long overdue. It is for lawn care services we provided to you in July and August 2000. We sent you our statement over 60 days ago, but you did not respond to it or to last month's reminder.

We value you as a customer, but you must pay your account in full if you want us to provide any more services. Paying now will help protect your credit standing.

Please send your check today for the full amount. Otherwise, call me as soon as possible to discuss an alternative payment plan.

Yours truly,

90-DAY LETTER

Dear :

Our books show that your account has a 90-day-old unpaid balance of $_____ for lawn care services that we provided to you over 90 days ago.

You have ignored my repeated calls and letters. If you do not pay this bill in full or contact me by December 1, 2000, I will turn it over to collection.

As you know, collection will damage your credit rating, and under our agreement you will have to pay all collection costs, including any attorney fees. Please call me, and let's try to work this out instead.

Yours truly,

Figure 6.4. Collection letters.

You could add a notation that a 1% or 1½% late charge will be added for charges not paid on time. This is a 12% or 18% annual interest rate, so you should check to be sure this policy will not conflict with your state's usury law. Also be careful about how large a discount you can afford.

Be firm with customers who don't pay on time. You will probably see them on the job. That is the time to ask them if they are having a problem with the bill. If the customer is not at home when you usually work on the yard, try to schedule the job for a time when you can see the customer. Otherwise, telephone and see what the problem is and if you can work out a solution.

Collections - If customers don't pay despite your best efforts you will have to take stronger measures. Figures 6.4 to 6.6 are collection letters you can use or adapt to suit your situation. Sometimes a letter from an attorney, which most attorneys will write for a very small fee, will shake the money out of a customer. If worst comes to worst, you can put the bills out for collection or bring a small-claims action to collect.

Your policy should be to spend no unnecessary time trying to collect money. Payment in advance is a great way in theory to reduce collections, but a lot of customers don't like it and won't give you their business if you insist on it. If you can't get paid in advance, the next best practice is to keep good customers and dump slow-pays fast.

Bad checks - Occasionally you will get a bad check. Telephone the customer and try to straighten out the problem. If the customer keeps bouncing checks, call your bank for advice on how to handle them. All states have bad check laws. You should familiarize yourself with your state's law in case you need to recover a penalty for a bad check. Go to a law library or consult a lawyer for information about the law in your state.

2. The Expense Journal

Expense records are very simple. Since the business checking account will be used to pay for nearly everything including your salary, you could almost use your check register for your expense journal. It would not be easy, however, to scan it for an idea of what your major business expenses are.

Tracking expense categories - The expense journal gives you a way to track expenses by listing major expense categories in columns across the top of a ledger sheet. Ledger sheets are available with between two and 25 columns. You will find them in all sizes at office supply stores. Most have a narrow column on the left for entering the check number or date, a wide space for listing the payee. You may want to enter the date in the narrow column under the check number and double-space the payees. You could enter an invoice number under the payee's name. A number of narrow columns for entering dollars and cents follow across the rest of the sheet. Above each column is a space to write the category of expense. Probable categories are "Amount," followed by those set out in IRS Schedule C: "Advertising," "Vehicle expenses," "Insurance," "Interest," "Legal and professional services," "Office expense," "Rent," "Repairs and maintenance," "Small tools and supplies," "Taxes and licenses," "Utilities and telephone," "Miscellaneous" or "Other," and, as mentioned before, "Non-deductible."

Set up like this, your books supply the information necessary to complete Schedule C of your federal income tax return. You may put some items into "Miscellaneous" or "Other." See figure 6.5.

EXPENSE JOURNAL

DATE	PAID TO	1 AMOUNT	2 ADV.	3 OFFICE	4 REPAIRS	5 SUPPLIES	6 UTILITIES	7 OTHER	8 NOT DEDUCT	9
JAN 4	FARM SUPPLY #714	52 38			12 50	39 88				
4	NEBS, INC (FORMS) #715	31 50		31 50						
4	SHOPPING GUIDE #716	23 –	23 –							
6	PACIFIC TELEPHONE #717	42 23					42 23			
6	CITY OF Y.B. (BUS. LICENSE) #718	27 –						27 –		

Figure 6.5. The expense journal.

Most of the columns are self-explanatory. You will probably want to use your own categories and change them once you have a feeling for which expenses need a separate category. The "non-deductible" column is for recording expenses that are not tax deductible, like personal draws of salary and parking tickets. Interest on business loans is a deductible expense, but repayment of principal is non-deductible. You will want your lender to provide you with an amortization table to show how much of each payment is interest and how much pays off principal.

Every time you write a check to pay a bill, enter the check number, payee's name, date, and the amount of the check in both the "Amount" column and the column or columns for each applicable category. Because one check may pay for different expenses, you can split the payment into as many appropriate categories as necessary and use the Amount column to confirm the correctness of your figures. At the end of the month, total the payments made in each column. When you do your monthly expense totals, you can check them for accuracy by comparing the sum of all expense columns with the sum of the "Amount" column.

Paid bills - Keep all your paid bills in a folder. When you write a check to pay a bill, write the check number on the bill. By writing the date on the bill you can pick out one month's bill from similar ones more easily. If you ever need to claim a credit or you have some complaint about something you purchased, you will need the bill or invoice to make your claim.

SAMPLE MONTHLY PROFIT & LOSS STATEMENT

```
Income . . . . . . . . . . . . . . . . . . . . $_________

Expenses
   Advertising . . . . . . . . . . . . . . .$
   Vehicle expenses. . . . . . . . . . . .
   Insurance . . . . . . . . . . . . . . .
   Interest and bank charges . . . . . . .
   Legal and professional services. . .  .
   Office expense. . . . . . . . . . . . .
   Rent. . . . . . . . . . . . . . . . . .
   Repairs & maintenance . . . . . . . . .
   Small tools and supplies. . . . . . . .
   Taxes and licenses. . . . . . . . . . .
   Dues and subscriptions. . . . . . . . .
   Utilities and telephone . . . . . . . .
   Depreciation (vehicles & other) . . . .
   Other (Miscellaneous) . . . . . . . . .

Total Expenses . . . . . . . . . . . . . . . $_________

Salary              $_________

Profit              $_________

Gain (or loss)                                $_________
```

Figure 6.6. Profit and loss statement.

Profit & Loss - Your income and expense journals will let you prepare a simple profit and loss statement at the end of each month. These statements let you analyze the exact condition of your business, make forecasts, and consider what steps are needed for improvement. Figure 6.6 shows a simple profit and loss statement. Notice that it includes an entry for depreciation. Being able to set aside a portion of income for depreciation lets you create a special expense account for building up money for new equipment as your old equipment wears out. You must include depreciation to calculate true overhead. Do not leave it out! We discuss the Depreciation Record below. Finally, notice that all you get for salary and profit are whatever is left over after deducting for all overhead expenses. Consider that an incentive to hold down costs.

3. Petty Cash

Handling petty cash is simple. Write a check for $20 or $50, whichever seems adequate, enter it in the "Miscellaneous" or "Other" column, and put the cash in an envelope with a sheet of paper that has columns for item, date, and amount. You can make this sheet yourself. You will probably carry the envelope in the truck with you locked up like the receipt book. Every time you pay for something from the petty cash envelope, write the information on the sheet and put the receipt in the envelope. There are some purchases for which no one will give you a receipt. Write your own receipt on whatever scrap of paper you have, including the bag the item came in or its wrapper. When you are low on petty cash, run a calculator tape of the receipts. If the tally doesn't give you $20 or $50 when added to left over cash, don't worry about a small discrepancy, just make an adjustment. You shouldn't have a large error if you keep your receipts. Then, staple the receipts to the expense sheet and tape, and store them with your records. Write a check to bring the petty cash back to $20 or $50, and put the money in the envelope with a new sheet.

4. The Annual Summary

The annual summary is taken from the total of monthly income and expense journals. You only do this once a year for taxes. It brings all income and expenses up to date. Post the twelve monthly totals for the appropriate columns to their counterparts in the year-end summary sheet. Record all expenses *whether paid or not*. Mark each unpaid expense bill "ACCOUNTS PAYABLE" and enter those amounts in the year's expenses. Next year, when you pay these bills, you will see the ACCOUNTS PAYABLE notation and put them in the "Nondeductible" column.

Add up the "Amount" column and all the other columns, then check that the sum of the other columns equals that of the Amount column. Record depreciation expense from the depreciation record to deduct from your taxable income. Happy new year!

5. The Depreciation Record

This is a list of equipment for which you will claim a proportional loss of value as an expense against income every year you use the equipment. Because the IRS lets you spread the expense of a new truck over five years, you'd charge one-fifth of its cost as an expense for each of the five years if you use a straight-line (S/L) depreciation method. You may want to consult a bookkeeper or a tax preparer for how to depreciate your long-term equipment. You wouldn't depreciate an existing truck, but instead would claim a standard mileage deduction (32.5¢/mile in 1999) for each business mile recorded from the beginning of the tax year. (Have you recorded your starting mileage yet?)

This list is essential for valuing your business's assets. If you sell the business, the buyer wants to know the value of its assets. If you need a loan, the lender wants to know what will secure it.

Figure 6.7 shows a simple depreciation record from Internal Revenue Service Bulletin 583 (*Taxpayers Starting a Business*), which summarizes the tax records the IRS requires. The IRS doesn't require any special kind of records. Those shown above are perfectly adequate, in that they're suited to the business and will state your income clearly.

Property	Date Put in Service	Cost	Section 179 Deduction	Balance for Depreciation	Recovery Period	Method	ACRS %	Depreciation Prior Years	Depreciation for Year
Lawn mower	1/4/00	$840		$840	7	S/L			$120
Office furn.	1/4/00	$350		$350	7	S/L			$ 50

Depreciation for year $170

Section 179 Deduction

Total Depreciation for Year $170

Figure 6.7. Sample depreciation record.

I do all of the above with *QuickBooks*. It's easy and fast, and it's designed to set up your books for you. If you're still hesitant, you can sign up for a course at your local community college or learn on-line at ed2go.com. *QuickBooks* lets you see profit and loss reports and the percentage of money spent on each expense category. It also helps prepare your taxes. I have never used other small business accounting programs, and you may wish to speak to others about their experience with them.

Other Records

Customer records - Once you do more than lawn mowing, you will have to keep records on other maintenance tasks for each customer. You need a calendar to remind you when to do each task, and a *record* that you did it. You don't want to do a job twice and you don't want to miss it. Each account needs a manila folder with basic information about the customer (name, address, and so on), notes about the property and landscaping, site plan, contracts, payment records, tasks scheduled for the property, and a checklist of tasks completed. It will also contain any correspondence, notes on telephone conversations, and everything else about your dealings with the customer.

When you transfer customer tasks from your records to the master calendar you will see that similar tasks bunch up seasonally, as they should. It's convenient. On the other hand, you;ll be doing so much of the same thing you won't be able to keep mental track of which sites you have and have not yet serviced; so keep the records. We take this up again in Chapter 8, on managing the business.

Vendor and supply lists - There are other items on which you ought to keep records. Keep vendor and supplier lists, and inventories of supplies in addition to an equipment depreciation schedule. Your list of vendors will have their names, addresses, telephone numbers and pertinent information about how they do business on 3 x 5 or 4 x 6 cards. You won't deal with every vendor often enough to remember its services or where you found it. You'll want to know whom you dealt with, company policies and the kind and quality of its products.

The Most Important Part

Don't get behind. Enter income and expenses into these records on a daily or other frequent basis, so that the entries don't pile up and become a chore. Remember that the more you do something the easier it gets. These are all the records you need for your ordinary income and expenses, unless you have employees.

If you expand the business and hire employees you will need a separate employee compensation record for each employee. It records the number of hours each employee works in a pay period and the employee's total pay for the period. You record Deductions withheld to show how you computed net pay. You'll also record monthly gross payroll, which will be carried to the Annual Summary. A brief discussion of the deductions to be made appears in Chapter 7, "Getting to be the boss." *QuickBooks* will do this for you. So will some bookkeepers, although most dislike payroll and refer it to specialists.

Further Reading

Those are the basics. If you need to know more about what underlies business bookkeeping and the tax system, there is no better place to start than with *Small Time Operator*, by Bernard Kamoroff, C.P.A., (Laytonville, CA, Bell Springs Pub. Co., 5th ed, 1997). The system outlined above was developed in part from Kamoroff's book. When last we checked, it cost only $18.95 and it will pay for itself far beyond that price. The above system was also developed using IRS Publication 583 (*Taxpayers Starting a Business*). All IRS publications on operating a business are free. That includes the IRS "big book," Publication 334 (*Tax Guide for Small Business*), which covers everything you need to know about federal income taxes. You can order them by telephoning 1-800-424-FORM.

Between *Small Time Operator* and the free IRS manuals, you will be able to develop an efficient, economical system of records for your business that can tell you everything you need to know about it. Furthermore, you won't have to ask a bookkeeper how your business is doing. You will know it completely from the records *you* built it up on. Or you can get a computer and do it with a lot less effort. Your choice.

Regardless how large or complex your business grows, it's important to keep the bookkeeping as basic as possible. If business reaches the point where it won't stay basic, consider the expense versus the advantages of using a bookkeeping service or accountant. Even with a service you should keep the basic numbers and let your numbers person crunch them. Never let yourself get separated from your income and expense figures. Bookkeepers often will set up a program for you to keep daily records that you can give to the bookkeeper every month. Then periodically you and the bookkeeper can review them.

Final words about taxes - Every business, including your own, must estimate and submit quarterly taxes to the IRS, and usually to the state taxing agency, by the 15th of every January, April, June, and September. There are penalties for late payment and underpayment, and there is no grace period. If you are unsure how this works, contact your regional IRS service center and ask for help.

Keep all your records for at least three years, which is the time in which the Internal Revenue Service may inspect them. The Appendix contains a list of how long you should keep many records.

Advertising and Interviewing

The Paperwork

Training

Firing

Enough Is Enough

Chapter 7

GETTING TO BE THE BOSS – GROWING WITH EMPLOYEES

Quick Start: *AS a quick-start reader, you aren't an immediate prospect for advice about employees. All you need to know for now is that if you pick up some part-time help when you get busy, your state and federal governments may consider you an employer for tax purposes. So, be careful. If you can't be careful, read on. Employees make your business at least twice as complicated as it was.*

DO ALL YOU CAN ALONE. First, by working alone you retain complete control of the business and the quality of the work. Second, becoming an employer means exponential growth in your paperwork—along with repair costs, insurance, and aspirin intake.

If you want to expand your business, however, you will need help. Go slow, look for the best employees you can find, and train them well. They will be what your customers see of your business.

There are no rules for what makes good landscape maintenance employees other than their diligence, reliability, enthusiasm, common sense, ability to follow directions, and the physical ability to do the work.

Hiring part-timers may be enough to begin with. One advantage of part-time employees is that when one leaves you can substitute another without disrupting your schedule too much. If you need only part time help, students are excellent candidates, especially for simple tasks that require little training or experience. If there is a local college in your area get to know the right departments, like landscape architecture, agricultural economy, business, and so on. Sometimes you can participate in student internship programs. Also consider older people.

They may already have the skills you want. They tend to be reliable workers and often want only part-time employment. Just make sure part-timers work full days, because time spent setting up and breaking down for a few hours' work is not profitable. Also, be careful, because hiring just a few part-time employees, even once in a while, can make you an employer for tax and other purposes.

Advertising and Interviewing

The best way to find employees is by word of mouth. You may know someone in the business or in a related one who is cutting back staff and has to lay people off. You may even know of a good employee who already works for someone else. It's all right to make that person a job offer.

You may have to hire through help wanted ads. List your business telephone number. Describe the work clearly in the ad. Be sure you describe the work as accurately as possible to each applicant, and don't make any promises beyond what the job has to offer.

If you get employment application forms at the office supply store, check to be sure the questions don't violate the federal civil rights laws. If any space to be filled in might suggest the applicant's race, color, national origin, religion, sex, marital status, age, or certain medical conditions, you had better cross it out. If there is a good reason why you need to know the information, such as an applicant's ability to do the physical labor involved, you may be exempt from the prohibition. Some states have additional civil rights protections, so you should contact the appropriate state agency. Just as a matter of courtesy, you should treat every applicant with consideration, not merely be conscious of legal rights.

Have the applicant sign the bottom of the form for checking on references. Always check an applicant's references carefully because some applicants "exaggerate." Listen for what the references do *not* say about an applicant. These days many employers are wary of being sued and won't come right out and speak ill of a former employee.

Make the job interview as comfortable for the applicant as possible. Take your time and talk about everything you think is appropriate to the job. Hire on the basis of ability, enthusiasm, and experience, in approximately that order. If you can't get an experienced applicant, hire the one with the ability and enthusiasm to do the work. You can follow up with on-the-job training. Don't discuss pay until after making an offer. To protect yourself, hire for a probationary period. And don't make the job "permanent" even after the probationary period.

It's a good idea to jot down short notes about what happened and what was said during the interview, whether or not you hire the applicant In fact, keep notes about all personnel transactions in case problems arise later. Store them with the rest of your records for at least four years, or longer.

The Paperwork

When you plan to become an employer contact the IRS for Form SS-4 to get an Employer Identification Number (EIN) and telephone 1-800-424-FORM for a free copy of publication 15, *Circular E, Employer's Tax Guide*. Also get W-4 forms for employee tax withholding and, while you are at it, a supply of W-2 forms. Before January 31 of the following year you must send one W-2 to the Social Security Administration, keep one for your records, and give the employee three copies.

You will need to set up a payroll sheet for each employee and comply with all the state and federal laws, rules, and regulations that apply to employers. This means carrying workers' compensation, either through your state or a private insurer, and complying with Occupational Safety and Health Administration (OSHA) regulations, with the Immigration Reform and Control Act (IRCA), and with the Fair Labor Standards Act (FLSA). You will have to pay for unemployment insurance and for half of your employees' social security. You'll need to buy and post employee information posters in a prominent location in your business. You will also have to comply with the following.

Hold your hands together and form a cup. That cup will only hold all that you yourself will ever be able to earn . . . Now add another person's hands and your earning capacity in-creases: More hands, more potential to earn more.

—*Andy Dicky, Cabinet Maker, the Author's Customer*

- **OSHA**. To maintain safe working conditions, the Occupational Safety and Health Administration, a division of the U.S. Department of Labor publishes minimum standards for each industry and inspects workplaces. It is very unlikely an OSHA inspector will ever come calling. Unless you are in a high-risk business, you will be exempt until you have ten or more employees. The agency publishes a self-inspection checklist that will help you spot hazards on the job. Write to OSHA for more information, including its checklist at OSHA, U.S. Department of Labor, Washington, D.C. 20210. Employees' have a right under OSHA to know about the health hazards of all chemicals, not just pesticides, that they work with. Train them to use chemicals safely. Obtain and keep written Material Safety Data Sheets (MSDS) available for employees to inspect, both at the shop and on the job, by putting it in the truck when they use the chemical. You can contact the manufacturer for a product's MSDS. It is faster, cheaper, and simpler to get a copy off the Internet. If you lack access or a friend who can get one for you, see if your public library will assist you. The best source for MSDS information appears to be the Cornell University Planning, Construction & Design site, which has abut 325,000 MSDS files. See http://MSDS.PDC.CORNELL.EDU (capitalized). If that appears to be too general to work, try again, adding "/issearch/msdssrch.htm" as an extension (not capitalized).

- **IRCA**. You and every employee you hire must fill out an INS Form I-9. The federal Immigration and Naturalization Act permits you to hire only U.S. citizens and aliens who are permitted to work here. For compliance with the Act you must review documents like birth certificates, drivers' licenses, social security cards, passports, visas, naturalization papers, and green cards. You must decide whether the documents are genuine and then record the evidence of your compliance on Form I-9. The form's instructions take you through the steps of filling it out. Each employee's Form I-9 must remain in your records for at least three years, or one year after a longer term employee leaves. Contact the nearest INS office or telephone 1-800-777-7700 for publication M274, its "Handbook for Employers."
- **FLSA**. The Fair Labor Standards Act sets the minimum wage and the standard work week, and determines overtime pay. There is no restriction on anyone over 16 years of age working more than 40 hours a week, but the act requires compensating at time and one half for work exceeding the standard work week. What exceeds the standard work week is fairly complicated. This is a special problem where you may have to reschedule crews for jobs interrupted by bad weather. Here also, you should contact the U.S. Department of Labor, Washington, D.C., 20210, about the application of the Act.
- **FUTA.** You must also pay federal unemployment tax on each employee and file it with an IRS Form 940 or 940 EZ if: (1) you paid $1,500 or more in wages in any quarter of a year or (2) had (a) at least one employee for (b) part of at least one day of (c) 20 different weeks in a year. The tax is calculated on the employee's first $7,000 of wages during the year, and any state unemployment tax is credited to your federal tax liability.
- **FICA**. You pay your portion of your employees' social security taxes directly and withhold the employees' equivalent portion from their gross pay. These are reported on Form 941.

  Refer to IRS Publication 15, *Circular E, Employer's Tax Guide*, which contains the withholding tax tables for figuring the amount of social security and federal income tax to withhold. See also Publication 937, *Business Reporting*.
- **Workers' Compensation**. All states require employers to carry workers' compensation insurance. The laws vary from state to state, and you should contact your state agency for details. As a sole proprietor you can't cover yourself with workers' compensation, but a partnership or corporation may elect to provide you with coverage as a partner of the partnership or officer of the corporation.

All of this may seem complex and forbidding, but if you need help to run your growing business, learn it and do it. Otherwise hire a bookkeeper at least part time to do it for you. Many bookkeepers dislike working with payroll information, but there are chain payroll services that specialize in it for reasonable rates. Let your bookkeeper worry about that if you already have one.

Do *not* ever pay your help in cash under the table. You won't really know the meaning of misery until the feds find out and go after you and your employees for fraud and tax evasion. It only takes one disgruntled ex-employee to blow the whistle.

Hiring, Training, and Firing

Once you have employees, keep them motivated by paying them a good wage, training them so they understand the work, and giving them all the responsibility they can handle. We include a job description in the Appendix. First, don't pay just the minimum wage unless you want minimum results. Second, employees have to understand a job to do it the way you want it done; so take the time to train employees so they understand each task. Third, employees with reasonable responsibilities and a chance for advancement are less likely to feel trapped in a job with no future.

Check with your local department of employment for wages for similar work in the area. The U.S. Department of Labor publishes wage rates for most jobs. If a living wage in your area is $8.00 an hour, pay $8.00 per hour. Some employees may be worth a higher wage, some less; but adjust their wages up or down from a reasonable level. When you hire for a probationary period you can pay a lower wage, but make clear it's temporary.

Quality. You must be sure your employees understand the importance of quality work. If they don't know what it is, and do it, that kid down the street will get the job. Out of about 100 employees—not applicants!—I have found only three who understood what "quality" meant and took pride in their work. That's what matters; that's what to look for in an employee.

Poor training will cost you in the form of employee turnover and lost business. Hold workshops, use videos, pay for extension and college courses, and encourage employees to pursue certification. The off-season is the best time for training, but don't neglect learning on the job. Reward training with better pay and more responsibility. It will reward you with satisfied clients, a stronger company, and more business. Motivate employees by praise, helpful criticism, bonuses, recognition, crew prizes. Peer pressure from a close-knit group is always a good motivator.

If you anticipate having a lot of employees, put together an employee handbook. Keep it simple. It should summarize rules, procedures, and standards of conduct and safety. It can list company benefits and routine things like work hours, pay, fringe benefits, vacations, travel reimbursement, grievance procedures, and discharge. There's an example in the Appendix.

Hold regular employee evaluations at least once a year. Tie them to company policy, job performance, and company goals. Keep evaluations a positive experience—a way to praise and encourage good employees and a gripe session. You could learn a lot from it. You can also prevent bad habits from becoming major problems. Be sure to put everything in writing. It's a way to keep a paper trail if you ever have to fire an employee. (See our evaluation sheet, Figure 7.1.)

EMPLOYEE EVALUATION

Name______________________________

Date:______________

1. Safety awareness ______
2. Productivity ______
3. Use of time ______
4. Quality of work ______
5. Customer satisfaction ______
6. Following directions ______
7. Initiative ______
8. Judgment ______
9. Problem solving ______
10. Equipment care ______
11. Equipment use ______
12. Work ethic ______
13. Company image ______
14. Reliability ______
15. Communication ______

Excellent = 4; Good = 3; Average = 2; Poor = 1; Unacceptable = 0.

Figure 7.1. These suggested categories for employee evaluation have worked for us. We don't advise averaging the ratings. They are to help guide your judgment.

Beware of employee "burnout," which used to be called boredom and overwork. If you take an interest in your employees, you will be watchful for any change in attitude or productivity. Don't let an employee's work problems slide by. Catch them early and try to resolve them. Watch out also for pilfering, false time sheets, and corner cutting. Make phone logs, equipment sign-out sheets, and other security devices a part of company policy before there is a problem.

If you need to fire someone, be as careful about it as you were about hiring. Lawsuits for wrongful termination are becoming more common these days, and even small businesses get zapped. It is not as great a problem in this business, where there are seasonal layoffs. When you have to fire someone, however, be sure that you have a good reason for it, that it is clear you hired that someone as an "at will" employee, and that you never made any promises or suggestions about tenure with the company. Make sure to document everything leading to the discharge and fire when someone else is present.

You should hold a fair hearing with the employee before dismissal. Keep it cool and unemotional. Use facts and the written record, don't let feelings get in the way, and never fire on the spot. When you're steamed up, send the employee home if you have to. Then meet later after things have cooled off. Make a record of every meeting, especially this one, and give the employee a copy.

Well-trained employees could become partners—or competitors—so treat them with the respect they deserve. The other half of the bargain is to set out clear company policies—see our sample in the Appendix—and insist that everyone complies with them. If you do that—in fact, if you do all of the above—you will have the kind of business other people find is worth working for.

Enough Is Enough

How many employees are enough? That's up to you. Some business people feel they have expanded too much when they become administrators and lose touch with the work that got them into the business in the first place. Others enjoy finding new challenges. Recognize the problem and watch for it. Then decide for yourself.

With two or three employees, depending on the stage of the gardening season, you can run several jobs at any given time and rotate among the crews. With more employees you might find yourself in the office more than you wish. It depends on if you want to spend only part of the day out on the job while increasing your income.

This brief chapter should make it clear that being an employer is a mixed blessing. There is no clear choice except to do what works best for you. If you're seriously considering hiring, we recommend that first you read Fred S. Steingold's *Employer's Legal Guide*, listed in the Appendix.

Customer Relations

Scheduling

Follow-up

Murphy's Law & the Weatherman

Controlling Costs

Insurance

Investing in Knowledge

Diversifying

Chapter 8

MANAGING – KEEPING IT ALL AIRBORNE

Quick Start: *WHEN you get customers do everything you can to keep them satisfied. That will get you even more customers to satisfy. A computer will ease your burden here too.*

Keep customer records carefully so that you do all the jobs they hired you for as scheduled. A master calendar will help you organize your jobs.

Keep your calendar flexible to adjust for bad weather, breakdowns, illness, and other mishaps. Good practice today may require a shift away from straight weekly mowing, making flexibility even more important.

Keep track of costs, inventory, and the condition of your equipment. Carry insurance, including liability and disability coverage, and an umbrella policy for any excess liability.

Keep learning about the business by reading all you can about it, talking to others in the business, taking classes, and joining trade associations.

ONCE YOU MASTER THE SKILLS and techniques of running the business, you have to combine them to manage successfully. This means not only good record management but scheduling jobs, ensuring quality work, maintaining good customer relations, and supervising any employees.

Customer Relations

Many businesses just stumble along or falter because they fail to recognize the value of a satisfied customer. A customer is not only a source of income today but of potential income tomorrow, from that customer and everyone the customer recommends you to. If you do your work well and provide the quality promised, you can anticipate almost a geometric progression from one customer to two to four to eight, and so on. As your business begins to prosper in this way you will find that the work seems to get easier and more satisfying.

When you open a new account, set up a customer record with all the information you need for handling the account. It's useful to keep customer accounts in 8½" x 11" file folders because they provide plenty of room for writing information about the customer and job. Your files should contain the customer's name, address, telephone number, the job location, a billing address, a description of the work, how long the tasks take, the starting date, frequency of services, and miscellaneous items like directions to the site, special plants or problems, notes taken from work, etc. The file folders should also contain any written estimate and bid. In time they make up a customer history.

When you are starting out, 4" x 6" cards and a file box may be sufficient for your records. When you must expand into the larger format later, switch *all* the accounts to a permanent system, which could be the 8½" x 11" files, so you aren't running two systems at once. You can staple the cards to the inside of the folders. Even better, get that computer and work with it.

Scheduling

Whether you have employees or work alone, careful scheduling is critical to managing well. Different landscape maintenance tasks have always had to be done at different intervals over the contract term. Weeding may come every other week or once or twice a season. You may fertilize monthly for southern grasses in the growing season, or only two or three times a year in the north. Seasonal tasks such as fertilizing, pruning, spraying for pests and weeds, leaf removal, and the like will continue to run on their own long-term schedule. And although lawn mowing typically has been a weekly task, there has been a growing tendency to vary mowing according to seasonal grass growth rates.

The once-a-week timetable may have to give way to bunching up and spreading out mowing with the growth cycle—to mulch-mow and keep cuts to ⅓ of leaf-height. (See Chapter 13's discussion.) If so, you'll have to think about scheduling seasonal tasks so they help even out your workload. Cutting grass once a week simplifies billing over a seasonal contract. We mow every 14 days unless the customer specifies otherwise. In spring and summer we mow every seven to 12 days. That's for our grasses in our climate. We've set up this book's estimating section (Chapters 19-21) on a standard weekly schedule. Billing for varied mowing won't be as easy. Ideally, the total number of mowings would not change over the contract term but there's no guarantee of that. To learn whether the total will increase or decrease in the average season, you might begin to vary mowing intervals gradually for a few years until you get a feel for them. In the process you'll have to make sure not to mow too many lawns for free while not short-changing the customer, either. To complicate things even more, yearly weather variations may upset your best-laid schemes.

Basic scheduling requires a master calendar and a weekly or daily list of each day's tasks and customers. The weekly list is a worksheet to take along for consultation. The list would include extra tasks like fertilizing, weeding, pruning, and so on, based on a seasonal schedule for filling in planned or unplanned gaps. The master calendar could be a wall calendar large enough to list each task you will do each day in the season. You can transfer master-calendar information onto the weekly sheets. With the right software you can schedule accounts daily or weekly.

The best time to calendar a job is when you analyze and estimate it. In the past scheduling could be confusing enough. It becomes more complex if you abandon a strict weekly schedule. By creating a season-long schedule for each job as you get it, however, the jobs will build up the layers of work that create your employment for the year. You'll interweave and integrate the tasks for efficient use of your time and equipment. It will never be like punching in and out with a local employer where you do the same thing every day. Some days may be much longer and others much shorter than eight hours. You may work six-day weeks during the busy season. This is the trade-off for your "dormant" winter months. You'll have to create your own work year. And you'll have to get used to it and learn to live with a fairly complicated, changeable calendar.

Here is one way to do it. As you analyze and begin to estimate a new job, look at the master wall calendar (even with a computer it helps to put things on paper) and write in the tentative dates for doing each task on your worksheets for a new customer's job. If you get the job, these will probably be the dates you'll enter in the customer file and on the master calendar. Each customer file will be reflected in the master calendar.

You want jobs to be easy to get to in order to cut down travel time. The neighborhood you work doesn't have to be close to you, but ideally all the jobs in it should be reasonably close to each other. If you work several neighborhoods, you would bunch up jobs in each for the same day or days. I save Fridays for book work. If a job comes up, I do the job on Friday and the bookwork gets done at night.

Selecting dates for extra tasks can be tricky. You may want to schedule them for the day you do the customer's regular work or, if it requires special equipment, you may do the extra task for all your customers in one neighborhood. That takes experience, planning, and judgment. Don't worry. When you're on the job, all your abstract scheduling becomes a real yard. You'll recognize its needs and see how your calendar system works. It will help coordinate the schedule. Above all, stay flexible right from the beginning. It's all right to change things when the time comes, as long as you don't forget and leave something out.

If you have to rent equipment but are unsure about getting it, leave some slack in the calendar in case you have to re-schedule. It's best, anyway, to check a few days ahead of time to see if the equipment will be available. Slack in the calendar is not all bad, although it may seem to be when you start out. As your calendar gets tighter, you will gain experience scheduling. It is something you have to play by ear and get a feeling for. Take your time, build slowly.

Subcontracting out specialized tasks is usually a good idea, and it is profitable. It gives the customer extra services at no cost to you. You should add a reasonable fee for bringing the sub to the site. If you've hired contractors yourself, you know that simply arranging for the work takes effort and often patience. Know your subcontractor. Learn all you can by word-of-mouth. Check references. Confirm reliability, the quality of work, insurance, and required licensing. Subcontracting can also complicate your careful planning, so flexibility pays here, too.

If the customer accepts your bid, enter mowing dates and each extra task's date on the big master calendar. (Even if you don't mow weekly, chances are everyone's mowing date will be at the same interval.) Use a pencil and—computerized or not—keep a large eraser tied to a string next to the calendar. You can change your print-outs, but using a pencil and eraser is cheaper than re-printing every time. Each week, enter the irregular tasks and mowing dates, on the daily or weekly list. Be sure to cross off each irregular task in the customer file as you do it. Review customer files regularly to be sure you are doing all the work.

There are specialized landscape maintenance computer software programs, such as CLIP (Clip.com, 800-635-8485), which start at $249 and go up to $3,000. I use Microsoft *Works*, which I had to customize but costs less than $100 and is often included with a new computer.

Follow-up

If you have employees, you will have to check the quality of their work. Contact the customers periodically to see how satisfied they are with the results. If you don't have employees, schedule an occasional walk-through together to see how satisfied the customer is and whether the work is improving the landscaping. It's a chance to educate the customer and see how you're doing. Make a note on the customer records of when you last checked the work or contacted the customer, as well as what you observed and discussed.

When you get customer complaints be positive. Try to solve the problem and get the job back on track. If you get a complaint on your telephone answering machine, call right back and keep calling until you reach the customer and work out a solution. Let's assume that when you lose an account it is not because of the quality of your work. It shouldn't be if you follow these procedures. Thank the customer for the job and state that you will be available to provide high quality service in the future.

Murphy's Law and the Weatherman

Be prepared for accidents and delays before they happen. When equipment breaks, a back-up, sometimes even a hand tool, will get you through a job without slowing down your schedule too much. If you have to do any digging or subsurface work, be prepared for buried pipes, rocks, concrete, roots—anything that can interfere with the time you allotted for the job. If a key employee is out sick or injured, have a plan to work around the absence temporarily. Managing means creating enough flexibility to absorb brief setbacks and dislocations.

If something can go wrong, it will.
—*Murphy*

The less you want it to go wrong, the likelier it will.
—*Rossi, seconded by Willis*

Planning your jobs and keeping a close eye on the calendar, as well as the weather report, is critical to managing a landscape maintenance business successfully. Try to leave enough flexibility in your schedule so that when the weather is not too bad you can put on rain gear and prune, rake out beds, haul refuse, or do other work. You build in this flexibility by working up a list of tasks that you can do anytime except during downpours, and sell the jobs to your customers as a task to be done at sometime within a contract period. Keep a separate list of odd jobs and which customers want them.

When the weather interrupts your schedule, rearrange it by telephoning your scheduled customers and setting up another time, unless the appointment is so routine they won't notice or mind. Your schedule should have enough looseness to let you catch up once the weather clears. While you are on the telephone ask your customers if they are satisfied with the service, or have any complaints or suggestions.

When you absolutely cannot get out on the job, use the time to catch up on your office work, check out, and maintain equipment. If it is a long spell of bad weather, and the office and equipment sparkles, drive around to check up on jobs assigned to employees. Or relax. You deserve some time off.

Controlling Costs

Estimating and bidding - A successful bid gets you the job and covers costs, profit, and salary. If you find yourself making a lot of bids, keep a record of them and how many are successful. The record should show the type of job and the figure quoted. It should have space for follow-up information, including whether or not the bid was accepted. You won't bid successfully on every job, but you should get a feel for your average after a while. If you're getting all your bids, you're bidding too low. Once you have a record of each bid, you can track their performance and adjust accordingly. If you begin to get more jobs than your average, you might be bidding too low, or, if your acceptance rate falls, you might need to cut costs. If your price seems to be in line, the winning bidder may have underestimated. Follow up lost bids by asking the customer why you lost it or just to see if the job is up for bid again soon. Anyway, be sure to write and say thanks for the opportunity to bid and that your charges are based on giving quality service. Be sure to read Chapters 19 through 21 on estimating and bidding so you understand the process and the importance of estimating.

Tracking purchases and operations - Keep a record of the cost of supplies, along with a record of suppliers. If you purchase supplies by mail, keep the catalogs and refer to them often. "Bookmark" suppliers you use on the Internet. Keep a record of what you pay local suppliers, either in the supplier record or in a record of your supplies. Keep a record of what you charge customers for the supplies to help determine whether you are marking up correctly.

Keep close track of the costs of running the office, including utilities, telephone, insurance, taxes, supplies. Also count expendable work items like gloves, tools, and incidental materials.

As mentioned before, since you are keeping records of income and expenditures, monitor your cash flow regularly. Get rid of slow paying customers and keep costs in control. You are in business to make a profit.

Keep your overhead low. As you make money, invest it in the business to make more money. Don't waste it trying to impress customers with your office or new trucks; high quality results will impress them more.

Insurance

Business insurance is for risks that are not problems for individuals, especially those who work for someone else. You won't be eligible for unemployment insurance and should insure yourself as the source of your own income. If you're injured and can't work, income stops, and medical costs make the need for coverage all the greater.

Whether you operate out of your home or own or rent business premises, you'll want comprehensive coverage against fire, theft, and vandalism for the business and its assets. Also, if operating out of your home, check to make sure your business activities don't jeopardize your homeowner's insurance. If they do, get insurance that will take care of you and your family, and the business.

Standard business coverage should cover your basic business needs. It usually includes public liability insurance and casualty insurance on your business vehicles and any commercial space. Look into insurance against loss of income and business interruption, which a standard policy doesn't cover. And it's worth inquiring about insurance against possible claims for toxic materials released accidentally on customers' premises if you apply pesticides. You can lower your premiums by having a higher deductible. Later, as your profile rises in the community, there's a greater chance of becoming the target of some legitimate or illegitimate claim. Most insurers offer umbrella coverage for claims that exceed other policy limits. The extra sum needed for an umbrella policy could in time be well worth the money.

If you have employees, state law will require you to carry workers' compensation insurance. It covers only employees for work-related injuries. The premium for workers' compensation coverage is based on total payroll expenses and the kinds of work performed. California recently deregulated its program, and we can shop for the best workers' compensation rates. See what your state does.

You'll need expert help for insurance. Salespeople will offer prepackaged products they will say meet your needs, but you're better off consulting an insurance *broker*, who gets a fee rather than a commission based on sales. A broker is likelier than a salesperson to give you an unbiased analysis of your insurance needs and will then take a flat fee for getting you the best deal available. Check the Yellow Pages.

Investing in Knowledge

Invest in yourself as well as in equipment. You have to know what to do with your tools. Take classes. Read the trade magazines. Use the public library. Look for the latest books at suppliers' stores. After reading everything you can, go back and read it all again with a critical eye. And keep up with new developments in techniques, equipment, supplies, plants, and design trends.

Get a 3-ring binder. Take notes, cut out articles and ads. If you're on-line, you can read and download information from scores of state agricultural college websites. Divide your binder into subjects like equipment, pruning, fertilization, and plant identification. If you don't know the plant, you can't possibly do your job. Write down what you hear from others in the business. Put anything in the binder that catches your attention. See what works and what doesn't. And leave lots of blank space for revision. Throw out the bad advice. The point is not to make binders full of horticultural information but to systematize your knowledge. You need a record of what works and what does not. Memory alone is not reliable enough.

If the local vocational school or community college gives courses in landscape maintenance or horticulture, sign up and take the courses. There is no end of learning this business. You have to learn if you want to be good. If this sounds like you are back in school, you are. As you acquire the knowledge you will notice yourself getting better and you will become more confident of your skill and the value of your services. Talk to others in the business, and join trade associations. This is one part of the business that you cannot afford to neglect. If you have employees and they show a willingness to learn, help them by paying at least part of their tuition for classes.

Diversifying

Once you are up and running, and you want to do a little more, you could consider diversifying. Before adding anything, think very carefully about exactly what you like about the work. You might find lawn care and landscape maintenance completely satisfying, as well as profitable, without adding anything to it. New tasks or specialties should grow naturally out of what you like best. Landscape contracting involves construction, some of it major, and you may have no interest in it at all. It also involves licensing, regulations, usually filing reports, often working under general contractors, and being very careful about the rules and fees. If none of this bothers you, you may decide to do it because you enjoy creating a landscape from scratch even better than maintaining it.

Profitable and less regulated sidelines include indoor plant rentals and maintenance, hauling, or exterior maintenance—including parking lot clean-up and striping, leaf and snow removal—even swimming pool maintenance. If you own or can rent a few acres cheaply away from the center of town, a small nursery operation could help augment your services with replacement plants. A composting business goes hand in hand with gardening. If you have access to even more land, with a good sandy loam, you may find sod production suitable. Always be sure to check with state and local authorities about licensing for any of these sidelines. Lawn aeration is a specialty all its own. Your town may be too small to support a lawn aeration business alone, so you might add that as a profitable service. For more information see the book on this subject by Robin Pedrotti listed in the Appendix. The professional organizations listed in the Appendix can provide information about some of these specialties, and there are usually informative books on most of them in a good public library.

Expand the business gradually. Control growth the same way you control costs. Remember that the best employees do not work as hard as the boss, so don't set yourself up to carry the burden of too big a business. Set a good pace and make the business an enjoyable as well as profitable experience.

Italian or perennial ryegrass. (USDA)

Basic Procedures

Clothing and Work Gear

Watch for Pests

Use Safe Tools and Equipment

Chapter 9

SAFETY – WORKING SMART, STAYING ALERT

Quick Start: *THIS chapter on safety is short. It is also very important. Read and learn it all.*

SAFETY ON THE JOB will save you pain, money, and possibly your business. An accident can cost you lost work time. It will cause loss of customers if you can't keep up your services, and loss of your business if you're permanently disabled. If you are insured and don't take reasonable precautions, your insurer could refuse to pay for an injury. It is just poor economic sense not to take every safety precaution you can. Chapter 13 on mowing discusses proper use of the lawn mower; Chapter 18 on pest control discusses safe use of chemicals. Here are a few words about other safety practices.

Basic Procedures

Safe work habits are essential. Safety gear won't protect you completely if you get careless running a lawn mower or other power tool. Learn to recognize your physical limits and don't use power equipment when you're tired, on medication—or intoxicated. Come back to finish a job later or on the weekend rather than risk an injury.

Have a good waterproof first-aid kit in your truck. If you need to treat someone else's cut or wound, do it wearing fresh rubber surgical gloves, then remove and discard them carefully wrapped, without touching the used surface. Blood-borne viruses like hepatitis C and HIV are serious and incurable threats, and the skin surface of hands is invariably broken and a potential entry for disease. If you're in an area with poisonous snakes, get a snake bite kit. Know where to find the nearest source of emergency medical care.

Carry a multi-purpose fire extinguisher. If you use gasoline powered equipment, fire is always a possibility. If you are in brush country, fire is a community hazard. Make sure your engines have spark arrestors. It's the law in some areas.

Watch out for vehicles when you load and unload equipment in the street. Don't count on the driver seeing you. If you are working in or very near a street or highway, wear an orange safety vest.

If you have to dig deeply, check in advance with the local public works department or utility companies for buried lines.

Clothing and Work Gear

Although careful work habits are essential, everyone makes mistakes and machinery breaks. Wear safe clothing, starting with heavy leather footwear with steel or Kevlar inserts in the toes and boot tops, and treaded soles that grip. A pair of shoes costing $100 or $150 could save you thousands in medical bills and lost work. Wear sturdy long-sleeved shirts and trousers.

Take precautions against sunstroke and heat exhaustion when the weather is warm. Wear loose clothing for good air circulation and drink plenty of liquids. A broad brimmed hat shields against ultraviolet (U-V) rays, and fair-skinned people should also use a sunscreen lotion. Tropical "pith" helmets shade well and let air circulate over the head.

Get a good pair of U-V blocking polychromatic glasses that adjust to the sun's brightness. Wear them all the time. Scrambling around among bushes is a continual threat to your eyes. Wear ear plugs if you are using noisy equipment such as backpack leaf blowers that sit up on your shoulders. Federal OSHA mandates ear protection for noises greater than 90 decibels; but don't go by the manufacturer's rating, wear effective expandable foam ear plugs anyway. You're around noise all day. While leaf blowing and string trimming, also wear safety glasses with side shields or goggles and possibly a dust mask.

If you do a lot of lifting and bending get a back-support belt to reduce the risk of lower-back injury. A bad back can end your gardening career quickly and permanently.

Watch for Pests

Learn to recognize poisonous plants in your region. Some are regular garden ornamentals. Every part of oleander plants, for example, contains a deadly poison. Ask the local poison control center for a list of poisonous plants. The poison center's telephone number is often listed in the front of the directory near the "911" information.

Learn to recognize and avoid your local variety of poison ivy, oak, or sumac. You can pick up their resin from tools, clothing, and pets, as well as direct contact. The entire plant contains the resin year around. Its effects are seldom fatal, but it is a leading cause of lost workdays nationwide. If you touch it, the best and simplest first aid is to flush the spot with gallons of cold water. That seems to neutralize the reaction a little. You can also daub off some of the resin with an organic solvent like paint thinner, gasoline, or nail polish remover for up to four hours after contact. They're as effective as a leading patent "poison-ivy remover" and cheaper. An over-the-counter blocking treatment, Ivy Block Lotion® from EnviroDerm Pharmaceuticals, has tested very high for keeping the resin off the skin.

If you have ticks in your area, they carry diseases. Some are incurable, as is Lyme disease if not treated early. Wear light colored clothing to see insects more clearly, and tuck your pant legs into your socks to block entry to the skin. Look for an insect repellent that repels ticks. Follow the label directions for applying it. Some repellents are applied to shoes, clothes, and exposed skin. Follow the directions for how often to reapply and check for bites at the end of the day.

Use Safe Tools and Equipment

Don't use damaged or worn out tools. Fatigue is the first step to an accident; defective tools hasten it. Dull blades will slow your work and tire you, as well as do a bad job. Broken handles can cause injuries; so replace either the tool or the handle. Power tools should have a keyed lock if possible. Disconnect the power cord from electric tools and the spark plug wire from gasoline engines before working on moving parts.

Use only ladders that are in good condition. Keep metal ladders away from power lines. A three-legged orchard ladder adjusts to uneven ground; make sure each leg is on firm ground and will not sink in, causing the ladder to tip. Ladder rungs should be evenly spaced. If necessary brace the ladder so it won't slip. Place it as close to your work as possible, so you don't lean or stretch out too far. Do not stand on the top rung.

Farm and ranch supply stores sell good outdoor work clothing, as do contractor-supply and industrial-equipment stores. We list mail-order safety outfitters in the Appendix. Many tools and much protective gear bear certification notices granted by testing organizations such as OSHA, ANSI (American National Standards Institute), and NIOSH/MSHA (National Institute of Occupational Safety and Health/-Mine Safety and Health Authority). Look for these certifications and ask what they mean when you shop for tools and equipment.

By putting safety first, you are much more likely to have a long, happy, and healthy gardening career.

Buffalo grass. (USDA)

Part III

Horticultural Concerns

Soil Texture and Structure

How Soils Nurture Plants

Water in Soil

Tillage for Better Structure

Chapter 10

SOILS – BUILDING THE GOOD EARTH

Quick Start:

SOIL is the earth's thin layer of decomposed rock in which billions of microscopic plants and animals per cubic foot have been living and dying for millions of years. It is very complex material that you have to understand in order to know how plants grow.

The rock particles are classified in size order from sand, the biggest, down to silt, then clay. Sand is too porous and clay is too fine for most plants to thrive in. The best mix, called loam, is mainly silt, with the remainder clay and sand. Moist loam contains organic matter that forms small clumps and bits that let in air to the roots but hold water. Like animals, plants die without air and water. Loam also has the best water-holding capacity; it's the soil of choice. There should be about 25 to 50 percent by volume of organic matter in good soil.

Clay and the organic matter form molecular structures called colloids. Colloids keep water from leaching the nutrients out of the soil before the plant can get to them. Colloids have a negative electrical charge that attracts and holds all the soil's dissolved nutrient particles, which have positive charges. The plant then trades its positive hydrogen particles for the positive nutrient particles attached to the colloids.

Soils can be acid or alkaline, measured according to the "pH" scale of 0 to 14. Most plants want soils around the neutral band, near pH 7. If the hydrogen ions from the roots build up, the soil gets acid, which eventually kills plants. If your soil is acid, which is common in the eastern U.S., or anywhere with heavy rainfall and sandy soil high in organic matter, you must add lime now and then to sweeten it. Alkaline soils in dry parts of the West need gypsum or sulfur and organic matter to neutralize them or they will kill plants, too. Labs will test for pH, but you can buy an inexpensive kit to do the job.

YOU need to understand soil to understand gardening. Soil is the thin layer of finely worn rock and organic matter covering the earth that supports all plant life. A soil's quality depends on its parent rock, the weather, surface water, the resident micro-organisms, and how long all of them have been working together. Soil changes continuously. A poor one can be improved and a good one depleted. How a soil begins and how it is treated will determine whether the plants growing in it will be vigorous and healthy.

Soil Texture and Structure

Texture - Most soil contains different sized decomposed rock particles classified as clay, silt, and sand. Clay is the smallest particle, sand is the largest. A soil's texture depends on how much of those different particles it contains. The perfect balance of clay, silt, and sand in a soil is called "loam," a loose, crumbly mixture that contains no more than one-quarter clay, with the rest silt and no more than half sand. Figure 10.1 illustrates the relative sizes of sand, silt, and clay.

Although only a laboratory analysis can measure a soil's textural mix accurately, you can gauge it by hand. Soil with a lot of sand feels gritty. Wet clay soil has a smooth, plastic feel and keeps its shape when you squeeze a handful of it. In-between mixtures feel less gritty or less slick. A fistful of good soil should hold together when wet but crumble easily.

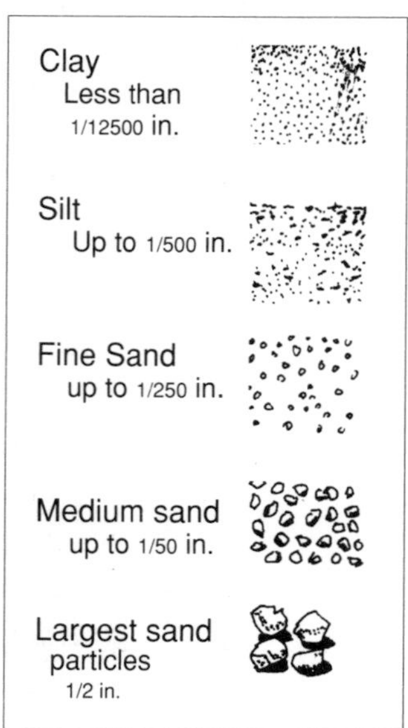

Figure 10.1. Size of soil particles.

Structure - A soil's structure, how it holds together, depends on its texture. All moist soils clump together more or less. Good soil structure, that of loam, contains clumps between the size of large beans and buckshot. The large pores between the clumps let excess water drain out, while air flows in, and the small pores hold onto water for the plants to use. Well structured soil will contain about 50 percent solid material, 25 percent water, and 25 percent air.

If soil gets compacted by heavy machinery or years of moisture and gravity, it won't have enough spaces for water and air, and very few plants will grow in it well if at all. That's because plant roots need to breathe. They give off carbon dioxide and absorb oxygen. Compacted soil slows the passage of carbon dioxide and oxygen through the soil. Too little oxygen or too much carbon dioxide in the soil will stunt a plant's growth or kill it.

Letting in air, water and nutrients - A clay soil has a dense, compact structure, with little space for air, and, if too wet, will drown a plant. Adding gypsum to neutralize an alkaline clay soil breaks it up temporarily by altering molecular structure. Many respectable texts tell you that adding sand, perlite, vermiculite, or calcined clay will lighten a clay soil. If you don't also add organic matter, however, what you get is a sort of clay-concrete.

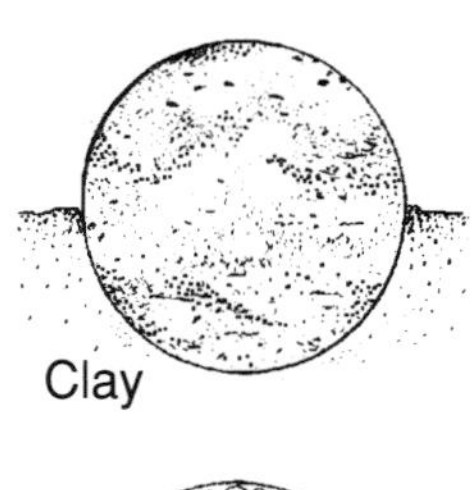

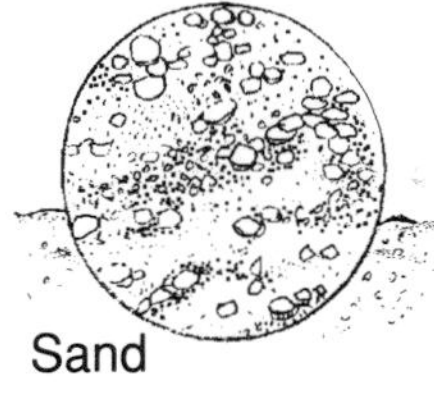

Figure 10.2. Soil structure.

For a more durable result, it's better and cheaper to add organic materials to loosen a clay soil. These organics include peat, well-rotted sawdust, straw, peanut shells, or rice hulls. Peat moss is expensive but takes almost 25 years to decompose. You should add a small amount of nitrogen fertilizer with these materials to help soil microbes break them down.

Organic matter makes the difference between a productive soil and a sterile layer of pebbles and dust. Good garden soil contains 25 to 50 percent of organic matter mixed finely with the rock particles. To keep this balanced soil, you need to add fresh organic materials in the form of plant residue from time to time. The added organic material not only provides food for soil fauna like earthworms, it is also dinner for the micro-organisms that break down and feed on the organic compounds. They store some of the compounds in their bodies. When they die they decompose and give off nitrates, which are nutrients that the plants can absorb. If the soil lacks oxygen, these good aerobic micro-organisms are replaced by anaerobic micro-organisms that take nitrates out of the soil. That is another reason why a good soil structure needs to have space for air.

As with all things use organics with moderation. Too much of it provides a home for pests that dine on seedlings as well as on rotting plants. Partly rotted vegetation can harbor harmful fungi and other pests. Unrotted manure contains weed seeds, and harmful ammonia and other salts, even dangerous bacteria. One excellent material is mushroom compost, which contains old mushroom parts and the partly used manure they grew in. Often you will see ads for bulk mushroom compost in the classified ads of your newspaper.

How Soils Nurture Plants

Cation exchange - This is complicated but worth it: Plants absorb nutrients by a micro-electric chemical exchange.

Humus and clay have molecular structures called *colloids*, which are the chemically active part of soils. Plants absorb nutrients in a soil-water solution that coats the colloids. Clay colloids are crystalline, while those in humus have no particular shape. Both are negatively charged, or *cations* ("cat-EYE-ons"). When water dissolves nutrients in the soil, the nutrients' positive ions attach to the clay and humus colloids. This electric bonding, keeps water from leaching the nutrients from the soil. Nutrients leach quickly out of sandy soils with little clay and humus. Plant roots, looking for food, exchange their positive hydrogen ions for the nutrient ions in the clay and humus colloids. This process is called *cation* exchange. The upper 1 to 2 feet supply about half of plants' nutrients and moisture, mostly from the upper 6" and progressively less from the layers lower down.

If hydrogen from the roots builds up in the soil, it becomes acid. This hydrogen build-up can be lowered by adding bases like calcium, magnesium, or sodium to the soil to keep it neutral or alkaline. Most soils in the eastern United States are acid and must be amended with lime now and then to sweeten them.

pH: How sweet it is - Acidity and alkalinity are measured on a "*p*H"* scale of 0 to 14. A *p*H of 7 is neutral, numbers less than 7 are acid, and those above are alkaline. Most plants grow best between *p*H 6.0 to 7.5. Some like azaleas and rhododendrons prefer acid soils—down to 5.5. An alkaline *p*H, common in much of the western U.S., can be lowered by adding a sulfate or gypsum and organic matter to the soil. (Unlike most people in the American west, we're in a coastal rain belt with acidic soil.) Adding pure sulfur to form a sulfuric or sulfurous acid takes skill to avoid over-acidifying the soil. Also, don't try to adjust the *p*H without first having the soil's complete chemical mix tested, as we discuss in the next chapter.

Water in Soil

Water is the most important environmental factor to deal with in this business. Sunlight and temperature are reasonably predictable, but water almost alone will determine what goes into a garden and how it prospers. For much of North America, water is becoming a scarce commodity. It is not a good sign that the U.S. has approached Canada about importing water—or that Canada doesn't think much of the idea. Many of us are beginning to recognize that future gardens will require drought resistant species in *xeriscapes*—dry landscapes—which we discuss briefly in Chapter 16. Even if you and your customers want traditional turfgrass and shrubs, proper irrigation will be central to good practice.

Begin now to think about drought-resistant grasses and irrigation programs for every customer and try to begin educating them. Probably few people in your region water their turf or surrounding gardens economically—or give it much thought. Timed sprinkler systems usually are set for a brief shower every few days. It wastes water and produces fragile, thirsty plants.

Soil is a reservoir for plants and can be the key to hanging on to the lush traditional garden most people want. Topography, surface cover, and soil structure govern how much water enters and remains in the soil. To supplement natural precipitation—rain, sleet, snow—we apply water artificially to wet the top 6" to 12" of root zone. How much water the soil keeps is up to you; it won't stay put. Plants lose

* This symbol measures the concentration of hydrogen ions as gram-atoms per liter of soil. It's a "negative logarithm" and it works for acidity and alkalinity.

water by transpiration, part of the process that moves nutrients to plant leaves and helps cool the plant. Water also leaves the soil by evaporation. Together this is "evapotranspiration." The two halves of good water conservation practice are to pick non-thirsty plants and to slow evapotranspiration. Mulches, which we also discuss in Chapter 16, will help slow evaporation. For lawns, aeration—punching small holes in the turf four to six times a year—decreases soil compaction, and improves water retention and drainage. New developments in turfgrass promise hardy, drought-resistant lawns. Sloped topography benefits from terracing if possible. But soil texture and structure determine how much water infiltrates the soil reservoir and is available to the plants in the first place.

Holding available water - Soil is "at the wilting point" when plants take so much water from it that they wilt. The amount of water in the soil between "full" and the wilting point is called its *available water holding capacity.*

The soil's structure, texture, and organic content determine its available water holding capacity. Sandy soils hold the least total water. Clays hold the most, but so tightly they won't give a lot of it up. They are slow to absorb it, too. The intermediate loams, however, hold the most *available* water. Most loamy garden soils can store about 1" to 2" of available water per foot of soil depth. The soil to aim for emulates the characteristics of good loam. If the soil lacks it, consider a program to improve its texture and structure for better water holding capacity.

How much water is enough - Gardens and lawns usually require about 1" of water a week when they are growing actively; a good soaking once a week replenishes the supply better than a lot of light sprinkles. This figure is an average that depends on how temperature, wind, etc., affect evapotranspiration. Most lawn and garden sprinklers apply about ¼" of water per hour. To learn the exact amount, put out straight-sided containers at increasing distances from the sprinkler and measure how much each collects. Ideally, you would time watering at a given rate, then dig into the soil to test for moisture penetration.

If water does not drain from the soil to let air in for the roots, dig it up and lighten it with amendments when replacing the plants. In the worst cases, the landscape may need drainage tiles. Design and installation of a tile system requires the technical services of a tile specialist or landscape contractor.

Tillage for Better Texture

Garden soil should be tilled in late fall or early spring by turning it over and working it by spade or a rototiller. Tilling mixes oxygen and plant remains into the soil and loosens compacted areas. Soils with good structure and already high in organic matter can be lightly tilled, just enough to cover the plant remains. Soils with infertile subsoils and compacted layers should be tilled as deep as you can go, digging in plenty of plant remains and nutrients. Tilling poor soils deeply creates a good root zone full of water and nourishment. It will probably also lower watering needs.

Tilling clay soils when they are too wet or too dry, makes large, dense clods. Dig up a handful of clay and squeeze it. If it crumbles, it is right for tillage. Fall is the best time to till. If the ground freezes where you live, fall tillage permits freezing and thawing to break up the clods even more. Unless you mulch the soil afterwards, however, you should avoid fall tillage where wind and water erosion are problems.

Blue grama grass. (USDA)

Chapter 11

FERTILIZING – HOW TO BUILD A PLANT

Quick Start: *OVER time plants never get enough nitrogen, phosphorus, and potassium from the soil, so these are called the primary plant nutrients. A balanced fertilizer has all three. Numbers like 10-5-5 on the bag mean that it holds 10 percent nitrogen, 5 percent phosphorus, and 5 percent potassium by weight. There is absolutely no standard for a suitable lawn mix. Every brand promotes its own balance. Usually, nitrogen will be the highest element, so that proportions like 5 or 6 parts of nitrogen to as little as 1 or 2 of phosphorus and 2 of potassium may be a good mix. We use 16-16-16. Elsewhere 18-6-2 or a 3-1-2 mix may be common. Your choice will depend on what works in your area.*

Once you arrive at a blend that works, you'll want to apply the right amount of nitrogen per 1,000 square feet (SF). The U. S. Department of Agriculture's fertilizer recommendations for different grasses are in pounds of nitrogen per 1,000 SF. You can calculate how much mix that means. Or you can follow the instructions on the bag. Either way, too much fertilizer is as bad as too little.

The mix should include iron, magnesium, and sulfur as secondary nutrients. Compare brands for trace elements, as well.

Select a fertilizer with at least 50 percent slow-release organic or synthetic organic nutrients (W.I.N for water insoluble nitrogen) on the label. It is less likely to burn the leaves and works over a longer period. Spreading a mix of low potency 10-5-5 blend evenly over a lawn is easier and safer than spreading concentrated 20-10-10, and doesn't cost much more.

THIS chapter is only an outline of how fertilizers improve plant growth, about how the different elements make plants healthy, and about how and when to apply fertilizers. Consider it a beginning. You will have to read more and talk to people in the business—nurserymen, extension agents, farmers—to improve your understanding of how to fertilize plants properly in your area.

What Makes a Fertile Soil

Fertilizer isn't plant food. A plant's only "food" is the solar energy it absorbs and uses to photosynthesize the minerals from fertilizer, soil, and the air into cellulose and carbohydrates. That's why most plants do poorly in shade; even shade-tolerant plants need sunlight. And photosynthesis—using the sun's energy to make living tissue out of minerals—is something no animal can do. It's why we all depend absolutely on plants for survival.

Fertilizers aren't a substitute for good soil, either. Soil is the medium or matrix in which photosynthesis drives the chemical exchange. You need good soil for an efficient, economical exchange of chemicals.

As we said in the previous chapter, a soil with good physical traits can retain and release the full value of the nutrients and minerals you put into to it. A *fertile* soil needs a balanced supply of nitrogen, phosphorus, potassium, calcium, magnesium, sulfur, and trace elements, as well as nearly one billion micro-organisms per cubic foot, to support the best plant growth. In the absence of one or more of these qualities photosynthesis falters, weakening the plant.

Scientists have concluded that there are 17 elements essential for plant growth. These are, in order:

1. Carbon
2. Hydrogen
3. Oxygen
4. Nitrogen
5. Phosphorus
6. Potassium
7. Calcium
8. Magnesium
9. Sulfur
10. Iron
11. Manganese
12. Copper
13. Zinc
14. Boron
15. Molybdenum
16. Chlorine
17. Cobalt

Plants take oxygen and carbon from the air. Microbes or chemical fertilizer manufacturers first fix atmospheric nitrogen in soluble compounds for plants to use. Plants get the other fourteen elements from the soil.

Nitrogen, phosphorus, and potassium are called the primary plant nutrients because farmers and gardeners have found there is never enough of them in the soil for the plants. Thus, good practice is that a "balanced" fertilizer's main ingredients are those three chemicals. A fertilizer bag labeled 10-10-10 contains 10 percent by *weight* each of nitrogen (N), phosphorus (P) and potassium (K).

Nitrogen

Nitrogen (N), the first number you see on a bag of fertilizer, is primarily responsible for plant growth and color. Adding nitrogen to plants has the most visible effect on plants. Too little of it causes yellowish leaves and weak roots. Too much, however, can make a plant over-succulent, turgid, and soft because of thinner cell walls. This makes it susceptible to cold, drought, disease, and pests. Plants lose nitrogen to competition by weeds, use by microorganisms, leaching, and volatilizing. Nitrogen comes in organic, synthetic, and "synthetic organic" formulas. It's the cheapest plant nutrient and buying combined fertilizers by the amount of nitrogen in them permits tailoring soil enrichment to specific plant needs. It also means a better price for the customer and a better profit for you.

Phosphorus

Phosphorus (P)—the middle number on the bag and an important part of DNA, RNA, and some enzymes—assists the plant's energy system and respiration, and plants can store it for later use. It shows up naturally in some soil minerals, and inorganic and organic compounds.

Ground rock phosphate can be applied as a fertilizer, but it dissolves slowly and may not help plants grow unless the soil is acid enough to turn it into phosphates. Superphosphates, first produced in England in the 1840s, were the start of the commercial fertilizer industry. Triple superphosphate is made by soaking rock phosphate with phosphoric acid. It works as well as ordinary superphosphates and costs less to produce.

Potassium

Potassium (K)—the last number on the bag and the third major plant nutrient—does not become part of the plant but regulates its life processes. It is a catalyst for water intake, transpiration, and enzyme actions. Plants need it to form and transfer starches, sugars, and oils. It also increases plant vigor and disease resistance. Most soils contain potassium but it is usually unavailable and is best added before planting and regularly after that. Adding too much potassium, however, can cause a magnesium deficiency, especially in sandy soils.

There are rich natural deposits of potassium chloride, called muriate of potash, that need only mining and purifying to make a cheap, high-quality plant nutrient.

Secondary & Trace Elements

Calcium, magnesium, and sulfur are called the secondary nutrients because, while important, there is usually enough of them in the soil, or they get added with soil amendments, so there is less need to include them in fertilizers. Calcium is important to cell construction and growth. Magnesium—it's in epsom salts—is the central part of the *chlorophyll* molecule, which makes plants green. It also seems to stimulate bud breaks in some shrubs. Sulfur works with nitrogen to build protoplasm for plant cells. Iron, zinc, and manganese may have to be added as *chelates* ("KEY-lates") of those elements for plants to absorb in low-rainfall, alkaline-soil regions. Chelation joins an element like iron to a non-nutrient to make it more available. Iron is essential for producing chlorophyll and gives plants a deep green color. Plants seem to need manganese and zinc to use the other nutrients. Often the so-called inert ingredients of chemical fertilizers contain some of these secondary and trace elements.

Soil Amendments

"Soil amendments" refer to minerals like lime, sulfur, or gypsum added to alter some chemical or physical soil trait. Amendments may also supply a few nutrients like calcium, magnesium, and sulfur. What matters is not the amount of plant nutrients in a soil but the *available* nutrients. What most affects the availability of nutrients is whether the soil is acid or alkaline. Normally, to adjust acidity and alkalinity, we add soil amendments.

The last chapter introduced the term *p*H to express the concentration of acid or alkaline ions in soil. The range of *p*H is from 0 to 14. A *p*H of 7 is neutral, with a lower *p*H representing an acid soil and one above 7 being alkaline. The USDA has graphed nutrient availability at different *p*H levels. See illustration 11.1. Soil acidity alone will seldom kill plants, but very acid soils can release enough aluminum or manganese ions to kill them. An acid soil may also corrode roots, lowering the plant's ability to absorb nutrients. Acid soils usually are also low in phosphorus. To counter high soil acidity, gardeners have to dig limestone and phosphatic fertilizers deeply into the soils. When you add lime to soils, the calcium in it replaces the hydrogen the soil particles absorbed from plant roots during cation exchange. That "sweetens" it.

As noted in the last chapter, a soil's cation exchange capacity, which depends on having sufficient clay and humus colloids, controls how well the soil can store nutrients and exchange them with plants. Soil *p*H determines how much of each element is *available*. Therefore, before beginning any program of fertilizing you must consider the soil's structure, organic make-up, and *p*H.

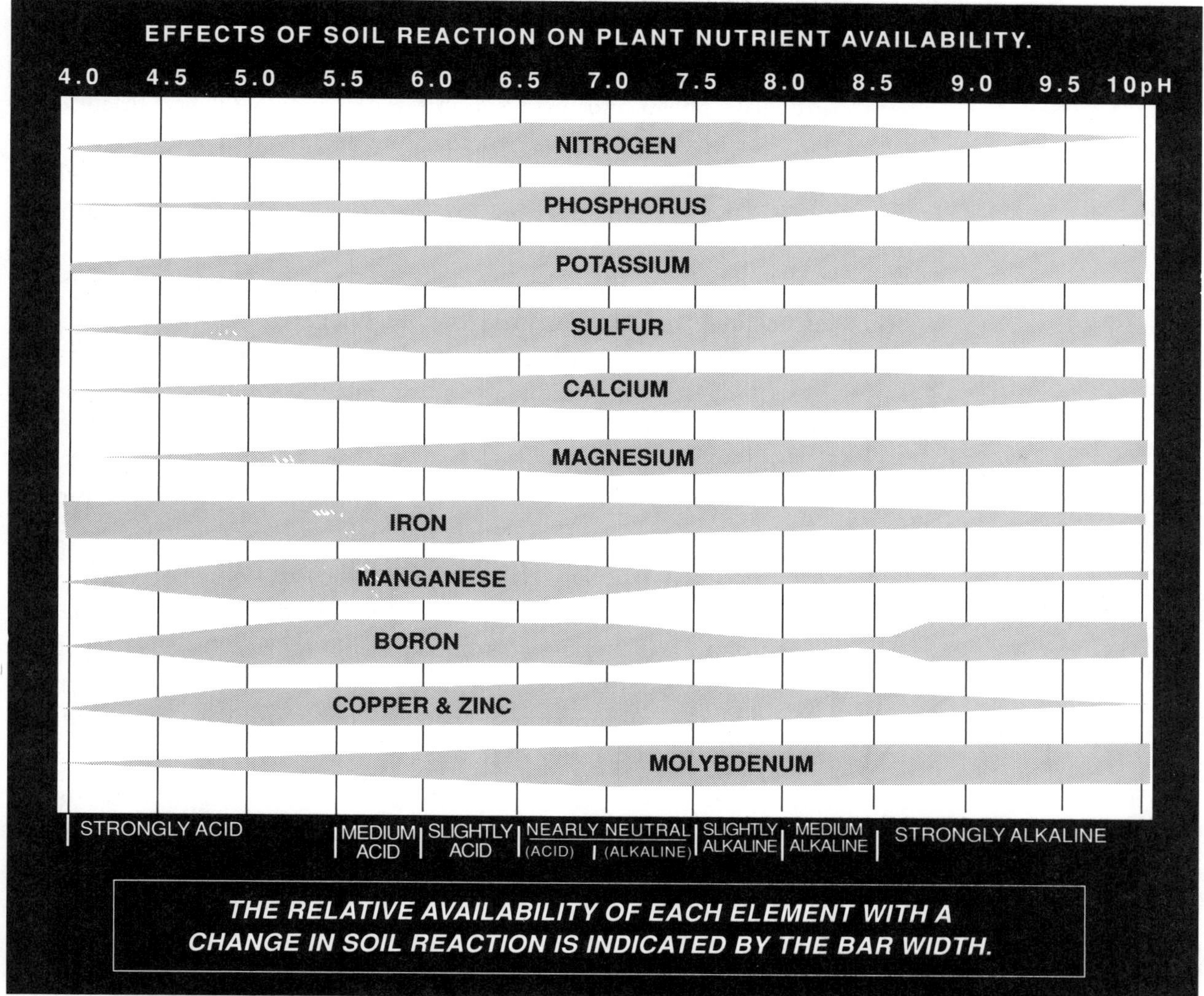

Figure 11.1. Nutrient availability at different *p*H levels. (USDA)

Maintenance Fertilizing

Fertilizing presents three problems: (1) When to apply fertilizer, (2) which to use, and (3) how much to apply.

First, fertilize when the plant is growing and needs it. A strong dose of nitrogen when a plant is dormant is wasted and applying it too late in the season could expose tender new growth to damaging frost conditions.

Selection of fertilizers - There is a wide choice of fertilizers available in as wide a range of prices. As with most things, you usually get what you pay for, but there are exceptions and qualifications.

Fertilizers come as powders, dry granules, solid pellets, tablets or spikes, and liquids or soluble powders. Powdered fertilizer, although usually low priced, is dusty. It gets damp and cakes. It is also likeliest to "burn" plant leaves if you don't wash it off right away. We'll discuss fertilizer burn later.

Mixed granular fertilizers are easier to handle. They reduce leaf burn, resist caking, and are usually worth the added cost. They are ordinarily cheap and most suitable for lawns and new garden areas. Slow- or controlled-release granules are coated with a polymer, wax, or the like to control how fast the nutrients dissolve. Quick-release granules work soon after application and may disappear in a season or less.

Solid, pelletized fertilizers are made up of compressed particles preformed into tiny beads, tablets, or spikes. They usually cost more than granular fertilizers but their slow release offsets application costs.

Liquid fertilizers are sold as concentrates or soluble powders to mix and apply to the soil or to spray onto the plants' foliage. Some liquid fertilizers contain nitrogen, phosphorus, and potassium. Others may be a single trace element like chelated iron. Liquids cost more but are handy "quick fixes" for chemical deficiencies.

Organic vs. synthetic fertilizers? - Manures and other organic fertilizers have been used for thousands of years and are still valuable for enriching soil. Organic gardening advocates are very vocal in rejecting most if not all synthetics. Both forms of plant food should be regarded as serving a useful function, however, which sensible gardeners should use to best advantage.

Organic fertilizers - Except in fish emulsion, which releases a quick shot of it,* nitrogen is locked up in natural organic compounds. Micro-organisms must break them down for roots to absorb. The organic camp argues pretty persuasively that having enough organic matter and fertilizer in the soil also makes the kind of soil a good garden needs. You can't fault that argument. The micro-organisms that do the major part of soil building and nutrient extraction are inactive, however, when soil temperatures fall below 55 to 60 degrees. This limits their use as cool weather fertilizers. Also, because complete organic fertilizer blends don't offer much nitrogen, they may need blood-meal or urea supplements to work well. Each organic mix is different, and you have to know the product to get the best results.

Despite any shortcomings, the reasons for using organics are that (1) it releases nitrogen more slowly and stimulates plant growth over a longer period, (2) large doses of it won't injure plants, and (3) some customers may want only organic fertilizers and amendments. It does cost more than chemical fertilizer, however, and often has less than the full range of nutrients.

Synthetic fertilizers - Chemical fertilizers—synthetics—release more nitrogen faster and are cheaper, but they can burn the plant (see be-

* It also attracts varmints like possums looking for a meal.

low) and often leach out of the soil quickly. There are two main groups of water-soluble synthetics:

The ammonia-based group—including ammonium sulfate, urea, and the ammonium phosphates—gradually acidify the soils. They attach to the soil and do not leach out readily. They need soil organisms to *nitrify* them; so, like organics, they will not work in cold soils.

The nitrates—ammonium nitrate, calcium nitrate, and potassium nitrate—act fast and don't need to be nitrified (they already are), but they leach right out of the soil. When dissolved these fertilizers release negative nitrate ions that the plants can take up immediately. They won't acidify the soil and they work in cold or sterile soils. As much as 30 or 40 percent may wash out, however, with no benefit to the plants and possible detriment to nearby fields and waterways.

Water-insoluble *synthetic organic* fertilizers are slow-release. They offer the convenience of a single, long-term application with less chance of burning the plant. Some contain up to 40 percent nitrogen, some of which is often identified as *Water Insoluble Nitrogen* (W.I.N.) on package labels. Look for a fertilizer with a W.I.N. index of at least 50-percent by weight for a good slow-release treatment. On the other hand, you may want a small amount of the quick-release variety for an immediate boost or while the soil is cold.

Fertilizers with less than 50 percent natural organics or so-called synthetic organics should be considered quick fixes with short-term effects. They cause rapid leaf growth, which encourages thatch build-up on lawns, and they require repeated applications.

The synthetic organics include organic urea, calcium cyanamid, urea-formaldehyde, and IBDU (isobutylidene-diruea).

The action of microbes in soil releases the nitrogen in some slow-release synthetics. Other slow-release synthetics are coated with waxes, acrylic resins or sulfur.

Fertilizer burn - Fertilizers contain salts just like ordinary table salt. When they dissolve in water they increase the water's *osmotic pressure.* Osmotic pressure is the force that causes a liquid to pass by *osmosis* through a semi-permeable membrane. Normally, high osmotic pressure in the plant causes water from the soil, with a lower osmotic pressure, to enter the roots through its cell membranes. Water always crosses the membrane from low to high pressure; it's as if the compounds or salts suck up water to equalize pressure. If fertilizer salts raise the osmotic pressure in the soil water above that in the plant, the plant loses water. Plant damage from this loss of water is called fertilizer burn.

Different fertilizers have different salt indexes. Table salt has an index of 114. Ammonium nitrate has one of 105. The synthetic organics have indexes of around 10, and the natural organics are around 5.

If a soil test indicates a high salt level in the soil, use a fertilizer with a low salt index.

Guaranteed analysis - State laws typically require a fertilizer's chemical content to be indicated clearly on the label, tag, or invoice for bulk amounts. The label, etc., has to display the three major values (N-P-K), like 10-4-6, and show the net weight, name, brand, or trade mark. It also has to show the potential acidity in terms of pounds of calcium carbonate per ton, along with the manufacturer's name and address. A "guaranteed analysis" from a fertilizer label appears in Figure 11.2.

GUARANTEED ANALYSIS

TOTAL NITROGEN (N)	15.0%
4.0% Water Insoluble Organic Nitrogen	
2.5% Water Soluble Organic Nitrogen	
5.0% Water Insoluble Inorganic Nitrogen	
3.5% Ammoniacal Nitrogen	
AVAILABLE PHOSPHORIC ACID (P_2O_5)	10.0%
SOLUBLE POTASH (K_2O)	5.0%
CALCIUM (Ca)	2.0%
SULFUR (S)	2.0%
IRON (Fe)	1.0%
MANGANESE (Mn)	0.1%
ZINC (Zn)	0.1%
Acidity ($CaCO_3$)	60 lb/ton

Derived from Ureaformaldehyde, Chicken Manure, Ammoniated Phosphates, Superphosphate, Muriate of Potash, Dolomite, Combined Sulfur, Iron Sulfide, Manganese Sulfide, and Zinc Sulfide.

Figure 11.2. Example of fertilizer label.

Besides giving the percentage of primary nutrients, the guaranteed analysis lists all the other essential nutrients in the fertilizer. These are the minimum percentages that state law requires the manufacturer to guarantee is in the product. The analysis also includes a breakdown of the total nitrogen percentage into the percentage of water-soluble and water-insoluble components. Sometimes it specifies the exact source of the water-soluble materials, such as urea or ammonium sulfate. The rest of the fertilizer is a combination of chemical impurities, inert natural materials, and fillers added for bulk and to prevent caking.

Acidity in fertilizers refers to how much they will neutralize an alkaline soil. Fertilizers that use urea, ammonium sulfate, or phosphate compounds for their nitrogen acidify the soil. Their potential acidity depends on how much calcium carbonate ($CaCO_3$) it takes to offset the amount by which a ton of a fertilizer lowers a soil's *p*H. It's a relative figure. Some fertilizers may be made alkaline by adding extra $CaCO_3$. Those sold in your area will probably be adjusted for local conditions, but it's something to know about.

Using fertilizers on the job - Since handling costs are similar for all fertilizer strengths, the cost of stronger grades tends to be lower per unit. While you can apply enough 20-10-10 fertilizer mix for about half the cost of 10-5-5, you must be careful not to over-fertilize with the higher strength. Easier application can make the low strength mix a better choice in spite of higher unit costs.

Specialty fertilizers for specific garden plants, cost more than all-purpose types but they are tailored for the job and do not add much overall cost for the average user. In addition, a specialty fertilizer for turf is usually a slow-release variety that won't burn the grass and requires fewer applications.

If you think of fertilizers in terms of how much nitrogen each contains, you can buy on the basis of nitrogen alone for price, easy application, and what's best for the site. It's a way to get a better profit for you and a lower cost for the customer. We use a balanced blend around here referred to as "triple 16," 16-16-16. This business is nothing if not local, so check to see what's right in your area.

How much mix to apply? - Our first edition provided calculations for applying the USDA-recommended amount of fertilizer to different varieties of turf. This edition will go easier on you by recommending that you follow instructions on the bag. Keep in mind, however, that over-fertilizing is a bad idea and that if you mulch-mow you can cut down on fertilizer by about half. For those of you who like to dot every "i," we've put a somewhat simpler method in the Appendix for figuring applications USDA-style.

Applying Fertilizers

Dry fertilizers, powdered or granular, are the cheapest and fastest to apply, using a wheeled hopper, called a "trough" or "drop" spreader, or a spinning or broadcast spreader. Drop/trough spreaders have holes in the bottom that adjust to control how much fertilizer it releases. Purchase a name brand spreader and follow the instructions on the bag of fertilizer. There's no need to calibrate the spreader since you've applied the right fertilizer amount when you run out. If you feel otherwise, we explain calibration in Chapter 18 on pesticides, since federal law mandates applying granular pesticides accurately.

To get a uniform application that won't create streaks of bright green and sickly yellow, apply half of a low potency fertilizer in one direction, and the other half crosswise to it. You may even find that four passes from each compass direction, with an even lower potency mix give a better result. The cost will be more time to apply it.

A spinning or broadcast spreader covers a wider area but covers less uniformly and may cast fertilizer into shrub borders. It is the spreader of choice, however, for large expanses of turf. Calculate its rate and time as you do for the drop/trough spreader.

Wash spreaders down thoroughly after using them, because the salts in fertilizers are very very corrosive.

Liquid fertilizer often goes on as a foliar (leaf) spray that may incorporate chelated iron to green up yellowed shrubbery. Liquid fertilizers come as concentrates, so the other calculation is how much to cut the concentrate for the right amount of fertilizer. We discuss pump sprayers and how to calibrate them in Chapter 18 under pest control, but the principles apply to fertilizers. To state the obvious, by the way, you should never use a sprayer for other than one kind of treatment, and you should NEVER, NEVER USE A PESTICIDE SPRAYER TO APPLY FERTILIZER!

Nutrient Deficiencies

Even in a good chemically rich soil too much or too little of just one element can hinder photosynthesis and stunt or weaken a plant. Some garden books show pictures of plants with chemical imbalances and they recommend chemical elements to correct the problem. Experienced gardeners learn to read plants' imbalances and determine what they need. A number of good guides on the market illustrate nutrient shortages in plants. Pale, yellow leaves, for example, are a clear sign of nitrogen shortage. Other shortages cause different problems.

A soil test is the best way to measure what a soil has or lacks. Your local Cooperative Extension Service* will test soils cheaply or recommend a private lab to do it. It's not a bad idea to get a soil test about every 5 years. The lab may want samples of a certain size, with a graphic record of where each came from, the soil structure, and if the soil is native or imported. It may request leaves or other plant tissue for analysis. Confirm how to prepare the samples, whether to

* The Smith-Lever Act of 1914 founded a national Cooperative Extension Service (CES) to help improve U.S. agriculture. It's an information network that links up the USDA with land-grant universities and county governments. Early on it began to answer questions from town and city dwellers about consumer affairs, food and water quality, and home gardens.

The typical office has one or more CES ("county") agents, support personnel, and trained volunteers called Master Gardeners. Advice is always free. Each university-trained agent will share scientific information on everything agricultural and horticultural. They refer tough questions to the state university or out-of-state universities—still at no charge.

Your County Extension's address and phone number is probably in the telephone book's county government pages as "cooperative extension" or under the state department of agriculture or education.

get leaf or tissue samples from healthy or weak plants or both, and how many samples to prepare.

Test results show a profile of the soil's chemistry and *p*H level, and recommend how to correct imbalances for each plant. Soil test kits are cheaper but less accurate, with less precise recommendations. Also, while soil test results are useful guides, a qualified local technician should interpret them. Technicians have conducted studies to match test data with plant response and they've have seen the results of farm and garden fertilization.

Soil characteristics in a region are often so similar overall that once you get a feeling for them you'll begin to recognize the deficiencies without the cost of a test. In time you can use your judgment about when to recommend one. First, get an idea of what a test costs and see how the customer feels about it.

Applying the right amount of the right elements is not always easy, and more than the right amount is definitely *not* good for the plant. It takes careful attention to the principles and a measure of experience to get it right. You will get it eventually if you study the principles and pay attention to how they work in practice. Using a mulching mower on lawns returns nitrogen, phosphorus, and potassium to the turf in just the proportions the grass needs; it reduces mowing time; it eliminates hauling off the clippings; and it cuts fertilizer needs in half.

Finally, consider this. Some sources estimate that nearly four times as much fertilizer is applied to lawns as to farm land in North America. The area under turf in this continent is about the size of the state of Virginia, and the run-off into our water supply is substantial—times four. Besides, if you apply too much fertilizer, you'll be encouraging thatch and mowing till the cows come home.

The Grass Plant

Turf Grasses

Watering Lawns

Fertilizing Lawns

Trends in Turf Grass

North American Turf Grasses

Chapter 12

GRASS – FROM THE GROUND UP

Quick Start: *GRASS is a highly evolved unique plant, all the parts of which grow from a crown at the surface of the soil. As long as the crown survives, grass will take a lot of punishment. If the leaves are cut moderately long, and the plant watered to grow deep roots in a fertile soil, it will do even better and look great.*

The list of roughly two-dozen North America turf grasses at the end of this chapter arranges them by region and notes their major characteristics. They all share one characteristic: that infrequent, deep watering and long leaves promote a healthy, relatively pest-free, and drought-resistant plant. "Infrequent" means to water just as the lawn starts to wilt. "Long" for leaves is relative and depends on the grass. Also, grass can't be cut long in places like putting greens and ball parks. Scientists, seed companies, and consumer tastes are changing the nature and mix of turfgrass as the search goes on for the perfect plant for every need.

Grasses should all be fertilized when they are growing fastest: fall and early spring for northern cool-region grasses; summer for heat-loving southern varieties. The recommended amounts of fertilizer vary widely and are listed in Figure 12.3. Fertilizers should be applied in several small doses and washed in to prevent burning the leaves. A slow release fertilizer works longer and can reduce the number of applications.

A LAWN is a plot of land covered with grass plants, usually a mix of several specialized varieties that are suited to the climate and are fine-textured, low growing, and tough. The result is *turf*, a tough mat of leaves, runners, and roots which becomes *sod* when it is cut out of the ground.

The Grass Plant

At this point we need to cover some basic botanical principles. Grass plants are known as *monocotyledons*, that is, only a single first leaf grows from its seed. The seed's first or "seminal" roots live only a few weeks until secondary roots grow out of the base of the plant's stem, or its "crown," which is at the soil surface. New grass plants develop later from the "nodes" on "rhizomes" and "stolons" of the parent plant. Nodes are joints on the stem where new growth starts. Rhizomes are horizontal underground stems from which new grass plants grow. Stolons are surface runners that root and grow where their nodes touch the soil. "Tillers," which are new grass shoots, grow at the crown from between the leaf sheath and stem.

What distinguishes grass from other plants is that none of the top parts grow out of the extremities but out of the crown, which is at the surface of the ground. If the crown survives grazing, drought, or fire, the plant will survive and re-grow. The root systems of healthy modern turf grasses enclose the soil in a dense, fibrous sod and are otherwise like roots on other plants. If the roots are damaged or weakened, grass that has been injured or stressed will have a hard time recovering.

Grass leaves grow up around the stem from the crown in overlapping sheaths. During growth, the stem stretches out between the first and second nodes, in what is called the second internode. The higher-up internodes stretch out even more and, if not cut, will flower and make seed heads. (See Figure 12.1.)

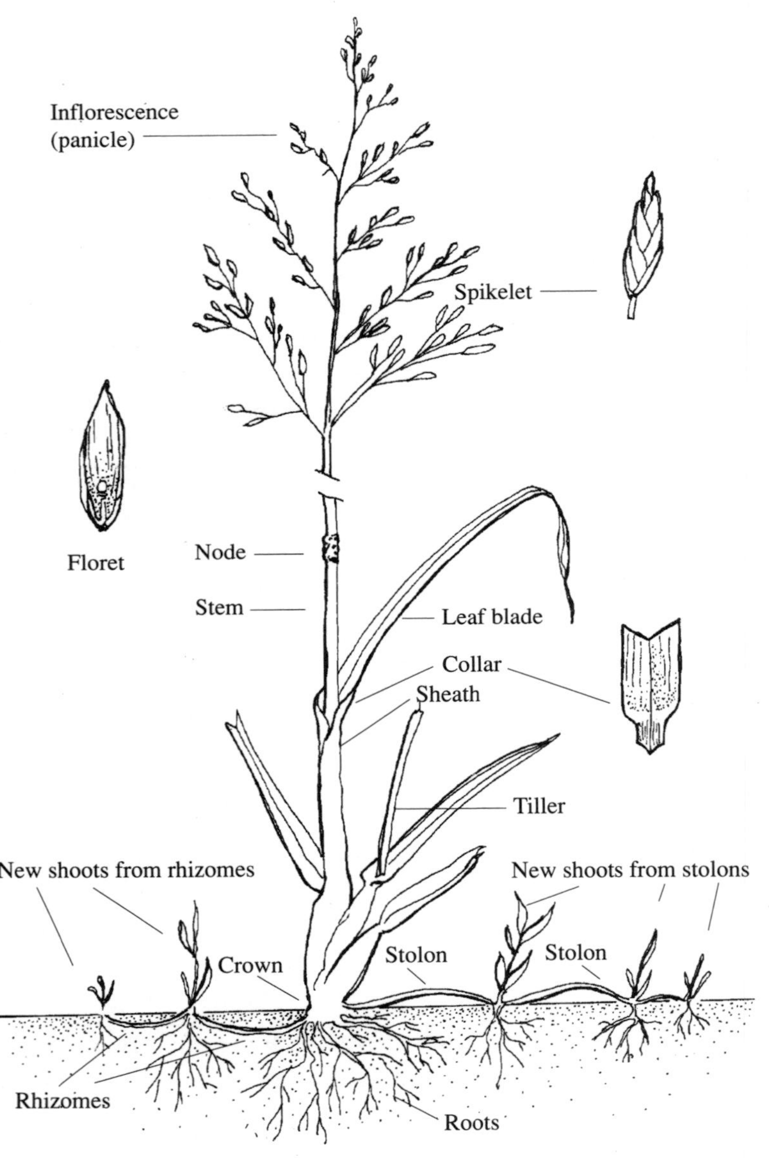

Figure 12.1. The grass plant.

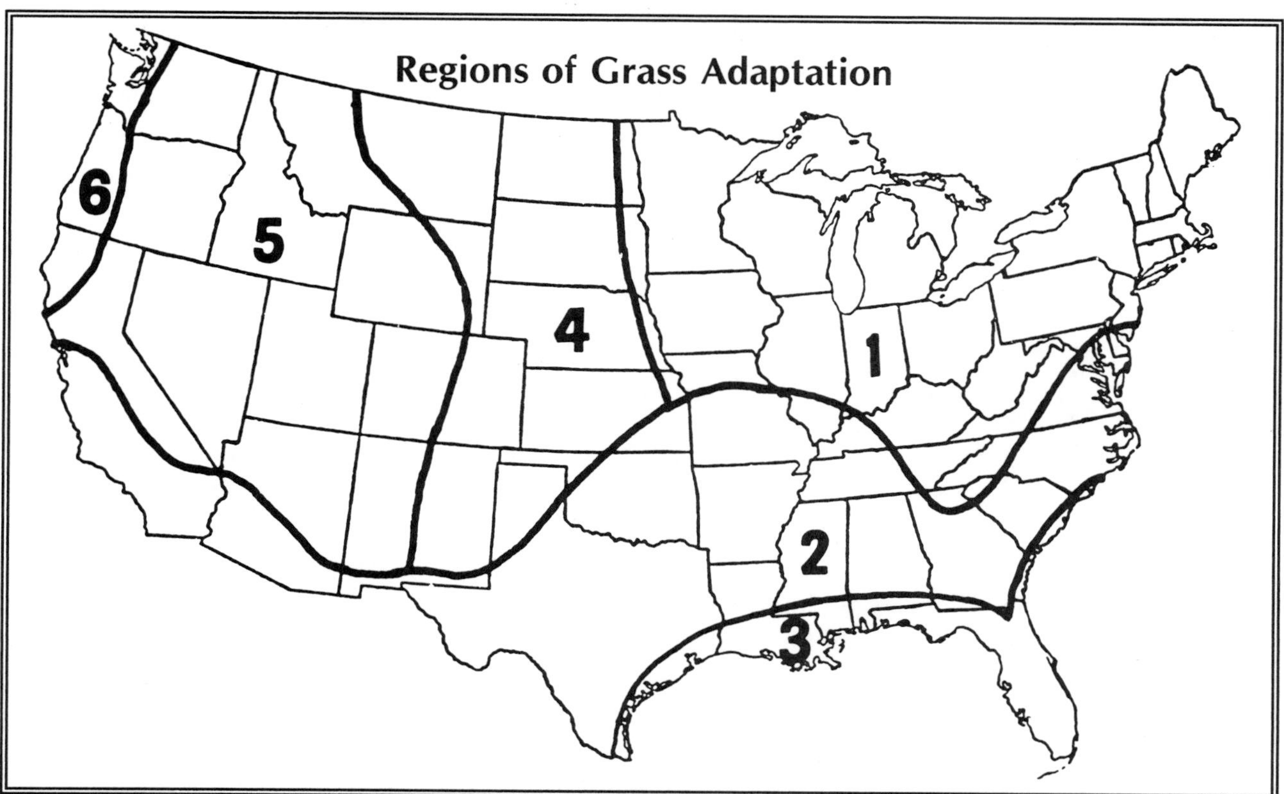

Figure 12.2. Regional suitability of grass for lawns. Region 1. Common and Merion Kentucky bluegrass, red fescue, and Colonial bentgrass. Southern portion: tall fescue, bermuda grass, and zoysia grass. Region 2. Bermuda grass and zoysia grass. Southern portion: centipede grass, carpet grass, and St. Augustine grass; tall fescue and Kentucky bluegrass in some northern areas. Region 3. St. Augustine grass, bermuda grass, zoysia grass, carpet grass, and bahia grass. Region 4. Unirrigated: Crested wheatgrass, buffalo grass, blue grama grass; irrigated areas: Kentucky bluegrass and red fescue. Region 5. Unirrigated areas: crested wheatgrass, buffalo grass, blue grama grass; irrigated: Kentucky bluegrass and red fescue. Region 6. Colonial bentgrass and Kentucky bluegrass. (USDA)

Turf Grasses

There are only about two dozen perennial grass species in North America that are suitable for turf. Some grow best in the northern cool regions, others prefer the warmer south, and a few even withstand the rigors of the Great Plains. The north-south transition zone roughly follows the line that weaves across the map in Figure 12.2.

The northern turf grasses, which grow best in the cool, humid weather of northern spring and fall, include bluegrasses, fescues, bent grasses, redtop and ryegrasses. The southern grasses include Bermuda grasses, the zoysias, St. Augustine grass, carpet grass, and centipede grass. These all grow best during the hot summer months. Lawns in borderline regions are often a mixture of northern and southern varieties, and some southern turfs may be overseeded with a cool weather grass to provide cover after the first frost. The best lawn grasses, northern and southern, spread by sending out rhizomes and stolons. A few bunch grasses are used where necessary but they give a rougher texture.

Grasses in the Great Plains and dry southwestern regions are usually hardy, drought-resistant native strains like buffalo and blue grama grass, which often adapt to otherwise toxic levels of salts, drought, searing heat, and arctic cold.

A list of the major lawn grasses with their USDA spellings, and arranged by their predominant locales, is at the end of this chapter. Meanwhile, here is how to care for and feed lawn grasses.

Watering Grasses

Plants need water for germination, growth, photosynthesis, and temperature control. They need enough of it to dissolve and absorb nutrients from the soil to assemble the food manufactured in their leaves.

About 90 percent of the water that plants absorb transpires into the air for temperature control. When they transpire more water than they absorb they take up fewer nutrients, and stop photosynthesizing. Then they wilt and eventually turn brown. Grasses have evolved to survive dry spells by going into dormancy. The shoots and foliage die, but if the crown and rhizome, or stolon buds survive, their tissues will start new growth when moisture returns.

As the list of turf grass varieties at the end of this chapter shows, grasses differ in drought tolerance. As a rule, however, tall grasses with deep, well fed roots survive droughts best. Deep, infrequent watering encourages root development. The ideal is a dry surface with the water table never more than about 2" to 6" below it.

How much water? - Deep watering takes the mechanics of soil moisture into account. Soil dries out from the top down. Good soils soak up water, hold it awhile, then let it drain down slowly. Clay takes a long time to absorb water, holding it so tightly that it does not drain away quickly and can even suffocate the plant. Sandy soils absorb water quickly, but it drains right out again. The best soil is a loam with enough clay and silt to hold moisture but enough sand to encourage good drainage.

If a lawn wilts fast as the ground dries out in spring, chances are that it has short roots, and the water has dropped below them after the top inch or two of soil dries out. A lawn like this will need water often and always have a damp surface, which favors weeds and fungus. If a lawn has deep roots, the top inch or so can dry out, discouraging weeds and fungus while the lawn draws water from deeper in the ground. This is often referred to as a "thick" lawn, which is healthier than a "thin" one and much easier to care for.

Vigorous spring growth drinks from deep down. It's better to keep the soil watered than to try recharging it after it dries hard and the roots begin shrivelling up to the "high water mark." Advise your customers to start watering as soon as the rain ends and to adopt a deep-watering program. It may take some persuasion to start the customers doing this, but the long term benefits will be worth it. It means watering thoroughly every 3 to 10 days, depending on the weather, to keep the soil deeply charged with groundwater. In very hot weather customers may have to soak deeply as often as every 3 days, but should *not* sprinkle lightly every other day as an unvarying routine. On the other hand, advise them not to cause run-off.

To control water waste from run-off, encourage the use of low-flow sprinkler heads and lawn aeration for better absorption. Because water flows downhill, sloped lawns won't need as much watering at the bottom as the top. On a slope or other high-runoff area advise "pulse watering." That means running the sprinklers five minutes, letting the water soak in for five, and repeating it for an hour to get a half-hour's irrigation, or two hours for an hour's irrigation. Pulse-water also in heavy soils that absorb water slowly. Your customers may be able to find an electronic lawn timer that will handle pulse watering. More likely they'll spend extra time at the faucet. Timers may be of little help and are probably best thrown away in a deep-watering program based on weather and soil mechanics. For slopes, getting enough water into them can be another reason (besides treacherous mowing terrain) to recommend a non-grass ground cover.

The rule for watering lawns is to water deeply and only when the grass needs it.

To get a deep-rooted lawn, keep watering from that first spring irrigation until it grows about 2" or 3" high. Then start mowing, but not too short. The leaves will be manufacturing plenty of food; so stop watering. Keep up the mowing schedule, but let the soil dry out so the roots will have to reach deeper for water. Don't water again until the turf starts to wilt. A wilting turf turns bluish green or shows footprints. When you water do it for a long time, perhaps an hour or two—or even more—to let the water soak deep. You want to put an average 1" of water in the lawn per session without any runoff. Don't water again until the lawn wilts again.

Water must be evenly distributed over the lawn for uniform growth and appearance. Measure water coverage in containers spaced evenly under the spray pattern. It may be necessary to hand water dry patches. You can use cans to measure output, and can also use them to time water flow and see how long it takes to lay down that 1" or even 2" of irrigation. It will take trial and error to get the best looking well-watered lawn—which, after all, is the whole point.

You can test for moisture penetration with an expensive electronic moisture tension sensor or by slicing into the lawn with a spade and feeling for dampness at the bottom of the cut. There are also soil coring tubes that let you extract a core of turf and soil to test for moisture penetration. It's a good way to inspect soil texture and structure, as well. The easiest way is to plunge a screwdriver in the ground and see how much resistance it meets. High resistance in a turf that you know is damp probably means it's compacted.

What time of day to water - For most of the country, morning—preferably well before sunup—is the best time of day for watering a turf. Low temperatures, high humidity, and low winds reduce water loss from evaporation, and the sun will dry the surface gradually.

In order to overcome the surface tension of dry soil, particularly a clay, some experts recommend putting a little detergent in the first spray of water. It won't hurt the grass, because it is washed in, and a major ingredient of many detergents is phosphate, an essential growth element for plants.

For regions with *extremely* dry, hot weather, watering at night will reduce the evaporative loss of water, which is probably a scarce commodity there anyway. By "hot and dry" we mean that open packages of soda crackers stay crispy all summer. The argument against watering at night is that grass left damp overnight is susceptible to molds, mildew, and disease. A well dried out lawn surface may have none of those problems, especially in arid conditions.

Contrary to some beliefs, water droplets will not cause scalding on grass at midday. Because of high evaporation loss, however, midday is a good time to water only if disease or molds really are a problem. Even then, it is a poor choice if the grass is used for playing fields and golf courses.

Over-watering, especially in warm, humid weather, promotes brown patch (Ryizoctonia solani) and grease spot (Pythium), common fungus diseases. But don't cut back on irrigation. Deep, infrequent morning or even mid-day watering helps counteract it. Cut down high-nitrogen fertilizing and aerate the soil to improve drainage if necessary. Use anti-fungus chemicals as a last resort. If the fungus is established, it's usually too late for chemicals to do much good.

Fertilizing Lawns

Apply fertilizer as uniformly as possible over the turf. Be sure to blow it off the sidewalks or driveway, as it may stain. Never fertilize wet grass, and be sure to wash in all fertilizers, especially quick release kinds, right after application in order to avoid burning the leaves. All grasses should be fertilized when they are at their maximum growth rate.

The exact amount of fertilizer to apply will depend: on the type of grass; on the length of the growing season, with more fertilizer needed in the south and less in the north; on soil leaching; on trees growing in the turf that also take up the fertilizer; and on the presence of other nutrients in the soil. See Figure 12.3 for basic fertilization rates.

In the North - Cool season grasses should be fertilized most heavily in fall, when they come out of summer dormancy. Use a high nitrogen mix as the days cool in September. Around late October, but a least a month before winter settles in, apply a high-potassium mix (say, 20-4-12) to build roots for spring growth. Turf grasses can be fertilized lightly in spring, but that may increase the need to mow. We find that following the instructions on the bag works well for us. The USDA recommends about 2 pounds of nitrogen per 1,000 square feet (SF) per year, but don't apply more than one pound per 1,000 SF at a time. Two applications are ideal, but you may need to apply three or even four doses to a starved turf which could want up to 4 pounds per 1,000 SF. Use a slow release fertilizer.

In areas with harsh winters, wait until the danger of severe frost is past before fertilizing turfgrasses in spring. Fall applications should be timed so that growth will have slowed before the first killing frost arrives. If you are unsure about local practice, consult your county agent or state experiment station.

Fertilization and Mowing Height for Selected Lawn Grasses

	Fertilizer (Pounds of Nitrogen per 1,000 SF)	Height of Mowing (Inches)
ARID REGION GRASSES		
Blue Grama	*	1-2
Buffalo (treated)	*	1-2
COOL SEASON GRASSES†		
Bentgrass (Colonial)	4-6	½-1
Kentucky bluegrass	2-4	1½-2‡
Red fescue	2-3	1½-2
Rough bluegrass	2-4	1½-2
Ryegrass	3-4	1½-2
Tall fescue	5-6	2
WARM SEASON GRASSES‡‡		
Bermuda grass	5-10	½-1
Carpet grass	8-10	2-2½
Centipede grass	8-10	1-1½
St. Augustine grass	8-10	1-1½
Zoysia grass	8-10	¾-1½

* ***Seldom required on most soils; plant in spring.***
† ***Fertilize in fall or early spring; plant in fall.***
‡ ***Mow higher during summer dormancy.***
‡‡ ***Fertilize from late spring to early fall.***

Figure 12.3. Lawn grass fertilization and mowing heights. (USDA)

In the South - Warm season grasses vary widely in their nutrient needs. Bermuda grass wants 5 to 10 pounds of nitrogen per 1,000 SF per year, most of it in the hot summer when it is growing fast. Give it a balanced fertilizer first, and apply the remainder in specialized mixes that are rich in nitrogen. Amounts to apply to other southern grasses are shown in Figure 12.3. Don't apply more than a pound per 1,000 SF at a time.

In the Plains - Grasses in the semi-arid or arid regions also have very diverse needs. Some may be in soils with excess nutrients in toxic amounts, or in which nutrients may be unavailable because of high alkalinity. The best practice is to check with the local county agricultural agent or state agricultural experiment station.

Trends in Turf Grass

Supergrasses - New grasses appear every year in the search for the perfect lawn. The old, traditional varieties often are less than ideal. Cool-weather turfgrasses are European and often ill-matched to our climate. It's drier here, and we have harsher summers and winters. The problem is less severe in the South where African and Asian grasses have met basic turfgrass needs. Many of those varieties need more water than is often available, however, especially in the southwest. Consequently, there has been major research into new drought-tolerant native turfgrasses.

Foremost among the promising natives is tough, deep-rooting, and drought-resistant buffalograss (*Buchloe dactyloides*). With roots that typically drive down 5 or 6 feet to tap subsurface water, it thrives in heat and drought. Dr. Terry Riordan, at the University of Nebraska, was one of the earliest to hybridize a buffalograss for turf suitable to a range stretching from the West Coast almost to the Atlantic. Other buffalograss hybrids have since arisen that can be planted from seed, plugs, or sod. Sod and plugs contain only female plants and don't have the male seedheads some people find objectionable in seeded buffalograss. Seeded brands are cheaper to install and look fine with regular mowing.

Buffalograss goes dormant with the first frost, however, and is khaki colored all winter. That makes it less than ideal for northerly latitudes. It also needs plenty of sunshine and may never do well in the shady, cloudy northeast. It is also unsuited to poorly drained and sandy soils. Varieties include Prairie, Tatanka, Bison, Cody, Stampede, and Dr. Riordan's Nebraska 609.

Compared to prairie buffalograss, Nebraska 609—a female cultivar for sodding or plugs—is denser with a deeper blue-green color. Mowing height is 1"-4" and it wakes up from dormancy three weeks earlier in the spring. Stampede, a semi-dwarf female cultivar, is native to Texas. Slow-growing and heat-loving but happy with four hours of daily sun, it wants water once a month or less, needs less mowing than other varieties, and is Kelly green. Its higher density and rate of spread let it compete better against weeds. Mowing height is as low as ¾ inches. Like all buffalograsses, Stampede takes half the water of traditional turfgrasses in its range. (For Stampede that's bermudagrass). Like all buffalograss varieties, it needs little fertilizer. The producer recommends two to four pounds annually per 1,000 SF. Department of Agriculture recommendations for none at all suggest the low end may be nearer the mark.

For the lawn care business, however, there are minuses. Because buffalograss is new to turfgrass settings, you must be careful which broadleaf herbicide to use. Find out the buffalograss variety you're working with and see what the producer recommends. With a few varieties use the Internet to access www.aggiehorticulture.tamu.edu/-plantanswers/turf/weedsinbuffalo.html. That's Texas A&M's website. Recommendations can change, so stay current.

The second drawback is a buffalograss strength: It grows slowly and needs less mowing. Some new owners of dwarf varieties have even stopped mowing altogether, opting for a short, shaggy green meadow. Wide use of buffalograss is still a few years off, but it's something to know about and anticipate with back-up gardening skills.

Lawns are the gas guzzlers of landscaping. They get even more fertilizer, water, and fuel-powered care than farm crops. Watch out for an environmentalist reaction against them and be ready with a knowledge of alternative landscapes.

Traditional turfgrass improvement hasn't stood still. Research centers on improving the old standbys, including six varieties of hard fescue. Fescues also root deeply; some reach 6 or 8 feet. Chewings fescue —Jamestown II, Banner, and Longfellow—did well in trials at Rutgers for the northeast. Red fescues, such as Cindy, Dawson, Ensylva thrive in the cool summers of Canada and the northern-tier states of the U.S. Improved hard fescues that also tolerate acid soil and low fertility are Reliant, Spartan, and Aurora. (These are "low-maintenance" grasses and take infrequent mowing.) Another low-maintenance northerner is Reubens, a Canada bluegrass from the Jacklin Seed Company, which takes very acid, poor soils, little water, and grows at 10,000-foot altitudes.

In the south, Stan Gardner of Gardner Turfgrass has developed a cross of Texas bluegrass (*Poa pretensis*) and Kentucky bluegrass with Texas A&M University, Kentucky bluegrass roots are only 5" deep. Reveille, the Gardner cross, is very drought tolerant and should be out in a few years. Gardner speculates that blue grama grass—a hard-wearing, drought tolerant bunch grass—will be the next native pursued in the search for the perfect turf.

New varieties of tall fescues for the south are tough and good looking. They include Hubbard 87, Shenandoah, Guardian, and Crossfire. Turfgrass producers, in cooperation with university agricultural departments, are developing drought-resistant strains of zoysias, salt-tolerant paspalums, and St. Augustines.

Experts predict also that genetic engineering is close to tailoring turfgrasses to any microclimate. It has already devised dwarf grasses that need mowing very infrequently. (Another trend; watch out and be ready for it.) By selecting desirable gene traits, scientists are close to blending the micro-mowing-height of bentgrass with the drought tolerance of buffalograss, or any combination in between. It will all happen much faster than with traditional breeding techniques.

Pest-free grass - Besides drought resistance, turfgrass companies and researchers are developing insect resistant strains. Some grasses naturally contain endophytes, microscopic fungi that repel insects. They're being bred into other grasses. If a parent plant is "infected" with endophytes, all of its seeds will be infected. When the seeds sprout the fungus infects the seedlings. Endophytic ryegrasses and fescues need almost no insecticides because they already resist aphids, armyworms, billbugs, cutworms greenbugs, sod webworms, and more. Endophytic grasses also tolerate drought and competition better than other plants. The best-known high-endophytic varieties are Repell II, Palmer II, Advent, Express, and Reliant, all of them fine fescues; Titan and Shenandoah are tall fescues.

The "ecolawn" - In about 1985 Tom Cook, associate professor of horticulture at Oregon State University in Corvallis, began to look for a lawn substitute that needed less mowing, water, and fertilizer. He settled on a blend of drought-resistant broadleaf plants and turfgrass. The grass provides a cover until the broadleafs emerge in spring, and drought-tolerant broadleafs mask the grass's summer dormancy.

For western Oregon, with about 40 inches annual rainfall and dry summer highs of 85-95 degrees, perennial ryegrass and Kentucky bluegrass mixed best with English daisies, clover, and common yarrow. Drought-tolerant yarrow gives a dense, dark green cover that nearly hides the dormant grass. It dies back to its crown about when the grass reappears for Oregon's mild winters. Clovers—which drink from deep roots and fix nitrogen from the air—are common in low-fertility lawns. English daisy, a common lawn weed in western Oregon, flowers best in spring but retreats in the hot, dry summer. Commercial varieties give good, colorful bloom from late March to mid-June, but they have daisies' paler foliage and die out after 3 to 5 years.

The typical ecolawn gets no fertilizer or one application at planting. Clover clippings left on the plots seem to provide plenty of nitrogen. Mowing every three weeks allows optimum flowering, although warm wet springs call for bi-weekly mowing to control growth. A 2" mowing height encourages bloom and gives the look and feel of a tended lawn. In summer Cook waters his plots deeply (1.5") once a month. This is about ⅓ to ¼ of a regular lawn's water. The Appendix lists a few books on "ecolawns" and sources for lawn/flower-seed mixes, some, like Fleur de Lawn, based on Cook's recipe.

Some North American Turf Grasses

Arid Great Plains

- **Blue gramagrass.** A low-growing perennial that is adapted to a wide range of soil conditions throughout the Great Plains. It is highly drought resistant. Its use as a turf grass is limited to cool, dry places with little or no available irrigation water. It is a bunch-grass that can be established from seed. Unless watered, it becomes semi-dormant and turns brown in severe drought.
- **Buffalograss.** A stoloniferous, highly drought-resistant perennial used in sunny lawns in the Great Plains. It is fine-leaved and dense during the growing season and turns from grayish green to straw colored when growth stops in the fall. It can be established by seed or sodding, and grows best in well-drained heavy soils.
- **Crested wheatgrass.** A perennial bunchgrass that thrives in most soils of the central and northern Great Plains. It is established by seeding. It will withstand long dry periods and is recommended for regions where irrigation water is unavailable. If not cut too closely it will take heavy wear. It makes most of its growth in the spring and fall; it becomes semi-dormant and turns brown in the hot summer months.
- **Weeping lovegrass.** A vigorous perennial bunch grass that thrives in the southern Great Plains. It is an excellent erosion control plant on nonuse areas but poor for home lawns because it will not withstand frequent mowing. It grows in any soil but does best in sandy loams.

Cool humid North

- **Bentgrass, colonial.** A fine textured, tufted grass with few creeping stems and rhizomes. It forms a dense turf when heavily seeded and closely cropped. Used chiefly in high quality lawns and putting greens, it is more expensive to maintain than ordinary lawn grasses, and is popular in cool, damp areas like New England, Oregon, and Washington. It requires fertile soil and frequent feeding. It is disease prone and must be mowed below about ¾" or it becomes fluffy and forms an undesirable spongy mat. Of the several strains sold, Highland is hardiest. Astoria is bright green compared to Highland's bluish green, but Astoria is not as drought resistant or as aggressive as Highland. Astoria, if well-managed, gives a better lawn than Highland.
- **Bentgrass, creeping.** Rarely used in home lawns but extensively found in putting greens throughout the United States. Its profuse creeping stems produce roots and stems at every node, and it develops a dense sod. It must be mowed closely (¼" to ⅛") and topdressed periodically to inhibit thatch formation. It requires highly fertile soils with low acidity, good drainage, and high water-retentive capacity. Maintaining good quality turf requires a regular program of fertilization, watering and disease control.
- **Bentgrass, velvet.** This finest textured bentgrass is used mainly in high quality lawns and putting greens in New England and the Pacific Northwest. It forms an extremely dense turf from creeping

stems and can be established by seeding or vegetative planting. It is adapted to a wide range of soil conditions but does best on well drained, fertile soils with low acidity. It is not as aggressive as creeping bentgrass and is slow to recover from all types of injury. It needs close mowing and periodic topdressing, along with a regular program of fertilizing, watering, and disease control. The only variety available is Kingstown.

- **Canada bluegrass.** Forms a thin, poor quality open turf in seed mixtures for playgrounds, athletic fields, and the like. It will grow in sandy or gravelly soil with low fertility, but does not tolerate high acidity or poor drainage. Although it won't long survive clipping below 2½ inches, it is very tough and wears well.
- **Kentucky bluegrass**, The most widely used lawn grass in the United States, where there is adequate irrigation for it, this is a hardy, long-lived sod-forming grass that spreads by heavy underground rootstocks. Common Kentucky bluegrass will not tolerate poor drainage or high acidity, put prefers heavy well drained soils of good fertility that are neutral or near neutral. It is highly drought resistant and can go into a semi-dormant condition in hot summer weather. It can be injured if mowed shorter than 1½ inches, and will not tolerate heavy shade. Because it is slow to establish itself, it is often planted with faster growing "nurse" grasses that provide cover and prevent weed invasion.
- **Merion Kentucky bluegrass.** This variety has proved superior to common Kentucky bluegrass in many regions of the country. It can be clipped more closely and is less susceptible to leafspot disease than the common variety, although it is susceptible to rust and stripe smut. It also appears to be more drought tolerant, vigorous, and resistant to weeds. For best growth it needs greater fertility and more maintenance than common Kentucky, and responds well to heavy applications of nitrogen. Other commercial varieties of Kentucky bluegrass are Newport, Park, Nugget, Pennstar, Windsor, Baron, and Fylking.
- **Orchardgrass.** A tall growing perennial bunch grass that forms coarse textured tufts but never a solid turf. It grows badly in poorly drained or very acid soils, but ignores soil infertility, resists drought and tolerates shade. It is sometimes used in poor quality lawn seed mixtures.
- **Red fescue and Chewings fescue.** These rate next to Kentucky bluegrass as the most popular lawn grasses in the cool, humid regions of the United States. Red fescue spreads slowly by rhizomes. Chewings fescue is a bunch-type grower. Both are established by seeding. They are used extensively in lawn seed mixtures, grow well in shade, and tolerate high acidity. They require good drainage but will flourish in poor arid soils. Red fescue and Chewings fescue are fine textured with tough bristle-like leaves. When seeded

heavily they form a dense sod that resists wear. They heal slowly when injured by insects or disease. Consistent mowing below 1½" can severely damage them. Improved strains of red fescue include Pennlawn, Illahee, and Rainier.

- **Redtop**. A short-lived perennial that seldom lives more than two seasons when closely mowed. It is common in lawn seed mixtures in the cool northerly regions to provide quick cover while permanent grasses are developing. It is often seeded alone in temporary lawns. In the southern United States it is used for winter overseeding of bermudagrass to provide year-around green color. Heavy seeding helps overcome its tendency to an open turf. It tolerates a wide range of soil and temperatures, grows in highly acid and poorly drained soils, resists drought, and needs little fertilizer.
- **Rough bluegrass**. A shade tolerant perennial injured by hot dry weather but useful in lawns in the extreme northern United States. It is established by seeding. Leaves, which are the same texture as those of Kentucky bluegrass, lie flat giving the turf a glassy appearance. Lighter green than Kentucky bluegrass, it spreads by short stolons. Its shallow root system limits its use to shady areas where traffic is light.
- **Ryegrass.** Italian or annual ryegrass and perennial ryegrass are propagated entirely by seed that is produced in the Pacific Northwest or imported. Much of the ryegrass in seeded lawns is a mixture of annual and perennial varieties. Many commercial lawn seed mixtures contain too much ryegrass which competes with the permanent grass seedlings for moisture and nutrients. Sometimes, however, it is advisable to include a small amount of ryegrass in lawn seed mixtures on slopes in order to help prevent soil erosion. Coarse clumps of ryegrass may persist for years. It often results in ragged looking lawns that are difficult to mow. In the southern United States annual or common ryegrass is used for winter overseeding of bermuda grass in lawns and on golf greens and tees. Fine textured varieties include Pennfine, Manhattan, Norlea, Pelo, and NK101.
- **Tall fescue**. A tall growing bunch grass with coarse, dense basal leaves and a strong fibrous root system. It is established by seeding. It is also used for pasture. Tolerant of moderate shade, it grows in wet or dry, acid or alkaline, soils but prefers well drained fertile soils. Because of their wear resistant qualities, two improved, highly drought-resistant strains of tall fescue, Kentucky 31 fescue and Alta fescue, are often used on playgrounds, athletic fields, service yards, and the like.
- **Timothy grass**. A coarse perennial bunch grass that grows best in northern humid regions, it is a forage crop sometimes found in poor quality lawn seed mixtures. It is sometimes suitable to provide cover for nonuse areas.

Warm sunny South

- **Annual Bluegrass.** An invasive weed. Little value as permanent turf because it dies suddenly in the hot summer months. Used chiefly to overseed warm season turf grasses during winter months. It normally begins growth in late summer or early fall from seed produced earlier in the same year, and will often grow through the winter. Requires a cool, moist, fertile soil. It produces large quantities of seed heads even when mowed as low as ¼ inch.
- **Bahiagrass.** A low-growing perennial that spreads by short, heavy runners (stolons). It grows best in southern Coastal Plains and is established by seeding. Common bahia, which has very coarse leaves, is recommended for forage only. Paraguay and Pensacola strains, with finer leaves make a dense and uneven turf and are useful on large areas like airfields where good cover is more important than turf quality.
- **Bermudagrass.** Bermudagrass grows vigorously, spreading by stolons and rhizomes, and can become a tenacious pest in other cultivated garden areas. It dislikes shade, poor drainage, high acidity, or low fertility. It needs heavy applications of readily available nitrogen. Although drought resistant, it requires moderate amounts of water during dry periods and must be clipped closely in order to form a dense turf.

  Each variety of bermudagrass has a fairly specialized use. Common bermuda, a coarse grass, is the only variety for which seed is available. Other varieties are established vegetatively. Common lawn varieties include Tiflawn, Everglades No. 1, Ormond, Sunturf, and Texturf 10. Tiflawn is finer textured than common bermudagrass and greener. Ormond is coarser and grows more upright than Everglades No. 1. Of the three varieties, Everglades No. 1 requires least maintenance.

  Bermudagrass varieties used in high quality lawns and in golf course putting greens and fairways include Tifgreen, Tiffine, Tifway, Bayshore, and Tifdwarf. These are medium green and fine textures.
- **Carpetgrass.** A rapidly spreading stoloniferous perennial that produces a dense, compact turf under mowing but is very coarse textured. It can be established most cheaply by seeding, or quickly by sprigging or sodding. Grows best in moist, sandy-loam soils or those with fairly high moisture content year around. Does poorly in dry soils or in arid regions. It thrives with limited fertilization in poor soils but is very sensitive to lack of iron. Although resistant to trampling, heavy wear, disease, and insects, it will not tolerate salt-water spray. Its tall, tough seedheads must be attacked frequently with a power mower.
- **Centipedegrass.** Spreads rapidly by short creeping stems that form new plants at each node, forming a dense, vigorous turf that is highly resistant to weed invasion. Although usually established vegetatively, some seed is available. It is considered the best low-maintenance lawn in the southern part of the United States, but can be severely damaged by salt water spray and lack of iron. An annual application of a complete fertilizer will improve its quality. Although drought resistant, it should be watered during dry periods. It is very low in nutritional value and should not be planted near pastures.

- **Manilagrass.** Technically Zoysia matrella, this is closely related and similar to the Japanese variety. It is stoloniferous and forms a dense carpet-like turf that resists weeds, wear, disease, and insect damage. It dislikes highly acidic soils and responds well to liberal applications of nitrogen fertilizer. It is established by sprigging and sodding, turns brown with the first killing frost and is dormant until spring.
- **Mascarenegrass.** (Zoysia tenuifolia) A low growing stoloniferous grass that is adapted to very few locations in the United States. It has the same requirements as manilagrass but is less hardy than manilagrass or Japanese lawngrass. It becomes sod-bound and humps up as it ages, encouraging weed invasion.
- **Rescuegrass.** A short-lived perennial bunch grass that grows best in fertile soils in humid regions with mild winters. It is used in the southern United States as a winter grass in large bermudagrass plantings like golf course fairways.
- **Seashore paspalum.** Native to tropical and subtropical North and South America, and common along coastal regions from Texas to Florida and South Carolina. A warm-season perennial grass that spreads by rhizomes and stolons. Forms dense turf mowed 1 to ⅛ inch. Outstanding tolerance of saline soils and brackish sites. Has grown at the edge of water containing 4,000 or more ppm salts. Adalayd, also called Excalibre, a variety found in Australia in the 1970s is distributed by Intersol, Palm Desert, California.
- **St. Augustinegrass.** A creeping perennial that spreads by long stolons that produce short, leafy branches, this is the number one shade grass in the southernmost United States. It grows successfully south of Augusta, Georgia, westward to the coastal regions of Texas. Seed is unavailable; it is established vegetatively. It will withstand salt water spray, and grows best in fertile, moist soils. It produces good turf in the muck soils of Florida, but liberal applications of high-nitrogen fertilizer are necessary, especially in sandy soils. It can be seriously damaged by diseases and insects.
- **Zoysia japonica.** (Japanese lawngrass.) A low growing perennial that spreads by stolons and shallow root-stocks, this grass forms a dense weed-, disease-, and insect-resistant turf. It grows best in a region south of a line from Philadelphia to San Francisco. Above that line the shorter growing season makes it impractical. It turns straw colored with the first frost and remains off-color until warm spring weather revives it.

  Common zoysia japonica is coarse textured and excellent for large areas like airfields and playgrounds; however Meyer zoysia is desirable for home lawns. Meyer is more vigorous, keeps its color later in the fall and regains it earlier in the spring. There is no seed, but the sod is available from nurseries. It will survive in low-fertility soils but responds well to liberal applications of fertilizers with a high nitrogen content. Emerald zoysia, a dense, dark green hybrid between zoysia japonica and mascarene grass seems superior to Meyer zoysia in the southern U.S.

Grass Is Made to Cut

Goodbye, Lawn Mower Bag?

Shopping for Mowers

Lawn Mower Safety

Start Your Engines

Mower Maintenance

Edging

Fertilizing

Aerating

Thatch and Dethatching

Re-seeding for Best Appearance

Finishing the Job

Chapter 13

MOWING – A CUT ABOVE THE ORDINARY

Quick Start:

MOWING is not good for grass, but luckily for us in the business, not many people want unmowed lawns. The sensible compromise is to remove as little grass as possible, consistent with good looks. This means slicing it with a sharp blade and removing no more than a third of its leaf surface at a time. That leaves it long enough to shade the lower leaves and crowns, and to keep photosynthesizing.

Many warm season grasses and all bent grasses can be shaved close, but bluegrasses and fescues want long legs. Mulch-mowing is becoming more common. It can complicate your schedule by requiring more, then less, frequent cutting, but it has other business advantages.

A low cost mower will keep you competitive when starting out, but eventually you will need an industrial/commercial (I/C) model to stand up to your heavier schedule. Get all the power they make, from a store that specializes in turf equipment and will service it if necessary. Choose a mower than can be adjusted easily without having to get near moving parts.

Power mowers are efficient cutters. Treat them with all due respect. Read about mowers in this chapter even if you are just skimming these capsules.

LAWNS USED TO BE CROPPED WITH SCYTHES, until around 1830, when Edwin Budding, an engineer in a Gloucester textile mill, invented a device for shearing the nap on piled fabric. He recognized that his device, somewhat modified, would work on lawns, too. Early models worked best with one person pushing and another pulling. The first gasoline mower is said to have appeared around 1902. There's more at www.artizan.demon.co.uk/mkm/menmow.htm, which is the Milton Keynes Museum on-line.

Grass Is Made to Cut

Mowing is the mechanical equivalent of grazing, and grass is well adapted to it. Regardless of what you may have thought or heard, however, mowing does not benefit grass. For one thing it wounds the leaf tops, increasing the chances for infection. More important, it removes part of the leaf area used for photosynthesis. Photosynthesis, remember, is how plant leaves use sunshine to make sugar, starch, and cellulose out of the 17 chemical elements that the roots extract from the soil and air. A healthy plant needs plenty of healthy roots to take in the raw materials and lots of leaf area to make food, which it puts back in the roots for something to grow on in the next season. Mowing shocks the plant, and root growth slows down every time grass is cut.

Damage control - The only reason to mow grass is for a uniform, good looking turf, or one that's a good sports height. To limit damage from mowing, grass should be cut in a way that removes as little green area as possible. All the experts agree that each mowing should remove no more than about a third of the grass blades. One seasonal program for northern bluegrasses and fescues does recommend cutting them short—down to 1½"—on the first spring mowing in order to clear out the dead matter, then gradually letting them get longer as the weather warms until they are as high as three inches, or even four where the summers are hot.

Keep your mower sharp. Dull blades beat and tear the grass leaves, leaving a grayish cast and making the lawn susceptible to diseases. Sharp blades cut cleaner and quicker. Zoysia, ryegrass, and fescue in particular require a sharp cutting edge.

It is uniformity, not height, that makes a good looking lawn. The reason why some lawns look good cut shorter than others is that different grasses require different cutting heights. Creeping bent grass, which spreads by stolons, takes close shaves and makes perfect putting greens. It can be mown below ½ inch. Canada blue grass can't be cropped safely below 2½" without falling into a decline. Fine grasses can be cut closer than coarse grasses. Stoloniferous creepers like Bermudas, etc., can be cut closer than upright growing ones. In fact, Zoysia and Bermudagrass build up excess thatch if cut too high.

Cool weather grasses especially will be weakened if you mow them too close in summer because, just when their growth has slowed in the heat, cutting makes them draw on food in their roots so they can grow back; but their short, slow-growing leaves can't photosynthesize food fast enough to make up for what they take out of the roots. The roots thin out and die, and the plants don't bounce back as well the next spring. For that reason, you should cut northern grasses higher in the summer to build good roots. As a bonus, keeping them at or slightly above the regulation length helps smother weed seedlings. Grass is not too long until it doesn't stand up straight for mowing.

If grass does grow so high that you have to take off more than a third of its height, don't cut it all off at once. Take a little off the top with each mowing until you work down to the right height. You may have to cut more often to do this, but if you don't, the lower shaded part will get sunburned. Also, long clippings left on the turf smell bad and promote shade-loving disease, especially when it's wet.

Finally, close cutting to get a really plush looking lawn can be hard on the plants and the gardener, too. You can get a dense turf by cutting low enough to destroy the top bud's "apical dominance." That encourages tillering, by which the plants bush out from the crown. It gives a finer, plusher turf than by clipping only the leaves, but it weakens the plant by stimulating top growth at the expense of the roots. Shallower, weaker roots need more care and maintenance than those in a rangier lawn, and they compete less well against weeds. They make you work harder and worry more.

How tall should grass grow to remove no more than ⅓ of its height and get the seasonal ideal?

Ideal Height	Height at Mowing	Amount to remove
1.0"	1.5"	0.5"
1.5	2.25	0.75
2.0	3.0	1.0
2.5	3.75	1.25
3.0	4.5	1.5
3.5	5.25	1.75
4.0	6.0	2.0

Notice that the taller you let the grass grow, the longer it takes to reach cutting height and the less often it needs mowing. Exactly how fast grass reaches its cutting height depends on the grass, the season, and the temperature. This information can be useful if you decide to use the varied mowing schedule we discuss.

Regional variations - Warm season grasses generally tolerate closer and more frequent summer mowing than cool-season grasses. They grow fast in hot weather, and you can lower their clipping height. There is more variation among the southern grasses than cool season grasses. See Figure 12.3 for their ideal heights. You should raise their cutting heights in the fall, however, to prepare them for winter. For example, Bermuda grass in its northern reaches winters over better if it can get shaggy before the frosts come.

In arid and semi-arid regions drought stress and cutting can kill some grasses. Except for buffalo grass, it is best to avoid mowing most of them, although cutting Kentucky bluegrass and red fescue at the normal height may be all right in the northern and mountainous parts of this region. When it gets hot, however, try to let bluegrass and fescue grow up to 3" or greater heights. The shorter the grass is, the more often you must cut it to remove only one-third. Because northern grasses grow slower in hot weather, they need much less mowing if you let them get taller. That applies to southern grasses in the cool season. See the table of ⅓-off mowing heights, above.

Goodbye, Lawn Mower Bag?

Lawn clippings make up 20% to 25% of the waste in many landfills, and some municipalities are beginning to prohibit them. Don't worry, they're too valuable to throw away. Professional grounds managers have never discarded them.

The best way to deal with clippings generally is to mulch-mow and leave them on the lawn to decompose. Lawn clippings contain all a lawn's nutrients in the same proportions as commercial "organic" fertilizers. And they let you use a slow-release fertilizer with about half the nitrogen and a high W.I.N. number (water-insoluble nitrogen; see Chapter 11 on fertilizer).

Customers' greatest worry about leaving clippings on a turf is "thatch"—the built-up mat of living and dead plants that can block water and air from the soil. Thatch, however, is largely roots, crowns, rhizomes, and stolons. All are high in decay-resistant lignins. Too much nitrogen fertilizer and over-watering encourage lignins. Turfgrass leaves have very little lignin. They're 98% water. They soon wither, shrink, and sift down to the ground, where soil organisms digest them and make their nutrients available to the lawn.

You could mulch-mow by blocking a standard mower's discharge chute so it re-chops the clippings and spreads them more evenly than if blown out the chute. A rotary mower blade's vacuum picks up the clippings and re-chops them, as do front-ejecting power reel mowers to some extent. A real mulching mower, with no chute or bag, chops them even finer, so there are no long clippings left behind to keep out sunlight or encourage disease.

Most authorities on the subject say flatly that you have to mulch-mow more often—every five to six days—in order to remove no more than ⅓ of the height each time. But the five- to six-day schedule is only for the peak growing seasons: spring and fall for cool-season grasses, and summer for warm-season southern grasses. When northern grasses slow down in summer and southern grasses are drowsy in spring and fall, you can probably mow less often. This is also when you may let the leaves grow longer, which would cut mowing frequency even more. You'll have to experiment here. It may take a season or two to set up workable schedules.

Let's complicate matters a little. If your contract is for the whole growing season, you can increase and reduce mowing frequency according to the season and try to aim for the same number of visits as if you mowed once a week. It makes scheduling harder, but if you use a big one-year wall calendar or the right computer software, you can do it. A variable mowing schedule is also an argument for getting paid the same amount for each month of your contract. You'll be busier mowing in the peak growing seasons, but it should give you time to do other gardening tasks when you mow less often.

General Lawn Mowing Rules

Tall grass in deeply watered soil has good roots.

Grass grows in cycles. Cool-season grasses grow faster in spring and fall, warm-season grasses in summer. Ease off them when they slow down, but let Bermudas get shaggy for winter.

Start to mow established lawns each year as soon as the grass greens and reaches the prescribed cutting height. keep after it as needed, cutting off no more than a third at a time. Too deep a cut exposes the lower leaves to sunburn.

Mow when necessary if possible. Base mowing on the grass's growth rate, not a set schedule. Short grasses need to be cut more often to avoid taking off more than a third of their height. You'll have to do a little figuring as you observe your jobs. You and your customer may want to abandon a regular weekly schedule.

In border-zone lawns with mixtures of warm- and cool-season grasses, frequent mowing in the hot summer months favors warm-season grasses and infrequent mowing, especially when it cools off, favors cool-season grasses.

If you can vary how often you mow and keep the same number of sessions over the whole contract, it won't cost your customers more than once-a-week mowing and it will be easier for you to sell them on mulch-mowing. As a small bonus, they'll need less fertilizer (an offset if you have to squeeze in a few more mowings). Finally, mulch-mowing may be the only choice where landfills prohibit grass clippings and you're not set up to compost them.

Not everyone will buy this new approach, however, and it isn't suitable for Merion Kentucky bluegrass, which grows leaves faster than the soil can break them down, or Zoysia grass, which is high in lignins. You'll have to haul these clippings off and compost them, along with those from customers who want their weekly mow-and-haul. If this forces you to set up a composting operation, you can sell it back to customers as soil amendment or your "factory" topdressing for reseeding the lawn each year. In effect, you'll be mulch-mowing with a step in between, and it ought to make you more money. See the introduction to composting in Chapter 16.

Shopping for Mowers

We will consider only walk-behind power mowers, either push or self-propelled. A push model is fine for when you start out. There are pros and cons about self-propelled mowers as with everything else. They take a lot of drudgery out of cutting grass, and we incline toward using them where possible. But they can be a nuisance when you have to make a lot of stops and turns. They are best for large turf areas. If you find you are getting a lot of large plots to cut, you may want to move up to a self-propelled model and use the push mower as a back up. Self-propelled models need plenty of horsepower because part of it goes to driving the mower. Take a test drive before you buy, to be sure it runs at the right speed for your pace. Some are geared to run at various speeds.

When you shop for any mower look for a heavy duty industrial/-commercial (I/C) model from a shop that deals in mowers and related turf equipment. It's a mistake to buy less than commercial quality. See that the shop also services its products. It should know good mowers from bad and steer you to quality equipment. Here are some pointers for shopping for lawn mowers.

A bigger mower will mow a lawn faster than a small one. That hardly needs stating. But first make sure the mower is the right size, weight, and design for you. Get the biggest you are comfortable with, one that won't tire you out too fast.

Besides buying a mower that fits you, consider what size lot you typically mow. A bigger blade cuts faster (so it makes more money) but may be less maneuverable on your jobs. Also, don't buy by brand name or sales pitch alone. A manufacturer may have one terrific model, while the rest are mediocre or even lemons. If you buy used—you may find a well restored high-quality machine—have a good mechanic check it out, ask to see the service and repair records, see what kind of warranty you get. If you have any doubts pass it up and buy new.

Also, go for power and durability. You need at least a 4-horsepower engine; 5 is better. Some newer mowers have powerful, lower speed overhead valve engines that should last longer. All power mowers look pretty similar on the outside. The cheaper ones, however, have cheap mechanicals. Whatever mower you select, it should have an engine with heavy duty parts, including cast iron cylinder sleeves that will not wear excessively and expand away from the piston rings when warmed up.

Get a machine on all-metal wheels. Check the potential weak points, like where the handle attaches to the mower housing. Be sure it is sturdy and won't break; otherwise modify it if you can. You want a short, thick power shaft to drive the blade. It should have a safety key that will shear on hitting a large rock or sprinkler head. Sometimes the keys don't break, and you will be grateful for the short, stiff shaft that won't bend. Some mowers have an offset engine that drives the blade with a belt. This eases stress on the engine when you hit that sprinkler head or surveyor's pin.

Look for a heavy, well-designed starter cord. The handle and cord should be on the side opposite the muffler. There should be guards to keep you safely away from the rear of the mower. Make sure all safety guards and controls work as intended.

New mowers have a number of safety features to look for:

- A deflector on the discharge chute against flying stones, etc.
- A blade housing and deck strong enough to resist puncturing by a projectile, and a place to brace the mower with your foot when you start it.
- A shield to keep your toes from sliding under the housing when the mower suddenly stops rolling or you slip.
- A muffler placed well away from the fuel tank, and exhaust directed away from the grass-catcher.
- A gas tank that can't leak or spill onto hot engine parts.
- Controls that don't force you to fiddle around near hot or fast moving parts.

Look for easy cutting-height adjustment that keeps your fingers away from the blade. Mowers built since 1982 have a "dead man" device that shuts off the engine or the blade when you release the handle. A better device is a Blade Brake Clutch that stops the blade within 3 or 4 seconds but leaves the engine running. That way, the blade is disengaged while you make adjustments and you don't have to keep yanking the cord to start up again.

Lawn Mower Safety

In 1995 power mowers injured 74,582 people, 75 of whom—including 15 children—were killed. The commonest injuries are amputations and injuries from thrown objects. Mowers are powerful cutting machines that make short work of dense grass, thick stems, sticks, wires, glass, and whatever gets in their way, including toes and fingers. The cutting blade can whip out projectiles like rocks and bits of metal or glass at 200 miles per hour. That's 300 feet—the length of a football field—per second. And, no, your reflexes aren't good enough for dodging, in case it crossed your mind.

Many of the thousands injured by power mowers were burned by a hot muffler or engine housing, or sometimes by explosions that resulted from gasoline touching the muffler or engine.

Start Your Engines

Wait! First, read and *understand* the operator's manual before you turn on your new lawn mower, and *always* follow the instructions.

- Keep the mower tuned up and in good repair.
- Dress for success. Wear sturdy long trousers. Use high-top shoes with steel toe caps for protection should an unexpected event put your feet under the blade. Shoes should also have steel or Kevlar reinforcements to protect your ankles and part of your shins from flying rocks, etc. Wear effective ear protection; and eye protection is always a good idea. If you absolutely have to mow wet grass to keep to your schedule, wear cleated or at least treaded shoes and make allowances for its being slippery.
- Fill the fuel tank before you start mowing. That sounds obvious, but if you forget that and it runs out, you have to remember to push the mower off the grass and let the engine cool for at least 10 minutes or until it is safe to pour in the gasoline.
- Always wait for the engine to cool before re-fueling and don't smoke while you do it.
- Refuel using the correct fuel mixture, either outdoors or in a well-ventilated area.
- Start the mower at least 20 feet from where you refueled it.
- When you pull the starter cord plant your feet firmly and brace yourself and the mower. Don't stand near the discharge chute. Start up close to the grass you're going to cut, but on a firm dry surface. Watch where you are going and expect the unexpected.
- Keep feet and hands away from the blade when starting or operating the mower.
- Before mowing look the lawn over closely to see if there are any "bullets" for the mower to shoot at you. If in doubt, rake the lawn first. It slows you down, so you have to balance risk against speed. If you don't rake, watch very closely and stop when necessary.
- Keep bystanders, especially children and pets, out of the way.
- Push. Don't pull the mower backward and risk getting your feet under it.
- Don't walk away and leave the mower's motor running.
- Remember to vary the direction and pattern each time you mow, otherwise, you will make ruts in the turf. Power mow across slopes, not up or down them. (Riding mowers should go

up and down slopes.) Slopes are tricky to cut even with old fashioned push reel mowers. If a slope seems too steep for a mower, and you get the willies every time you do the job, talk to the customer about a low-maintenance ground cover, at least over the steepest part. Or consider a good hand mower for that part of the lawn. Scott® makes a 20"-wide mower with a 3" maximum cutting height. You can buy it through at least one Web site: www.cleanairmowing.com/scottclassicreel.htm.

FINALLY–

Turning a mower's cutting blade with the spark plug wire connected can start the engine. Always disconnect the spark plug wire when adjusting any moving part on the mower.

Better: Don't connect the spark plug wire *except* when you are mowing.

Mowing - Begin mowing a lawn as follows:

1. Pick up any debris in the lawn, roll up hoses and remove toys, dog bones, or other small objects.
2. Check mower height.
3. Start the engine on a hard, flat surface as close to the lawn as possible.
4. Mow the lawn area's outside perimeter, circling once or twice to give yourself room to make turns.
5. Mow the remainder in straight lines, overlapping the previous line slightly.

Be aware of your surroundings and watch for tree limbs, holes, and other dangers high and low. If you are hauling the clippings take along a tarp or trash can to remote areas like the back yard, so you won't have to walk back and forth to your truck to empty the mower bag. Finishing off, don't mow across your nice straight lines to make a bee-line for the truck.

Basic Mower Maintenance

Disconnect the spark plug wire if you haven't already. Clean the mower by scraping the blade and housing at the end of each work day, and more often if needed. The glucose in grass is a pretty good adhesive and will build up a tough, thick coat of dead grass.

Keep the blade sharp by running it over a grinding wheel daily; but don't overheat the edge and destroy its temper. Balancing the blade with a $5 balancing weight is a cheap way to prolong mower life and stave off "white finger," a lingering injury caused from vibration that shakes the circulation, feeling, and grip out of your fingers.

Keep the oil and air filters clean. Dirt will wear down engine parts just as it will in your car, and a clogged air filter reduces performance. Change the oil and filter often—at least once a week for the oil, monthly for the filter. Oil breaks down fast in a hot, high-revving mower engine. Keep the cooling fins and the rest of the engine clean so they dissipate heat well. Using an air compressor periodically helps clean out engine parts. Check all nuts, bolts, and other fasteners for tightness and condition. Use a torque wrench if the manual gives torque specifications.

If your season ends, empty the fuel tank by siphoning and run the engine till it dies. Try starting it a few times to be sure the tank is empty. This protects the tank and carburetor from condensation and rust. Clean accumulated mud and grass from the blade and deck one last time for the season, then sharpen and balance or replace the blade. If there is any rust on the blade or housing, remove it and prime the clean metal. Then spray the blade and deck with a moisture displacing fluid like WD-40.

Next, pull the spark plug and drain the oil. Squirt a few ounces of oil in the spark plug hole. Refill the crankcase with fresh oil and crank the engine with the starting cord a few times to lubricate the cylinder walls. Clean, regap, and replace the plug, but don't connect the wire. This is a good time to replace filters. Next season, before you start, drain and refill the crankcase. We recommend also learning how to repair your own equipment and take that up in Chapter 17.

Edging

Crisp edges normally improve a lawn's appearance. Edging is a job that demands power tools for efficiency. You should edge with a string trimmer where a lawn edge is already established; it makes quick work of the job. Old-fashioned power edgers are much too cumbersome for commercial use and are a bad investment. Always use the cutting string as long as possible, with cleanly cut ends. A short string won't cut as cleanly and vibrates the operator. If the engine bogs down or struggles, the string is too long. Stabilize the trimmer by holding it close to your body with the cutting head vertical, and walk along the pavement at a steady pace. Run the string in the edge line between the pavement and turf. Always walk forward to see obstacles in your path, and *stop* trimming if anyone is approaching you from ahead or behind.

String trimmers throw rocks with enough force to break the windshields of cars parked across the street. Always use extreme care when trimming near rocks or gravel!

Some lawns don't have to be edged every time, but may require touch up with a hand edger or the string trimmer. A sharp hand tool, like a half-moon edger—even a spade or square shovel in a pinch—will slice off errant grass blades. Don't depend on lawn shears, even the long handled stand-up kind. They slow you down needlessly, unless you are just spot trimming.

Aerating

Aeration does for soil under turf what tilling does for other garden soils. It involves lightening the soil by extracting 2" to 4" plugs of it from the lawn 2" to 6" apart in each direction. The plugs or "cores" lay on the surface where they decompose a little before being raked away. The process is called aeration because it makes spaces in the soil for the roots to get air, water, and nutrients.

When the soil is damp you can aerate manually or with a power aerator. Forget manual aeration. The worst kind of aeration, called spiking, just pokes holes in the soil and compacts it more around the holes. The best quality aeration is done with a heavy-duty machine that pulls up cores ½" to ¾" thick and 3" deep. It is something you should either subcontract or refer out. Good aerators cost from $2,000 to $4,000. You can rent less expensive models from rental agencies, but try one out before adding aeration to your list of professional services. Unless it makes sense as a sideline or you'll use it enough to justify buying, it's better to refer the job out and let an expert do it. See the Appendix for Robin M. Pedrotti's book on the aeration business.

Post-aeration fertilization, amendment, and watering encourages deeper root growth. With lots of little holes all over it, the lawn soaks up water better, too, so it's a good way to reduce water loss on slopes. The only soil that should not be aerated is a sandy one, which has too much aeration.

The consensus is now that lawns should be aerated from at least four to as many as six times a year. A lawn that is regularly aerated needs it less often than one that has been neglected, and excess thatch, as well as compaction, may call for aeration.

Thatch and Dethatching

As we said, lawn clippings you haul off after mowing take nutrients away with them. You can replace them with fertilizer or you can leave them on the lawn to decompose and return the nutrients to the soil. When the lawn is a variety that inclines toward thatch, there is little choice except to remove the clippings. They'll never reach the soil and will just add to the thatch. Always check for thatch, and consider dethatching if it has become excessive.

If you stick your finger down between the grass blades and feel bare soil, there is no thatch at all. Either all the clippings were caught and taken away in every prior mowing, or they decomposed on the ground where they fell and became part of the soil again. It would indicate a live, fertile soil that needs much less added fertilizer. But it's so rare that it's almost gardening folklore or fantasy.

In most lawns thatch isn't all bad. About ½" of it helps even out temperature swings and cushions the crowns against wear. Some authorities recommend slicing a V into the turf and prying up the point to see now much thatch there is. If you pry up a whole spadeful of sod, you can check for earthworms, which help decomposition. If there aren't any, they may be the victims of heavy pesticide use along with other organisms that consume vegetation on the soil. That's another reason to cut down on pesticides.

Grass leaves by themselves usually won't cause thatch to build up. Too much nitrogen or over-watering hastens thatch, however, and some bred-up turf grasses make leaves faster than the soil can decompose them. Vigorous growers are prone to this kind of over-production, and stoloniferous grasses are even worse because the stolons tend to weave around each other. Fibrous grasses like zoysias and fescues decompose slowly. If a lawn has a thatch problem, don't leave clippings on the ground after mowing.

Just so you can't say we've ignored the problems of southern grasses, here's how to reinvigorate Bermuda grass: Wait till the weather warms to about 55 degrees. Then shave, verticut if necessary, aerate, feed, amend, and topdress.

If the mat of tangled dead straw, stolons, and roots exceeds ½ inch, the lawn has too much thatch and may show it. A thick thatch, like that on the roof of English cottages, keeps water off the lawn's roots; but unlike the inhabitants of English cottages, the roots need and want the water. Some thatches even keep air from the roots. Thatch also provides a good home for insects and usually goes along with serious insect damage. A mower's wheels will sometimes sink into a soft thick thatch and "scalp" the lawn, causing a brown, stubbly patch.

The only real fix is to remove the excess and keep it under control. If it's only moderately thick, a power rake with tough steel tines that spin over the ground can claw it out. Even hand raking may work. If it's too thick for a power rake, the next step is a vertical mower or "verticutter." A verticutter has sharp blades that chop through and under thatch, and lift out little clumps of it. If it seems to be chopping the lawn out of the ground, turn it off. The lawn's roots are too shallow. Set the blades higher in order to break up the thatch. Then try to get the lawn rooted more deeply in the next few months before trying to verticut again. Use a power rake or verticutter when the ground is slightly damp but not wet.

Verticutting is a pretty drastic cure; lawns need a chance to recover from vertical mowing. Dethatch cool season grasses in early spring or in late fall while there is still at least a month of growing season left. Dethatch warm season grasses in late spring at the start of their growing season. It's likely that, even without excess pesticide, soil micro-organisms beneath thatch have suffered from lack of air and water, and the soil is probably as poor as the grass that grows in it. Coordinate dethatching with a program of fertilization, amendment, and deep watering to give the soil proper *p*H, good drainage, and to promote a fresh supply of earthworms and micro-organisms. It helps to follow dethatching with a topdressing of about ¼" of matching topsoil, compost, humus, or even well-rotted manure to encourage natural decomposition and help build a good soil. Be careful to limit mulch-mowing until the rate of decomposition catches up.

Frequent aeration has the same effect as verticutting, with lower stress on the turf. You might instead consider regular aeration to revive a lawn with heavy thatch, although it may not work in every case.

Re-seeding for Best Appearance

In the fall of every other year or so, at the time when you fertilize, you may want to re-seed northern grasses with a good bluegrass/fescue seed mix (you don't need the cheap cover grasses). You use the same kind of trough/drop spreader as for fertilizer. Then topdress the turf with a topsoil to keep birds from dining on the seeds. Most experts recommend using the same topsoil as is already there. That's usually not possible, but try to match it as best you can. In the spring the new grass will regenerate the lawn and promote a thick, healthy appearance. For more information about reseeding, see the next chapter on lawn installation and renovation.

Finishing the Job

You have come on the jobsite, set up the mower and string trimmer, put on your ear protection and safety glasses, and mowed and edged.

Now get out the broom, blower, tarp, and a bucket or large trash can, and clean up the site. If you mowed with a grass catcher, there may be little if anything to pick up. If you used a mulching mower, there may be a few bits strewn on the pavement to blow back onto the lawn.

Regardless of how little debris you think the job made, load the mower, edger, and other mowing equipment securely on the truck, then check the site over. Remember you came to leave it better than you found it. If there is time, clean the edging beds to make that final good impression. Use the tarp and bucket for things pulled from branches or raked up and pitched into them. When you are sure you did the best job possible, pack up and go on to the next job.

Preliminary Considerations
Installation
Renovation

Chapter 14

LAWNS – INSTALLATION AND RENOVATION

Quick Start:

WHILE installing a lawn is beyond the scope of this book, knowing how one is installed right can help analyze problems that watering, fertilizing, and spraying for pests won't fix. If you are skimming for basic information, this chapter goes beyond the basics, but someday you may need to renovate a lawn and you need to know about installation to renovate well. Proper installation involves good drainage, soil structure, pH balance, and nutrient mix, then planting the right grass. Any corners cut will make an inferior lawn, and no amount of watering, feeding, or dousing with sprays will make it better.

So, if all else fails, don't forget the lawn's installation.

THE MORE YOU KNOW about installing or renovating lawns successfully, the easier lawn care gets. You may never install a lawn, but, as with any craft, any job that relates to it matters to those who pursue it. This isn't an exact science, and the more you learn about good practice, the better you'll become.

Preliminary Considerations

Licensing - Lawn renovation can mean a complete overhaul—that is, installing a new lawn—or re-seeding small bare patches. The contractor's license laws in your state may prevent you from installing even the simplest lawn. In California, for instance, a landscape contractor is defined as anyone who constructs, repairs, or installs landscape systems and facilities for public and private gardens, or who subcontracts for someone else to do it. A landscape contractor is defined further as someone who "prepares or grades plots and areas of land" for any horticultural or decorative treatment. If you are unlicensed in California but do work that requires a license, the customer can legally refuse to pay you, and the state can charge you with a misdemeanor if the customer complains. So, unlicensed contracting can be risky.

In any case, it is worth knowing how to install and renovate a lawn if your state allows you to do some or all of it without a license. Also, knowing how a lawn is installed properly will help you analyze and correct problems that lie beyond routine maintenance. Analyzing the problem is the first thing you must do to know what steps to take and whether to take them or refer the job to a landscape contractor.

What's the problem? - There are some preliminary issues to consider before tackling lawn problems, including the following items.

Lawn diseases caused by fungi can strike quickly. sometimes overnight. Many make a pattern of rings, patches, and colors. If you can diagnose it, it's too late. Fungicides prevent diseases better than they stop them and cost more than minor repairs. It's often better to strip away the damaged areas, fix any soil problems, reseed with disease resistant strains, and prevent new outbreaks with healthy cultivation practices.

Insects can ravage a lawn. Surface feeders can chew off blades or pierce grass shoots and suck out fluids. Subsurface insects, like white grubs (beetle larvae) eat the roots and may kill large areas of lawn by fall. To check for grubs, reach into a patch of dead turf and try to pull it back. If it rolls back like a rug, grubs are probably at work. Insecticides can control insect damage, but in all but the worst cases it makes more sense to take better care of the lawn after repairing the damage. A well watered, drained, aerated, amended, and fertilized lawn normally will outgrow hungry insects.

Grass wants four to six hours of sun each day. Even shade-tolerant varieties do poorly without a few hours of direct sun. The best solution for a shady spot is to replace grass with a shade-tolerant ground cover. Licensing laws may prevent you from doing even this.

Grass won't grow well in hard-packed soil. Neither roots nor oxygen can get in. You can try switching to grass that tolerates heavy traffic but it makes more sense to lay a path or make everyone keep off the grass. If the whole lawn suffers from compaction the best fix is to aerate regularly.

Excessive thatch is usually caused by grass varieties that grow too densely, from over-fertilization or sometimes too much time between mowing. Long clippings take longer to decompose. Control thatch by choosing less thatch-prone varieties, by fertilizing less, and by mowing more often. In severe cases de-thatch regularly.

Weeds are at home in a thin, shallow-rooted lawn. The reasons for sickly lawns vary. We've discussed a few of them. Usually it's a local problem that a good nursery or your county extension can best advise about. Be sure your renovation plan addresses local problems.

Poor subsoil drainage may require the installation of a drain tile system. The system should be designed and installed after consultation with a tile dealer, county extension agent, or other professional.

Installation

For easy reading this section will proceed like instructions on installing a lawn, whether or not you ever do it. So put yourself in the contractor's shoes and follow along.

Seedbed preparation - After considering and taking care of the above steps, installation proceeds as follows.

A good lawn begins with the subsoil. First, remove all debris such as bricks, stones, cans, concrete, boards, paper, wire, and the like from the proposed lawn site. Do not bury debris; it will interfere with plant development. (Often an unscrupulous building contractor may bury construction debris and let the landscape subcontractor install a lawn over it.)

Loosen the subsoil with a rototiller, a spade, or otherwise so that it can be worked. Slope it away from the house. Don't slope it to drop more than one foot in 16. One foot in 50 is adequate for good drainage.

When you finish grading the subsoil, test for *p*H level. If local soil testing facilities are not available commercially or through the state or county extension service, ask a farmer or nurseryman in your area whether your area's soil is acid or alkaline. Using an inexpensive kit to test for *p*H is okay, but it won't tell the whole story or give recommendations.

Mix in lime or gypsum, if needed, and phosphate fertilizer before covering the grade with topsoil. The amount of lime or gypsum will vary with the soil's original *p*H and the type of soil. Clay, with more particles per cubic foot, needs more lime. Usually you want 50 pounds per 1,000 SF. Once the soil is balanced, it should get about 35 pounds per 1,000 SF every three years, but not all at once. Dolomitic limestone, which contains magnesium and calcium, is best for eastern soils but is not available everywhere. It is often unnecessary in dry western soils which usually have enough magnesium and calcium. (That doesn't apply where we are on the cool, wet coast.)

Spread a 4" to 6" layer of topsoil evenly over the subsoil. Use a hand rake to level and spread it, and try to avoid making low spots. Tying a rope to the ends of a ladder or long plank and dragging it across the surface is a good final check for evenness.

Before buying "topsoil" inspect it for its quality. Some is just spiffed up subsoil and may contain debris, toxic salts, noxious weed seeds, or other unwanted surprises. You can make a fairly decent topsoil by adding an equal amount of plain sawdust or similar organic material to the first 6" of existing soil. If the sawdust is fresh, it will need a little extra nitrogen to help break it down. Add 10 pounds of iron chelate or iron sulfate, and mix it in with 55 pounds of ammonium sulfate or 35 pounds of ammonium nitrate per 1,000 SF to help the micro-organisms digest the cellulose. The ammonium sulfate will acidify the soil, the nitrate will not. Check to see what is used locally.

You may have to add about 25 pounds of a superphosphate per 1,000 SF, too, but check with your county agricultural extension agent about that as well.

Do another *p*H test before seeding. If you need more lime or gypsum after you spread the topsoil, apply it while you work the soil to a finish grade. If the soil is too sandy, gravelly, or mostly heavy clay you will have to incorporate soil additives to improve its organic content or structure. Remember that a desirable soil contains 7 to 27 percent clay, 28 to 50 percent silt, and less than 52 percent sand. There are laboratories equipped to test the content of soil. Essentially, the test consists of stirring up a thick soil-soup in a straight-sided jar of water and letting it settle out. Sand, the heaviest settles out first, followed by silt, then clay. The proportions are estimated by measuring the levels with a ruler. There is also the fistful-of-squeezed-mud test that works pretty well for experienced gardeners. You can add silt, clay, or sand in order to balance the soil's characteristics. A heavy clay soil can be lightened by adding sand, perlite, vermiculite or calcined clay, but remember organic amendment is essential and better.

Good topsoil should contain 25 to 50 percent of organic matter by volume for good ion exchange and nutrient retention. Likely additives are eight- to 10-year-old decomposed sawdust, spent mushroom soil, and rotted manure. You can also add rice hulls, peanut shells, cocoa shells, and similar cellulose materials if they are composted. If not, add a little extra nitrogen to help the soil micro-organisms break them down.

Another way to add organic matter is by turning under a "green manure" crop four to six weeks before planting the grass. In northern regions a spring planting of soybeans, sweet clover, red clover, sudangrass, or ryegrass will give you green manure to turn under in August. In the South fall plantings of crimson clover, hairy vetch, winter rye, or ryegrass will provide a cover through the fall and winter to be turned under before a spring planting.

Two to four cubic yards of organic soil additive per 1,000 SF are usually enough. Combine these additives into the soil very thoroughly so that you don't create layers. Layers of clay often stop water movement, while layers of organic matter get saturated with water and

Figure 14.1 Grass seeds. (Facing page.)

Lawn seeds

Production, transport, and sale of seeds in this country are subject to strict state and federal laws to control quality and limit the spread of noxious weeds. The Federal Seed Act (Title 7 of the U.S. Code, beginning at Section 1551) has a counterpart in every state. Among other things, these laws govern what goes on the seed label.

The *statement of purity,* "pure seed," gives the percentage by weight of the seed varieties. If the seeds are Merion Kentucky bluegrass with 90-percent purity, that means a 100-pound bag contains 90 pounds of bluegrass seeds of the Merion Kentucky strain. The 10 pounds (10%) of impurities are other seeds, inert matter—chaff, dirt, sand, seed parts—and weed seeds.

The amount of impurity is less important than the kinds of impurities. No one wants a bag of 99% pure seed if the 1% impurity is perennial sowthistle seeds. Seed laws make producers list noxious weed seeds separately on the label, and most states prohibit the sale of mixes that contain certain of them.

The *germination percentage* states how much of the pure seed should sprout. A 90-percent germination rate means that 90 percent of the, say, 90 pounds of pure seed in the bag will germinate as of the date on the label. This percentage drops as the seeds age, although seeds stored in a cool, dry place should last better than those that aren't. Generally, the heavier a bag, the likelier the seeds will germinate well and grow vigorously.

Sometimes you see the terms *pure live seed* or *real value.* They refer to how much of the selected seed is expected to sprout. Ninety percent germination of a 90-percent-pure bag of bluegrass seeds has a real value of 81, that is, 0.90 x 0.90 = 0.81, which means 81%, or 81 pounds, of all the seeds in our 100-pound sack will sprout and grow as bluegrass plants.

Seed mixtures. Since most lawns consist of two or three grass varieties, a seed mixture should be simple, with grasses that give a uniform appearance. Kentucky bluegrass and red fescue blend well, with bluegrass predominating in the sun and fescue taking over the shade. Most mixtures also contain a fast growing annual or perennial grass to cover the bed until the slower bluegrass and fescue get going. There is a tendency away from using such "nurse" crops because they often compete too well with the selected varieties, and you don't need them when re-seeding.

SEEDING RATE	NET WT. 64 OZ. (4 LBS)
OVERSEEDING LAWNS	1 LB. PER 700 SQ. FT.
NEW LAWNS	1 LB. PER 350 SQ. FT.

PREMIUM GRASS SEED MIXTURE

PURE SEED		GERM.	ORIGIN
48.53%	CREEPING RED FESCUE *	80%	OR
25.01%	MERION KENTUCKY BLUEGRASS *	80%	OR
23.21%	KENTUCKY BLUEGRASS *	80%	OR
0.96	CROP SEED	75%	OR
2.12%	INERT MATTER		
0.17%	WEED SEED		

LOT NO. 47308-GT-11105678 NOXIOUS WEEDS: NONE
TEST DATE 8-93 * VARIETY NOT STATED

EXEMPLARY LAWN & TURF CO., P.O. BOX 43,
BEAVERTON, OR 97000

Example of a seed label.

drown the plants. Even at best, grass will do poorly in these conditions because both layers lack oxygen for the roots.

Preparing to plant - The best way to prepare soil for planting is to rototill or spade it, then disk or hand rake. Excessive rototilling can destroy some of the soil structure because it "floats" the finer soil particles to the surface. You need to finish by hand raking in order to level the soil and eliminate hollows and low spots. Water the soil to sprout weed seeds, and spray with a non-residual herbicide (*e.g.*, glyphosate) or pull by hand.

Just before planting apply a complete slow-release inorganic fertilizer and rake it into the soil. Try to base the proportions of nitrogen, phosphate, potassium, and other elements on a competent professional analysis of the prepared soil. This step can make the difference between an "okay" lawn and a great one. For northern grasses, apply the fertilizer so that it will provide two pounds of nitrogen per 1,000 SF unless the test shows it needs more. Many soils lack phosphorus, which is important when grasses are getting started. You can overcome this deficiency by mixing 25 pounds per 1,000 SF of a superphosphate into the first 3" to 5" of soil before planting, if you didn't do it when making topsoil out of sawdust.

Tree wells - Trees can be killed by suffocation when their roots are covered deeply by soil. If the new lawn level will be higher than existing soil surface, trees should be protected by a brick or stone well around the tree. The well should have been three to five feet larger in diameter than the tree trunk. A 6" layer of crushed stone or gravel should have been spread around the well and extended 6 to 10 feet outward. The new lawn level should be over the stone or gravel to the well's edge. This lets air reach the tree roots.

Planting northern grass seeds - Mixtures of seeds, mainly bluegrass and fescue with a fast growing cover species, are usually planted in the northern region. Single species are planted in the south. Consult your extension agent, nurseryman, or seed dealer for the best mix.

Choose the right grass. Select high quality seed of a type or types that are suited to your soil and climate. Go back and read the list in Chapter 12 on grasses or ask your cooperative extension agent for a list of varieties the state university recommends. Plant a mix of three or four of them. If one fails the others will fill in.

The transportation and sale of seeds are controlled by federal and state law, and the information on their labels or tags is strictly controlled. The labels give the percentage of each grass seed in the container, the purity, the germination rate, and the date of the germination test. A sample tag is illustrated in figure 14.1. Read the label of any seeds you buy. "Bargain" lawn seed often contains "trash" varieties like redtop. The price of lawn seed will probably be around 5 percent of the total cost of installation; so it is a false economy to buy anything but the best quality seed.

You can sow seed by hand, but for even coverage you need a mechanical seeder. For a more uniform distribution, mix the seed with small amounts of topsoil or sand as a carrier. Divide the mix evenly in half, and sow one part in one direction and the second crosswise to the first sowing. Or divide it in fourths and spread from the four points of the compass. Cover the seed by lightly raking it in. Cover large seeds ¼" to ⅜" deep, and small seeds ⅛" to ¼" deep. Firm up the surface with a light roller or other packing tool. The soil surface should be watered several times a day to keep it moist. The new seedlings once germinated should be kept moist until well established. In many places, saturating the soil at this point can encourage a fungus blight called "damping off." In hot, dry climates you have to saturate the soil before the final seedbed preparation in order to create a "reservoir" of moisture to keep the seed from drying out.

To help hold in moisture you can mulch the surface with a light covering (⅛" to ¼") of straw or peat moss also prevents rainfall from washing out the seed. Don't use sawdust. A 60- to 80-pound bale of straw will cover 1,000 SF. Evenly spread, it will eventually rot and need not be removed. You will have to use open-mesh sacking or commercial mulching material on a terrace or slope to prevent erosion as well as to mulch.

Sodding - Unless the customer wants a new lawn in a hurry, the expense of sodding can't be justified except on steep slopes or terraces where the seeds may wash out. You prepare the subsoil and top soil the same as for seeding, then firm it with a roller after the final hand raking.

The thinner the sod the better. Sod cut ¾" thick will knit to the soil faster than one cut 1" thick. Sod should not be thicker than an inch.

Lay the sod pieces in a staggered pattern like bricks. After laying the first strip along the edge of the lawn, place a broad piece of plywood on the sodded strip. Kneel on the board and move it forward as you progress. Don't trample the prepared seedbed. After laying out the sod, tamp it down or roll it lightly and apply a little topsoil as a topdressing, working it into the cracks of the sod pieces with a stiff broom or the like. Keep the sod moist until well established.

Vegetative planting - Many grasses, primarily bentgrass in the north and those common to the southern region of the United States, are not grown from seed. They are planted by spot, plug, or strip sodding, sprigging, or stolonizing. Centipede grass, velvet bentgrass, and buffalograss may be either seeded or vegetatively planted. With some, like buffalograss, the result is different from seeding.

Spot sodding is planting small plugs or blocks of sod at about one-foot intervals. You can set them closer for faster coverage. Fit the plugs tightly into prepared holes and then tamp them firmly into place.

Strip sodding is done by planting 2" to 4" wide strips of sod 6" to 12" apart. Again the strips should contact the prepared soil firmly.

Sprigging requires planting individual plants, runners, cuttings, or stolons obtained by shredding solid pieces of established sod. Sprigs or runners may be planted end to end in rows or at spaced intervals. How densely to plant the sprigs depends on how fast you want coverage. Sprigs come by the bushel, or you can buy sod and pull it apart carefully. Some people recommend inserting each sprig in prepared furrows and firming the soil around them. Excess handwork is costly; so buy by the bushel, scatter the sprigs over the seedbed and roll them in with a special cleated roller.

Stolonizing is done by mechanical equipment that spreads shredded stolons over an area that is disked or rolled and topdressed. It is done only for large or specialized areas like golf courses.

Renovation

Renovating a lawn may involve complete reconstruction, or it may be a matter of re-establishing grass without destroying the surviving turf. Sometimes a lawn needs reconstruction because of poor drainage or faulty subsoil, and the work is the same as for a new installation. If the lawn needs total reconstruction, a contractor would have to tear it up with a spade, rototiller or plow, and establish a new one following the procedures set out above.

Lawns that can be renovated without moving lots of earth are those that: lack plant nutrients; have acid or alkaline soils; or suffer from surface compaction, too much shade, insects or disease, or too many undesirable grasses or weeds. Most often the cause is just general neglect.

Early fall is the best time to renovate a northern lawn. Summer heat is hard on new, less well-established plants. Also there is less competition in fall because most weed seeds germinate in the spring. Spring is the best time to renovate a southern variety. For spring renovation plan on following up with plenty of water and careful weeding.

If less than 50 percent of the lawn is in desirable grasses, the best approach is to tear out everything and replant. If more than 50 percent is in good shape, you can usually replant without preparing a new seedbed. First find out what caused the deterioration. You will have to coordinate renovation with a corrective program, otherwise the lawn will have to be renovated again within a few years. Probably not by you.

Have the soil tested before beginning to renovate. Then add topsoil, lime, sulfur, organic matter or fertilizer as indicated by the test. In some cases, you may want to aerate the soil to enhance the application.

Your next step is to get rid of all weeds and unwanted grasses. Either dig them up or apply an herbicide, such as a broadleaf selective kind like Weed-B-Gon®. (Check with your local ag department about licensing or certification.) A glyphosate like Roundup® is non-selective and will injure or kill any plant it touches. Mow closely, rake to remove clippings, and other debris. Consider running a dethatcher deeply over the bad patches to pull out the remains of any old lawn. What you cut out can go into the compost pile. Finish by using a chemical weed killer to knock out the remaining weeds. Bermuda grass is particularly stubborn and will have to be sprayed a lot to kill the stolons. We discuss chemical weed killers briefly in the next chapter on lawn diseases and in Chapter 18 on pesticides.

There are two kinds of lawn repair with seeds. For dead patches, rake the area vigorously and thoroughly, or cultivate it to loosen the soil surface. This makes a rough seedbed for planting. For areas that are failing but not dead, simply overseed.

Even overseeding takes preparation. First rake the lawn vigorously with a stiff rake or de-thatching rake. Pull up whatever thatch you can and sow the seeds by hand or with a spreader cross-wise in two directions. Rake again to make good seed-to-soil contact. Cover with topsoil so you're not just feeding the chickadees.

If a patch of grass is dead, start by digging up the dead turf. Work in topsoil and a soil amendment if necessary. Spread a few handfuls of seeds over the soil. Rake the seeds lightly into the soil or scatter on topsoil and tamp the whole area with your feet. If the soil is dry, mulch with a weed-free straw to help retain moisture. A mulch can also control erosion, and protect the seeds from being washed out by heavy rains. Apply fertilizer and amendments according to the soil test.

Keep the seeded area damp. Water lightly and often if there is no rain, but avoid flooding the area. Water less often after germination (one to two weeks) then mow when the seedlings reach the height of surrounding grass.

Renovating a warm-season lawn

The best time to renovate a warm-season lawn is just before the growing season and after the last frost. Again, consult with your extension service about the best grasses to use. Many improved hybrids of warm-season grasses won't set seeds and must be vegetatively propagated. See above. Sod gives immediate results but is very expensive. For a small repair, plugs or sprigs are cheaper. Prepare the seed bed as before—including needed fertilization, amendment, and aeration—then water the soil in advance, usually the night before. Make holes as deep as the root balls with a special plug cutter or a bulb planter. Space the plugs 6"to 12" apart in a checkerboard pattern. It will take four to six months for them to fill in. Like plugs, sprigs won't fill in for months. After a reasonable wait, however, you and the lawn should be back in business.

Zoysia matrella. (USDA)

Fungi

Moss

Weeds

Insects and Others

Chapter 15

LAWN DISORDERS – COMMON ILLS AND A FEW REMEDIES

Quick Start: *EVEN correctly established, well maintained lawns have their bad days. Among the pests that afflict turfgrasses are fungi, mosses, weeds, and critters. This chapter does not list them all but hits the major pests and afflictions. References to chemicals can soon go out of date, and we have not provided anything like a complete list. You will have to consult a local supplier or agricultural extension service for what is currently recommended. This chapter is intended only to help you recognize the major infestations and how to respond in a general way. It suggests some answers and, we hope, gives some guidance. Otherwise, you can skip it now and read later to fill in the gap.*

IMPROPERLY established or maintained lawns, those with poor soil aeration or drainage, or improper fertilizing, watering, or mowing are likelier to have diseases than those without these problems. The following are a few of the commoner lawn diseases. Consider any references below to specific chemicals as suggestions, because products registered with state and federal government agencies constantly change. New products enter the market and old products are withdrawn. Also, registration with the U.S. Environmental Protection Agency (EPA) doesn't guarantee the product is available in every state. So you will need to check your garden center or agricultural extension agent to find the newest killers and fastest guns.

Fungi

Brown patch is a fungus disease of nearly all turf grasses, but is worst on Kentucky bluegrass, bentgrass, ryegrass, centipede grass, St. Augustine grass, and fescues in the west. It causes irregular brown spots 1" to several feet in diameter. There is a dark "smoke ring" outer edge where the fungus is active. Excessive nitrogen fertilization aggravates the disease. Control by cutting back nitrogen, minimizing shade, irrigating deeply, and applying a recommended fungicide.

Dollarspot is a fungus disease most severe on Kentucky bluegrass, bentgrass, ryegrass, centipede grass, and St. Augustine grass. It causes wet looking, straw-colored spots the size of a silver dollar, which often merge to form large irregular areas of damage. Dethatch, water deeply, and apply a high-nitrogen fertilizer. Fungicides can help control it.

Fairy ring appears as growing rings of dark green grass, with or without mushrooms, which leave dead grass behind them. Aerate, apply a high-nitrogen fertilizer, and water heavily for up to five days. Fungicides don't work here.

Fusarium patch is common in the central and northeastern U.S., showing up as 2" to 12" tan spots with thin white threads in thatch or dewy grass. Reduce shade, aerate, and improve drainage if possible. Cut down high-nitrogen fertilizers and apply a fungicide in early fall.

Grease spot makes dark and matted leaves in greasy streaks across the lawn. It prefers new lawns. Minimize shade and cut down on water. Check on the best chemical control.

Leafspot causes reddish-brown to purple-black spots on Kentucky bluegrass, and may reach the crown and cause serious damage. To limit damage mow no shorter than 2 inches, fertilize well, overseed with Merion Kentucky bluegrass.

Red thread is a cool, moist weather fungus that causes small patches of dead grass snarled in bright pink threads, which spread out in 2" to 12" yellowed patches. Reduce shade and apply a high-nitrogen fertilizer in late fall.

Rust looks like its name and comes off as an orange smudge if you rub the grass with a white cloth. Water, apply a high-nitrogen fertilizer and the right fungicide—the labels will tell.

Snow mold is a fungus disease common in the northern region in late fall, winter, and early spring. The fungus cause of the disease likes the cool moist conditions of melting snow. It first appears as a white cottony growth on the leaves, which will kill and turn them brown and matted. Treat by providing adequate drainage, less fall fertilizer, and raking leaves, etc, from the lawn. Winter applications of fungicide will help prevent the disease.

Slime molds are bluish gray, black, or yellowish masses of molds that may show up in wet weather. They smother the grass. Break up the masses by sweeping them with a broom. They disappear in dry weather. In long wet periods, after sweeping, dust lawn with a dry fungicide.

A lawn disease caused by fungi often strikes very quickly. By the time you diagnose it, it's usually too late to stop it. Fungicides prevent diseases better than they cure them and cost more than prevention based on disease-resistant strains and healthy cultivation practices. Because many fungi have reproductive cycles of around 7 to 10 days, the labels on fungicides often will recommend how soon and often to reapply the chemical. The best cure is still to eliminate the conditions that provide fungi a home.

Moss

Low fertility is the commonest cause of moss in lawns. It never develops in a healthy lawn. Poor drainage, high soil acidity, too much shade and soil compaction or a combination of the above cause moss in lawns. Get rid of it by hand raking or burning it with ferrous ammonium sulfate applied at a rate of 33 pounds per 1,000 SF. Sometimes what looks like moss is algae. Ferrous ammonium sulfate will kill that too, but improve drainage and, if possible, light to keep it out for good. Otherwise, consider a non-grass ground cover.

Weeds

Weeds are the *result* not the cause of a poor lawn. Make your goal a thick, well fed, deeply rooted turf. Most people's first response to a weed-choked lawn is to turn to a weed killer—an herbicide. Herbicides come as either "post-emergent," the kind you spray directly on the weeds, or "pre-emergent," which you apply before the seeds germinate, so the weeds won't start in the first place. We'll discuss pre-emergents later. But always remember that herbicides alone are not the answer.

Every year Americans pour 3 percent of the world's entire herbicide output on their lawns. In an era concerned about organic food and poisons in the atmosphere, lawns get up to 10 times more herbicide proportionally than farmers apply to crops. Glyphosates, the newest, don't sterilize the soil and are reputedly harmless to animal life. They are very toxic to aquatic life, however, and runoff from rains, etc., carries them for miles. Glyphosates break down into formaldehyde among other things. It's a known cause of cancer.

One of the most widely used post-emergent broadleaf herbicides—a "diethylamine salt," known as 2,4D—is a deadly neurotoxin. It attacks the central nervous system. It and its kind can also cause cancer, and damage the liver, kidneys and reproductive organs after too much exposure. Nobody knows how much is too much, but kids playing on chemically treated lawns, anyone handling grass clippings, even dogs and cats, are at risk. While no one knows how much exposure is life-threatening, the build-up of toxins over time is a serious concern for landscape professionals, who should never use them routinely.

It is true that "lawn treatment" companies will spray a liquid fertilizer with high levels of herbicide on a lawn and get it looking great in a few days. Some people want that. But it's excessive and potentially dangerous. If people don't want pesticides on their strawberries, they shouldn't have it on their grass. The trade-off is between good health and the "quick and dirty" way.

When you fertilize a lawn, and it has a few weeds, ask if the customer wants the weeds sprayed. Then use a squeeze spray bottle or dauber of broad-leaf herbicide on each plant. By touching just one green cell in each plant, the weeds grow themselves to death. You'll kill 90 percent of them with less than a tenth of the herbicide in "weed & feeds" and spray-company dousings. It will probably also take less time and be cheaper, although you may have to educate your customer in advance. Don't forget about hand weeding. If there are just a few weeds, reach for the dandelion weeder that should be in your pocket or on your belt and root them out. You must dig out dandelions and other deep-rooted perennials, but pulling works best for annual weeds.

Mowing is a good weed control in slow growing turfgrasses like buffalograss. Annual weeds generally grow faster than buffalograss, especially in early spring, and, although the turf may not need it, you can mow to control upright weeds. "Sanitary practices" also help. That means keeping weeds and undesirable plants away from lawns, and taking care that a sprig of zoysiagrass or other vegetatively rooting grass doesn't drop off your mower to colonize a bluegrass turf. Finally, when reseeding use the best quality certified seed you can find—one that tells how much weed seed it has, if any.

When you use herbicides to control broadleaf weeds and crabgrass or whatever, always read and follow the directions and warnings on the label. Compare brands, too. It's usually cheaper to buy an herbicide concentrate with the higher percentage of active ingredient, but sometimes you have to do a little figuring. A diluted "store brand" mixture may cost less than a concentrate and need less or no preparation. A concentrate may cost less per-unit-applied but cost more to store, prepare, and dispose of.

Post-emergent broadleaf weed killers for lawns usually combine two or more herbicides. They work better than a single herbicide that may be effective against one weed but less so against others. Herbicides come as liquids, granules, or a fertilizer/granular combination. Use the granular kind when the turf is wet, so that the weeds absorb it. Liquids are easier to work with and provide the best coverage.

When you spray liquid herbicides, you want to avoid drift on windy days and volatilization on hot days to keep them off nearby plants. Typically, herbicides are esters or amine salts. The amine salts are less volatile and easier to control than esters. Cool days and mornings are best for spraying. Ideally the temperature should be below 75 degrees with a moist soil and a wind less than 5 MPH. Apply the liquid in a coarse, low-pressure spray. The best times of year are early spring and early fall when weed germination and growth are highest. This is also when the weeds are small and actively taking in nutrients. As they age they take in fewer nutrients, so you need to apply more herbicide. By then, too, their invasion is starting to make a thinner,

Learn Weeds' Life Cycle to Control Them

Annual weeds live one year, just long enough to produce seeds. They're best controlled before germination or when still small. Winter annuals (henbit, shepherdspurse) germinate in fall, winter over, and finish in the spring. It's best to control them in fall. Summer annuals (crabgrass, prostrate knotweed) die with the first frost and next year's seeds are best controlled in spring.

Biennials (e.g., thistles) form a rosette in year one and flower the next. They are best controlled in fall or the spring rosette stage. Perennials (dandelion, ivy, quackgrass and yellow nutsedge) live indefinitely. Many grow from seed, others from tubers, roots, and rhizomes. They are most vulnerable before a hard freeze when nutrient movement to the roots speeds up. Next best is before flowering, when food reserves in the root system declines.

Crabgrass, an annual, grows from last year's seeds. New plants keep sprouting through the growing season, and their purplish seed heads give a lawn an ugly, smoky cast. Several years' pre-emergent control will cut down on viable seeds. During the season rake the lawn to lift immature seed heads within reach of the mower; then use a grass catcher to collect them. Crabgrass won't tolerate a thick, dense turf that is at least 1½" high.

Other grasses—orchardgrass, timothy, quackgrass, nimblewill, and the like—are perennials. Use an all-purpose herbicide, such as a glyphosate like Roundup®, Kleenup®, or Knock-out®. The treatment will also kill lawn grasses. That means limiting the spray and re-seeding the sprayed area.

less competitive turf. The herbicide has to stay on the weeds' leaves, so don't water afterwards and be sure no rain is expected for at least 12 hours.

Fertilizing just before or after treatment can encourage the grass to crowd out the weeds. When weeds creep into a thin turf, reseeding alone may crowd them out again. A lawn that had a lot of weeds may end up with bare patches and need reseeding. But don't reseed until after the waiting period recommended on the herbicide label—usually three to four weeks.

Hold off on mowing the weeds before spraying so they offer plenty of leaf surface; and delay mowing afterwards so the herbicide moves to the roots. With six or seven days between mowings, grasses may exceed their ⅓ growing height limit. When you do mow, you may have to lower turf height gradually with several cuttings, in order to remove the right amount of leaf surface each time.

The best defense against weeds and pests in lawns is a well established, healthy turf.

Herbicide on the clippings can last for three weeks or more. Left on the lawn, its residue can wash into the soil where it may provide additional control. The clippings can go into a compost pile, but don't use them as mulch around sensitive plants until after about four mowings. And remember to keep herbicide and insecticide spraying equipment clearly marked and separate.

Pre-emergent herbicides, when wetted with ¼" to ½" of rainfall or watering, form a chemical blanket at or just below the soil surface that keeps weed seeds from germinating. Pre-emergents work best when watered within at least 24 hours of application, and the sooner the better. Already sprouted weeds escape contact with the barrier and keep growing. Pre-emergents typically last on the soil from 8 to 12 weeks and should be applied just before broadleaf weeds emerge. Even so, they can be applied in late winter—even as early as January—because the chemicals usually degrade more slowly in cool weather. They become effective when night temperatures rise to around 55-60 degrees and forsythia is in bloom. Residues of these herbicides will retard or prevent lawn grass seeds from germinating too, which means holding off on re-seeding when you plan to use a pre-emergent.

You need to prepare a turf for the best pre-emergent control. Up to 95% of pre-emergent herbicide has been shown to stick to grass leaves and never reach the soil. So mow to lower the turf height, then rake it and remove trash, thatch, leaves, and old dead grass. This will also help warm the soil to encourage new growth. Apply the pesticide according to label directions, but cut the amount in half and apply it crosswise in two directions for better coverage. Water the pesticide into the soil right away, otherwise heat and sunlight will soon degrade it.

Pre-emergents pose much the same health problems as post-emergent herbicides. In the 1980s, however, an Iowa State University researcher, Dick Christians, stumbled on a safe, effective organic pre-emergent control that was a natural byproduct of one of his state's economic mainstays. It was corn gluten meal. Corn gluten meal is entirely safe for people and pets, and the EPA exempts it from all herbicide regulations. Christians had used the meal to test a plant disease on a golf course. His experiment failed, but he noted that the gluten's protein inhibited emerging weed seeds. It has since proven effective against dandelions, crabgrass, smart weed, purslane, lambsquarters, foxtail, and barnyard grass. What's more corn gluten meal contains 10% nitrogen by weight and is a pretty fair "weed and feed."

The gluten meal goes on before weed seeds sprout, at 20 pounds per 1,000 SF. It's watered into turfgrass and can be worked into the first 2" to 3" of garden beds. Then there's a four- to six-week waiting period before seeds can be planted. It isn't quite as effective as some chemicals and costs close to three times as much (about $9.00 vs. $3.00 per 1,000 SF). Christians estimates 55% to 65% pre-emergent weed control in the first year, rising to 80% and 100% in the two years following. Seven or eight companies now market the product under a variety of names. Ask your local supplier. If you have Internet access, just use "corn gluten meal" as a search term.

Ultimately, the best weed-control strategy is proper lawn care, period. Your job is to bring the turf up to a better standard, so that the question of which controls to choose and use seldom ever arises.

Insects, Nematodes, and Related Creatures

The list of animal lawn pests, other than moles and rodents, is about as lengthy as the one for weeds. It includes lawn moths, cutworms, skippers, Lucerne moths, vegetable weevils, flea beetles, snails and slugs, leafhoppers, chinch bugs, leaf bugs, fruit flies, scale insects, mites, white grubs, billbugs, and various nematodes, which are microscopic worms that infest plant roots suck nourishment from them.

Inspect lawns regularly for localized insect attacks that cause stunting, die-back, and yellowing leaves in order to prevent them from spreading to the whole turf. Good control depends on detecting and identifying the pest early, and knowing its habits and biology. Most pests prefer only one or a few types of grass. Some like warm, dry conditions and others like it cool and moist. Often just changing shade and watering can eliminate many of them.

Insects, grubs, and the like attack grass in three places: the roots, crown or leaves. Blade-eating insects will hop up when you run your hand over the grass. Usually they do little damage. If you see more than 20 spring from a square yard of turf, use an insecticidal soap or pyrethrum ("pie-REE-thrum," see Chapter 18). Grubs—whitish insect larvae—live underground and eat the roots. Enough of them will create a brown patch of turf that you can peel off like an orange rind. If you suspect their presence, cut a foot-square patch of sod, lift it back, and inspect the roots. If you see more than six grubs, apply an insecticide with carbaryl or neem in late summer or early fall. You can also use milky spore, a safe bacteria that sets up in the soil and dines on grubs for many years.

Many insects are night feeders but can be flushed out by sprinkling a gallon of water containing a tablespoon of a 1 or 2 percent pyrethrum insecticide on a square yard of partly damaged and undamaged grass. Even flooding them with a water hose left running 5 or 10 minutes can bring many to the surface. Once they are in the open, use a good pest control guide to identify them. Some grubs and larvae ignore the pyrethrum and flooding tests.

Crown dwellers are especially hard to find. One source suggests sinking a coffee can with both ends cut out into a hole in the lawn and filling it with water. If more than a dozen of the suspected insets land in the water in half an hour, treat the turf with insecticidal soap or a pyrethrum.

Before applying an insecticide for leaf-eating insects, irrigate a lawn deeply. Let it dry. Then spray the insecticide and don't water again until the grass begins to wilt. That keeps the insecticide on the leaves longer. To treat pests that attack roots, wash the insecticide into the soil by a deep watering after application.

The first defense, as always, is that healthy turf—sunny, properly watered, mowed, fertilized, amended, aerated, and dethatched. A healthy lawn will outgrow hungry insects. A weak turf is prey to every passing ill, needs constant first aid, and recovers more slowly than a healthy one. Some pests begin on weeds, then move on to lawn grass; so keeping the turf weed-free can help control pests. Until it is well established, new turf is especially subject to insect attack and needs close attention.

There is no room in this chapter to catalog and illustrate all the pests. Treatments for them change continually. Your best strategy is a book with an illustrated chart of each pest and the kind of damage it causes. Often the popular books published by Time-Life, Sunset, Ortho, and so on will do. We list our choices for good pest-control books in Chapter 18. See the Appendix for where to get them.

Crabgrass. (USDA)

The Elements of a Garden
Mulches
Compost
Water in the Garden
Principles of Pruning
Introduction to Trees
Some Encouraging Words

Chapter 16

THE REST OF THE GARDEN – PRUNING AND MAINTENANCE

Quick Start: *IF your basic service expands into general landscape maintenance, you will want to read this chapter and then move on to speciaized texts, some of which we mention here.*

Everything in the earlier chapters about soils, fertilizing, and watering applies to the rest of the garden. You should also know about mulches in the garden and how to compost yard waste. The preferences of plants, from annual flowers to trees, are as different as the plants themselves. There are some general principles, however, that can steer you in the right direction.

Plants depend on good pruning just as grass needs proper mowing. Remove only enough of the plant to improve its health and looks. Thin out dead, weak, and unsightly growth. Let in light and air. Don't chop it to fit a pattern. Only the standard hedge plants tolerate shearing. Prune when or just before the plant grows fastest, late winter or early spring. You will have to learn whether flowers grow on new or old growth so you can prune for heavy foliage or blossoms.

The same principles of thinning apply to trees. Cut back to the next biggest branch if you need to reduce the volume of a tree's crown. Open it up, rather than stub it back. Make it look good. Serious tree work will require a specialist called an arborist.

ALTHOUGH LANDSCAPE MAINTENANCE beyond lawn care is stuck alone here in a short single chapter of its own, all of the information on soils, fertilizers, and pest control apply to it. The work involves planting and maintaining bulbs, annuals, and perennials; pruning trees, shrubs, and ground covers; mulching; and fertilizing and amending the soil under all those plants. We have already covered most of the basics, except for work involving groundcovers, bulbs, annuals, and perennials. So here is a short introduction.

The Elements of a Garden

Most bulbs are planted in the fall and bloom in the spring or summer. In the right climate and location, some bulbs will reappear year after year and even multiply with no human help other than weeding and maintenance fertilizing.

Annuals are plants that grow from seed or bedding plants for one year and have to be planted again the next year. The soil where annuals are bedded needs amendment and mulching each time they are planted. Methods of preparing the beds, and fertilizing and watering them vary substantially from species to species.

Somewhere between annuals and shrubs is a class referred to as perennials. Except for some mild-winter varieties, these go dormant in the winter and grow again the next year.

A Short Plant Glossary

Groundcover, low-growing or prostrate shrubs, near-grasses, or perennials planted in extended areas, sometimes in place of turf. These include vines like ivies, stoloniferous greens like strawberry leaf, and shrubs like junipers.

Annuals, grown from seed, complete life-cycle in one season. Examples are petunias, marigolds, and pansies.

Perennials live several years. Some are tender, others hardy. They include geraniums, asparagus, peonies, and hosta.

Shrubs are long-lived with woody multiple stems or a single stem with branches. Some are evergreen, others are deciduous and bare in winter. Forsythia, English laurel, holly, azaleas, rhododendrons, and roses are shrubs.

Bulbs have multiple layers around a central bud, all wrapped in a papery "tunic." Onions are bulbs, so are tulips, hyacinths, and daffodils.

Corms are solid but also with tunics. A corm shrivels as the plant grows, but new corms grow from the old one, spreading the plant. Crocuses and gladioli grow from corms.

Rhizomes are horizontal stems that grow near the soil surface. Irises and calla lilies grow from rhizomes.

Tubers are plump food-storage roots that grow eyes or buds on their surfaces like potatoes, a well known tuber. Tubers include dahlias, and begonias.

Everything noted earlier about soils, watering, and fertilizers applies to groundcovers, bulbs, annuals, perennials, shrubs, and trees, except that individual plants have different tastes about the acidity or alkalinity of their soil, about what mix of nutrients makes them grow or flower best, and about when to feed them. We will not even generalize here. Plants' individual tastes are the subject of encyclopedic treatments, and specialized texts. If you want to maintain the rest of the garden, read about these plants and see what they need in your region.

Mulches

Mulches, especially organic mulches, are a basic ingredient of soil building. By shielding the soil surface, mulches increase water intake, lower water loss, prevent erosion, aid physical structure, control weeds, and even out soil temperature.

Water from rain or irrigation is lost by runoff, by transpiration from plants, by evaporation from the soil and by percolation deeply into it. Mulches cut losses from runoff and evaporation, leaving more water for the plants. Mulches also make plantings look better by providing a dark or light ground for leaves and flowers, and keeping mud from splashing on foliage, walls, and fences.

Drops of water hitting the soil often break down the soil surface and compact the large pores that soak up water. This can lead to erosion. A mulch absorbs the impact of falling rain or irrigation, and the water seeps through it into the soil without sealing the surface or running off. Mulch also slows the flow of water, giving more time for absorption. To get the most from mulch, work up the soil surface before spreading it. Once mulched, a soil needs less tilling.

On bare soil, some of the water entering it flows back to the surface by capillary action and evaporates. Mulches that soak up little water dry out quickly once the air dries. Once dry, they don't act as capillary conductors. They also shield the soil surface from the sun and wind, slowing down evaporation further.

A mulch of 2" of pea gravel, for example, may reduce evaporation by 75 percent. Organic mulches are more readily available than gravel, they weigh less, and they all reduce evaporation, particularly when the soil is in direct sun. A good mulch can often double the time between watering. The actual time between watering will depend on the weather conditions, the soil's water holding capacity, how deep the roots are, and how far apart the plants are spaced.

To prevent root rot and damage to the bark, don't pile mulches around plant bases; leave space or use a porous covering. Mulches also cut weed seed germination, and the few weeds that come up can be pulled easily and left as more mulch.

When selecting a mulch, consider cost, durability, and appearance. Nurseries and large discounters sell bagged shredded wood, coarse bark chips, fine bark mulch, wood shavings, and gravel. Check classified ads for local mulch materials: salt marsh hay, cottonseed hulls, wheat and other straw, pine needles, chipped bark, etc. Look for a bulk supplier of landscape materials such as gravel, stone, bark, and the like. Ask what others in your area use. You may be able to gather mulch at cost or no cost for resale to customers. Your municipal maintenance department may have more pruning chips than the public works department can use. Many organic mulches are crop residues or food byproducts that would otherwise be a disposal problem. Mulching recycles them. Farms can supply straw. It doesn't last long, but that could be an advantage if you want it to increase a soil's organic content. Straw is a recommended mulch for newly seeded lawns. Alfalfa straw will return nitrogen to the soil as it breaks down.

Dark gravel mulches will warm light soils where organic mulches will keep them cool. You can use this principle to speed or slow plant growth. Organic mulches are insulators because of their low heat conductivity and have a big influence on soil temperature.

Organic mulches gradually improve soils' fertility and structure. Tiny tunnels in soil, the "pore structure," let water drain down, while harmful gases vent out and let in fresh air. Humus helps hold the pore structure open; but without a cover of mulch, excess cultivation, bare soil, hot soils, and drought speed up the breakdown of humus. As organic mulches decay, they release chemical compounds for nutrients and meld soil particles into less water-soluble units. Woody organic materials that are high in carbon may cause a temporary nitrogen deficiency that limits plant growth. The microorganisms at the soil's surface need nitrogen to break it down. Adding a slow-release fertilizer can help offset this deficiency. Organic mulches need replenishment as they break down—more than once a year for grass clippings and shredded leaves. Climate affects breakdown; long lasting mulches in the North may seem to disappear in the heat and humidity of the South. Digging in also hastens decay.

Mulch and composted soil amendments are basic for sound irrigation practice in modern gardens.

One drawback of organic mulches is that they sometimes provide a home for slugs and cutworms. Too much of any mulch—over about 2"—invites rodents. Too much can also cut off air to the soil, which slows nitrification, also creating a nitrogen deficiency. It's a good idea to loosen mulch now and then, to aerate the soil and remove weeds. Try out mulches sparingly at first to see where they work and where pests are a problem. Some organic mulches are even fire hazards if left to dry out.

Polyethylene sheeting has been used as a mulch, but its disadvantages for garden use outweigh any advantages, except for very brief periods. Somewhat better, if not much better looking, is a water permeable "landscape fabric," which you also roll out, cut holes in it for the plants, and cover with a decorative loose mulch.

Deep mulching for winter can reduce physical damage to plants by lessening soil heaving during frosts. Mulch also helps protect the roots and crowns of perennials and shrubs in winter. But deep mulches should come off for new growth in spring. At the start of the growing season wait until the soil is fully warmed before replacing or adding mulch.

Compost

Compost is usually low in nutrients but a good soil amendment. "Cold composting," the simplest and laziest way to get it, involves mixing grass clippings, dry leaves, kitchen vegetable scraps with dirt (for the micro-organisms) to let them rot for six weeks to six months into a valuable black, fluffy crumb. It works but won't kill weeds seeds or bacteria.

"Hot composting" works faster and cleaner. Seeds, and any bacteria in manure, won't survive hot composting beyond about 60 days—or longer in cool weather. It uses a pile 4 to 6 feet high and wide inside an enclosure with air spaces—ideally a slatted or wire-mesh bin—that you can open on at least one side. Green vegetation, such as grass cuttings and garden trimmings, add nitrogen to the mix. Decomposition time depends on temperature, moisture, the size of the pieces, and your own labor. A chipper/shredder helps cut materials down to size. (These machines require hearing protection, goggles or face shield, heavy gloves with high wrists, padded pants or chaps, and a thick jacket.) The pile needs frequent turning to aerate it and to get everything into the center where the temperature should be 150° or 160° F. Piling mixed-size pieces on a wooden pallet will improve air circulation. Keep the pile damp but covered and shielded from rain. Finally, a few cups of all-purpose fertilizer speeds the process, as does manure.

THE ELECTRONIC COMPOSTER

Cornell University's Web page on composting is probably the most extensive treatment online (and possibly off) that you will find on the subject. You can sign up for an online newsletter, too. The site is at www.cfe.cornell.edu/wmi or /compost.

The best way to compost is with three bins—one for new materials, the next for decomposing material, and the third for the finished product. Compost involves plenty of work and overhead cost, so don't feel guilty about charging when you sell it for topdressing.

Here's a recipe that uses the recommended 3 parts brown to 1 part green materials: In a composting bin, wire-mesh cylinder, or the like, add straw with manure to get the right brown/green ratio, then 15 lbs cottonseed meal per cubic yard, 5 lbs gypsum per cubic yard, 3 lbs of bone meal per cubic yard. Turn about every 4 days, mixing thoroughly and keeping slightly moist. Use a compost thermometer with an 18" to 24" probe to make sure that the center is hot enough to sterilize weed seeds and bacteria. You must age finished compost to leach out soluble salts. Test for doneness by putting a little in a jar; then add water and cover it. If it smells bad when you open it a week later, it isn't done. For Web information see www.cfe.cornell.edu/wmi.

If you add leaf removal as a sideline, the 8 to 45 bushels per load from commercial vacuum collectors, or even from hand power tools, may exceed your capacity to compost. Many municipalities provide compost disposal sites and may pile collected materials 8 to 12 feet high in stacks or windrows, making a finished product in 60 to 90 days, which they often sell cheaply.

Water in the Garden

The rules for watering a lawn apply to the rest of the garden, so there are only a few points to add here. The whole garden needs an irrigation program, just as the lawn does. You and your customer have to decide and make very clear who does what. Except for commercial jobs, the customer usually handles watering. Even then, you can educate the customer about an irrigation program that balances the best plant growth with optimum water conservation.

Since you aren't a landscape contractor, you'll have to work with the existing irrigation system. And although the residential customer usually maintains the system, you should inspect it as well as the landscaping for problems. Sprinkler heads get damaged, plugged, corrode, and crack if they're plastic. Drip irrigation emitters become stopped with silt, algae, bacterial slimes. The wrong head, bubbler, emitter, or soaker line may have been installed in the first place. Undrained pipes and fittings may have frozen during the last winter.

All plants show the lack of water by wilting, but many have specialized early warnings of thirst: shiny leaves may turn dull, bluegrass fades from green to bluish, rhododendron leaves at the branch tips stick up. Most trees and shrubs depend most on moisture in the top 6 to 18 inches of soil. You can purchase expensive equipment to test for soil moisture, but even if you do, learn to recognize the signs by eye. Then, as with a lawn, budget water according to the soil's water-holding capacity, so that you regularly replace the water lost at the evapotranspiration rate, but no faster.

Periodically flooding parched soil to water it probably does more harm than good. The microorganisms that process nutrients die off in dry soil; then, flooding suffocates the survivors. Even after the water drains down, the bacteria take awhile to return. So there's a lag before the root hairs can begin feeding and by then the soil is probably drying out all over again. Except for drought-loving species, plants prefer a soil that is always airy and slightly moist.

Before sprinklers, the irrigation of choice was by watering moat or ditch. Sprinklers and moats tend to flood the pore structure, however, drowning root hairs and microorganisms. Flooding also sends water to deeper airless soil, away from the root hairs that need the moisture.

You could compensate by manually cycling the water on and off to let the soil drain. But you'd have to keep checking drainage.

Drip irrigation avoids these problems. As emitters drip onto the soil, capillary action pulls some moisture sideways to make the soil damp, not sodden. Drip systems give the best control over the how often to irrigate and at what rate. And they'll use 15% to 50% less water, depending on how bad the old system was. Gardens with well-designed drip systems get more foliage, increased bloom, and fewer diseases like mildew, crown rot, and rust. Drip irrigation can also help maintain the right moisture between summer rains.

That's especially important today. Increased utility rates and water rationing may soon affect the lushest gardens and stimulate an interest in *xeriscapes*—dry landscapes. At least half the residential water in North America is used for landscaping. Most states, particularly in the West and the Southern tier, have started xeriscape programs. Xeriscaping includes: using low-water-use plants, of which most regions have lists; hydrozoning, grouping plants by their water needs, with plump thirsty plants out where you can see them; mowing higher, cutting nitrogen rates, and controlling weeds; deep watering and reducing leaks; water retention methods, including mulching; and (watch out!) reducing turfgrass. Xeriscape methods have trimmed 30 to 60 percent off water bills. Contact your local extension agent to learn what's going on. Do your customers know about the problem?

Keep an eye out for irrigation problems when you are mowing, or walk through all of the landscape in order to spot damage from over- or under-watering. If you see your customer while on the job or during a regular walk-through inspection, it never hurts to ask about water and other problems. It's one partnership that pays off.

Principles of Pruning

There is good pruning and bad pruning. Healthy plants depend as much on good pruning as on good soil and pest control. Knowing the basics of good pruning will take you far past the average start-up gardener, even if you don't yet know precisely how to thin a photinia or rhododendron.

Prune the way the plant wants - Pruning should be no more than removing enough of the plant to improve appearance and vigor. To do so you need to see the plant's framework and understand its growth and flowering patterns. With a few major exceptions, pruning should just thin or open up a plant rather than chop it off below its natural size. Stunted plants are no healthier than stunted people or animals.

Plants in nature are not pruned except when twigs and branches fall off; so no pruning at all is better than intense cutting. Browsing animals often make a meal of trees and shrubs in nature, but, like mowing, every cut injures the plant and must be made for a reason. Most plants need only minor cosmetic cuts. Even formal hedges, once trained, are trimmed carefully to stay in good condition.

A Little Plant Biology - Typically, plants have a terminal or *apical* bud at the end of each shoot. Below it there are lateral or *axillary* buds arranged in one of four patterns: opposite, alternate, circling the shoot (whorled), or spiral. The buds or shoots are also called nodes. Their pattern determines how later branches will form.

The terminal bud exerts *apical dominance* over the lower buds by oozing a chemical that gravity pulls down the shoot. Apical dominance varies from plant to plant. Young trees show a lot of it, while bushy shrubs have little. If the shoot bends down or the tip is cut, the chemical stops flowing and the lateral buds will grow. That is why when you pinch off or bend down the tip of a shoot, the lateral buds bush out. This process is known as *stopping*, and the lateral buds are said to be *breaking* as a result.

When you prune a branch, therefore, plan to cut back to a strong lateral bud facing in a direction that will improve the plant's appearance. Your cuts should be just above the bud, or node, and sloping down from it.

Prune just high enough above the lateral bud to give it some cover and sloped down from it just enough to shed water.

To keep a plant healthy, thin by cutting off only deadwood, damaged parts, diseased parts, and weak growth. Also remove crossing and unsightly branches. In other words, open the plant up to sunlight to clear out potential disease pockets and let the vigorous branches develop good leaves and flowers. Your customer may like to see you use a pruning paint on all cuts bigger than ½ inch, but a plant's sap provides all the protective coating it needs. Paints are unnecessary, except to reassure some customers.

A rule: prune branches that are dead, damaged, diseased, too big, too small, crossing, and ugly (the three fatal D's, and big, small, cross, and ugly).

When to prune - In general the time to prune is in late winter or early spring just before vigorous growth begins and the plant can best recover from pruning. Flowering fruit trees, whose buds will break robustly after spring pruning, are an exception. Summer pruning is stressful to plants; so confine it to removing suckers and water sprouts. Fall pruning is all right if you leave time for tender new growth to harden before frosts occur. Pruning in winter stimulates some growth in mild climates but not as much as spring pruning.

Next you need to know whether the plant will flower on new growth or growth from last year or earlier. Some plants can be pruned either for heavy foliage by pruning hard in the spring, or for flowers by cutting after it has already flowered. Which plants flower or fruit on new or old growth is beyond this introduction. It is enough to know the difference exists. You will have to learn more by reading a detailed treatise, like *American Horticultural Society Pruning & Training*, by Christopher Brickell and David Joyce. In the meantime, here are a few more basic observations.

Canes, roses, etc. - The major exceptions to not cutting a plant back severely are the vase-shaped shrubs that grow from ground-level crowns like grass. These are canes. The best known canes are raspberry and blackberry plants. Some shrubs like roses, forsythia, and quince resemble canes by growing multi-branched trunks. They will sprout new canes from the crown every year. You must prune the old and dead canes back to the crown to make room for the new ones. The best way to prune very old, badly overgrown plants like these is often to shear them right back to the crown. When the new shoots sprout you thin out all but the desired number of the strongest shoots.

When it takes less than major surgery to prune a cane, visualize the ideal plant with a balanced spread of young, straight, leafy shoots. Cut out everything that doesn't fit your mental picture and take the remaining ones back to a correctly facing bud at the right height. If you can't draw the mental picture, consult a good pruning guide.

Other shrubs - Shrubs like small trees and bushes are subject to the thin-don't-head-back rule of pruning. Heading back means cutting a branch so it leaves a stub. Knowing a plant's growth pattern can eliminate the need for major pruning or raise a question about a plant's place in the garden. A shrub that will grow to be 12 feet high with a 7-foot width, should not be planted in a 4-foot square space. Pruning it to fit the space will create an ugly, weak plant.

For shrubs up to small ornamental trees, do not remove more than one-third of branches at one time. As with lawn mowing, the plants need leaves to photosynthesize. If a plant needs major thinning, do about a third of the job each year.

When you prune old, bulky, upright shrubs try to see the underlying shape and prune to make it more interesting. Open it up and layer it.

Many plants are naturally symmetrical and you have to remove only the occasional maverick shoot. When a plant gets unbalanced, with strong branches growing on one side and weak branches on another, resist your impulse to cut back the healthy parts. Cut off the *weak* branches to the lowest good bud. Cutting encourages vigorous new growth, and that should balance the plant so you can thin it normally.

If you have to prune prostrate growers like some junipers and creeping ground covers, you can go in from the bottom and cut off the long lower branches. That leaves fresh new growth on top within smaller confines. Prune other ground covers like the rest; thin so you can't see where you cut. Snip from behind the greenery that shows.

Hedges - Shearing hedges is pruning to encourage natural hedgers to break buds within pre-set contours. Formal hedges are labor-intensive and need to be trimmed regularly to keep their shape. Informal hedges need pruning only enough to keep them from getting overgrown or too straggly. To start a hedge off right, the young plants are pruned hard at some early point to encourage bottom growth. How hard and when to shear them depends on the plant. Once established, hedges, whether rounded, squared off, or informal should be tapered wider at the base than at the top so that the sun shines on the lower branches.

Most plants should not be sheared. A few like pyracantha, yew, holly, box, hawthorne, tamarisk, and privet are tough enough to be sheared and come up green. Shearing others eliminates flowering, causes die-back and crossing branches, and begins a slow decline.

Two tips:

Don't prune coniferous (needled evergreen) hedges past the green part. They won't fill in.

Cut the handle on a leaf rake down to one or two feet for raking cuttings off the top of pruned hedge.

Climbers - Architectural mistakes are saved by growing ivy on them, and even the best house, wall or fence can be improved by growing something on it. Climbers include clingers that support themselves by aerial roots or suckers, twiners whose tendrils need a support to grow on, ramblers that grow long and flop on things, and ordinary shrubs that can be pruned to grow *espaliered* (es-PAL-ee-aid, that is, arms growing from shoulders) along a wall or fence.

These should be planted about a foot away from the supporting structure. Don't hesitate to prune shoots that don't follow the plan, which is to say up against the wall and spaced to cover. Pruning should be based also on whether flowering is on new or old growth. Some climbing roses flower on horizontal branches, or laterals, and pruning should encourage more of them. Some are so vigorous that they need aggressive pruning.

Introduction to Trees

Trees are a specialty all their own which is the business of professionals called arborists. This is only an introduction to maintenance of these complicated, valuable plants. Pruning trees usually has a major impact on a garden, so we have included some basic illustrations. Figure 16.1 illustrates the parts of a tree.

Now, a little tree biology - A tree's trunk and branches grow in four layers. The protective *bark* is outside. Below the bark is the *cambium* through which water and nutrients flow. Next, the *sapwood*, made up of *phloem* and *xylem*, conducts somewhat less fluid and fewer nutrients. Inside, the darker *heartwood* is made up of older phloem and xylem that may or may not be active.

Cutting through the cambium layer completely around a tree or branch (*girdling*) will kill it. The next worst thing to befall a tree is any injury to the cambium layer.

Tree anatomy consists of the trunk, out of which main the branches known as *scaffolds* grow. Side branches, called *laterals*, grow

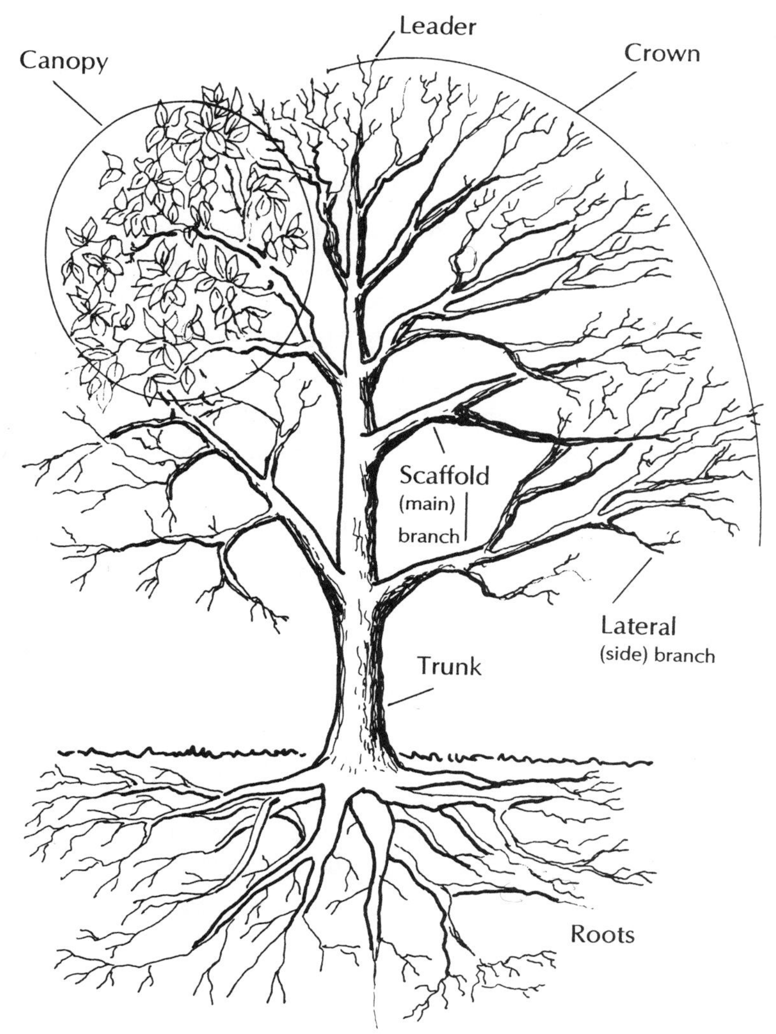

Figure 16.1. The parts of a tree.

out of the scaffolds. The trunk of some trees grows all the way to the top as a central *leader*. Occasionally, damage to an apical bud will result in a *double leader*. The weaker leader should be pruned from a tree that follows the central leader form. Other trees are roughly umbrella shaped, with several scaffolds branching from a low trunk. The scaffolds and laterals make up the tree's *crown*. The leaves make up its *canopy*.

A scaffold that forms an angle usually less than 45-degrees with either the trunk or another branch is a *narrow crotch*. It captures excess bark in the angle. The captured bark is a weak spot where the branch can break. Such branches should be removed for safety of the tree and whatever or whoever is under it. Just which crotches are narrow depends on a tree's normal branching pattern.

A double leader, one that rises from a narrow crotch between two branches, is usually the result of *topping*. One, if not both, leaders should be removed from a young tree. Trees from nurseries often have been topped to make them bush out, and you have to thin them to remove surplus leaders. If an existing tree needs major thinning, including removing the weaker of two branches or leaders, do it in stages, cutting back over several years to let the canopy fill in.

Fertilizing trees - Refer to specialized texts if you agree to fertilize your customers' trees. In general, for most soils and moderate tree growth, it's easiest to apply 2 to 4 pounds of nitrogen yearly per 1,000 SF of soil beneath the crown area. Fertilize in a circle extending slightly beyond the crown. Reduce fertilizer somewhat for any applied to turf and shrubs under the tree. Trees in a well maintained turf or garden may not need more fertilizer. Also consider soil structure and organic content. Trees in sandy soil with plentiful rain would need more. Evergreens use less fertilizer than deciduous trees. Needled evergreens take even less, but fertilize them in a radius roughly equal to the tree's height. Where roots are confined or under pavement, cut back applications to match the exposed root area, otherwise there will be a salt build up. Compensate for the reduced application with a foliar spray or injections into the trunk. Young trees respond best to annual fertilization; preferably in two applications. Trees with nutrient deficiencies need more treatments until the problem is corrected. Older mature trees may get by with fertilizing every three or four years.

Figure 16.2. Heading and topping a tree.

Fall seems better than spring for fertilizing, even as late as October and November if soil temperatures are above 40 degrees. Don't fertilize in late summer or early fall if winter temperatures will injure new growth. These are all generalizations. Keep an eye on the tree's health, refer to specialized texts, check with experts, and adjust your program as necessary.

Pruning trees - When pruning a tree to shape it, remove weak and unnecessary, branches. Prune to reduce bulk and clutter, to eliminate diseased and dead members, to admit light and air, and to increase safety and security. As an ideal, aim for a tree with scaffolds growing from the trunk at angles of 45 degrees or wider, and circling evenly around it at big, evenly spaced intervals.

The worst tree pruning comes from a misguided belief that trees can be cut to any size or shape. Trees are not lumber. They're programmed to grow in a certain way, despite what people do to them. They respond to excessive or bad pruning by trying as best they can to grow as programmed—but with thick, ugly crops of straight, weak shoots.

Having said that, we will point out that there is an accepted style of formal pruning for sycamore trees called *pollarding*, which creates a parasol of leaves on thin, weak shoots that grow from the trees' chopped-back top lateral branches. Sycamores appear to withstand pollarding well enough, and some are actually "topped" (see below) for a lollipop crown of shoots. Pollarding is an artificial look that sometimes appears along with topiary hedges in formal gardens. But it is still bad for the tree, no matter how it fits the decor.

Figure 16.3. Thinning a tree.

Trees should be pruned by *thinning* or, occasionally, *drop-crotching*. Good drop-crotching practice is skilled work that involves lowering the crown somewhat by pruning a tree back carefully to a healthy branch at least half the pruned limb's thickness and leaving the smallest amount of cut surface, with no stump or snag. Thinning is the removal of branches in the same way to improve a tree's appearance and health. In addition to *thinning*, you can safely *lift* a tree's crown by removing lower scaffolds and laterals.

The commonest forms of tree butchery are *heading*, *stubbing*, *topping*, and *lion-tailing*. Pruning like this is not only in poor taste, it is bad economics. It lowers the plant's long-term health and locks the owner into a cycle of high maintenance costs. A heading cut is one that arbitrarily shortens a branch and leaves a stub. A severe heading cut is called stubbing, and severely heading the tree is called topping it. See figures 16.2 and 16.3. Lion-tailing is stripping out all the inside lateral branches and leaving foliage only at the tips of the remaining branches.

Heading and the rest are destructive and stressful to mature trees, reducing their vigor, and causing their decline and even death. Tree structure never recovers afterward. New branches—usually formed in the thin cambium layer—are weakly attached and snap off easily. The trees need constant (and hopeless) maintenance to try to keep this from happening.

The many weak, poorly attached adventitious (surface) shoots that result from stubbing, etc., are called *suckers* when they grow from a trunk and *watersprouts* when from branches. The tree's lateral buds that produce suckers and water sprouts are invisible under the bark. Growth from them is the tree's response to a wound. Lion-tailing seems to produce fewer suckers and water sprouts, but, like the other sins of bad pruning, it reduces a tree's canopy for photosynthesis.

Bad advice about trees: If a tree root is severed, cut off enough branches to balance the tree.

NO! Remember what we said about grass; the roots need all the green a plant has to make food and build strong healthy roots. You should not only **not** prune a tree whose roots are cut, you should not even touch it for a year or two until the roots have a chance to grow back. If the soil around the root has been removed, replace it with a mix of soil and peat moss, or soil and sand, to encourage root development. Some people also recommend adding, vitamin B-1 (rooting hormone) to the soil, but opinions are mixed about that.

Trees die slowly from a succession of wounds and stress. They do not heal, but set up a barrier against rot and grow around the wound. If you inspect trees in lawns you may see thick bark growth over gashes left by mowers. When a scaffold is stubbed, the barrier may grow far down the cut. The decay that begins in the stub will eventually penetrate the barrier and in time can kill the tree.

Scaffold branches grow out of a *collar* on the trunk. Collars may or may not be clearly visible. A branch should be removed slightly outside the collar, not to the surface of the trunk. The collar will help the tree grow over the cut. If the cut is too far from the collar, the stub can rot and may kill the tree. If you cut the collar the tree will not grow over the wound properly, and it will introduce rot into the trunk. Use a sharp saw to cut the branch cleanly, and pare the edges of the cut with a knife if necessary.

Most trees will have limbs you can remove or reduce without hurting their size, shape, or vigor. The first rule for trees is *Always Underprune*. The second is *Use the Right Tools*: a pruning saw, pole pruner (very useful in thorny trees like hawthorns), loppers, and hand pruners. Clear out clutter from the center first. Cut back to a lateral branch that is ⅓ to ½ the diameter of what you're removing. Stand back and look at the tree every so often to see the principal framework. It's better to leave questionable branches and remove them later when you're sure. Small cuts heal faster, so pruning often is best. Use pruners to thin growth on branch ends and reduce their weight. Pruning to a downward facing bud will encourage horizontal growth; pruning to an upward facing bud will favor upright growth. Heavy pruning promotes heavy new growth—suckers and water sprouts you'll have to remove next year.

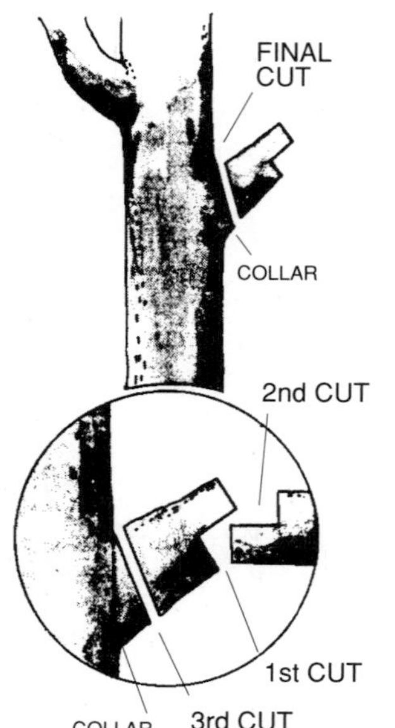

Figure 16.4. Three cuts to remove a tree branch.

You should remove all but the lightest tree branches with at least three cuts. First cut the branch about a foot from where your final cut will be. Then cut upwards at the final cut line to prevent the falling limb from tearing the bark and cambium. Finish with a downward cut. Large branches may need several preliminary cuts to bring you near the trunk. See figure 16.4.

If you're faced with rehabilitating a tree that's full of suckers and water sprouts, don't touch new ones for a few years. Removing fresh suckers will only produce more. Make sucker removal part of normal tree thinning. Even then be careful. Pines take well to thinning. Cherry trees will sucker with even light thinning. Dogwoods, magnolias, crab apples and plums are almost as bad. After making the major cuts, remove all the vertical water sprouts except those that would leave large holes in the canopy.

Palm trees are slow growers that need a well-nourished start and a balanced fertilizer mix. A newly planted or transplanted palm takes time to establish itself—a year in warmer climates like southern Florida or Hawaii, up to two years in cooler places like coastal California. While getting established, the plant wants special attention and care as the roots grow into the surrounding soil. They suffer quickly from inadequate or faulty fertilization and prefer controlled release to quick release mixes. Nutrient deficiency problems can dog a badly planted or poorly cared for palm. Some experts recommend a 3-1-3 NPK ratio along with ⅓ magnesium. Check with the local extension service for special palm formulas. Palm roots are very compact. Fertilizer goes right around the base but not directly on visible roots. The only pruning most palms get is removal of dead fronds. The fronds remain on a few varieties to protect and humidify the trunk.

There are good one-volume guides to tree care. The Ortho garden book *All About Trees*, like all the Ortho books, costs less than fifteen dollars, doesn't push the company's chemicals, and is a great introduction. The definitive text is Pascal P. Pirone's *Tree Maintenance*, up to its seventh edition under the direction of John R. Hartman. If you encounter an old tree with bigger problems than you can handle, contact a certified arborist to correct them. (If your state doesn't certify arborists, ask your prospective subcontractor if the tree should be topped. Reject whoever gives an unqualified yes.)

Finishing the job - As with all gardening, haul away your cuttings and other debris when you go. Leave your workplace neater than you found it.

Some Encouraging Words

The gardens in every neighborhood differ widely. Some are very formal, with cropped hedges set in geometric patterns around symmetrical lawns, while others are as close to nature as they can get and still be a garden. The principles just discussed work easier at the natural end of the scale, but can serve you well in a more formal garden. If the customer wants closely pruned geometrical plants, do them that way. As you learn your craft, remember that you will do what your customer wants but that you are the expert. If you see how to improve the lawn or some shrubs without opposing the customer's wishes, talk about how the improvement will work and see what your customer wants. Your business is better gardening, but it is the customer's space.

Second, as you work on a yard, think about how to make your work easier. Prune plants according to their natural shapes when you can. Mulch to cut down weeding. Try to get the lawn to grow and smother weed seedlings. Plant or mulch around lawn trees so you won't need to use a string trimmer and gash the tree. You will improve the garden's health and probably its appearance as the work gets easier.

Third, take time on each job to look at the whole garden. Start from the plants on the ground, up to the shrubs, and further up to the trees. Look for which levels are strong, which are weak, and how they all work together. You will begin to see where to make improvements and balance the whole. Developing that kind of skill will take time; but if you can do it, you will have your customers for life.

Transporting Tools
Gloves
Earth Moving
Hoses
Weeding, Pruning, Shearing
Ladders
Clean-up
Fuel, Service, Repairs

Chapter 17

TOOLS OF THE TRADE – GETTING WHAT YOU PAY FOR

Quick Start: *YOUR truck will be fine for hauling tools and equipment when you first start out, but as you acquire more of them you will want a sturdy steel rack and lockable cabinet to make your tools secure and accessible. For shovels, brooms, and spading forks, attach some 2x lumber to the rack and low on the truck's bed with holes to accept the handles. Tool racks on the side interfere less with rear vision. Ladders can ride on the rack.*

Know the best quality tools, but buy cheap ones if you tend to lose them. What generally distinguishes a good quality tool on close inspection is an absence of cheap construction like: rivets, bent mild steel, dull edges, weak welds, pressure fittings, imperfect wood handles, and "streamlining" that conceals joints. Never use anything that starts out broken or dull unless it is good quality and you know you can restore it.

Keep tools in working trim by cleaning, oiling, and sharpening them regularly. It's a good idea also to learn how to repair small engines and the rest of your power tools. A little extra work on hand and power tools will not only ease your work on the job but also save you expensive repair bills.

THIS CHAPTER will cover tools and equipment not already discussed in the chapters on bidding, lawns, mowing, or pest control. Descriptions of most equipment appear with the tasks involved, along with a discussion of what to look for in each item. Keep your overhead low by buying only the tools you need. If it is an expensive piece of equipment, like a verticutter or aerator, rent until you need to use it so much that buying is cheaper than renting. Don't forget about subcontracting, either. Done right, subcontracting can be profitable. When you do "sub" jobs out, however, you must know and be confident about your subcontractor's skill and reliability.

Let's talk about tool quality and real life. When we first started out, my husband insisted on a $40 pair of lopping shears. He used them on one job and left them at the site. The next day they were gone. Now we buy the best equipment but mid-priced to cheap tools, depending on the tool. We'll give some pointers on what makes a tool work well, so when you shop for bargains you'll recognize a good deal and steer clear of junk. If you're sure you (or your employees) will *never* lose a tool, go out and buy the best. Otherwise be smart, be a cheapskate.

Transporting Tools

Start off with a light pickup truck. Then, when the scope of your work and the equipment you haul increase, don't get a larger one. Get a trailer. A larger truck means a larger gasoline bill. It's a good idea to have a welding shop build a rack for the truck as soon as possible. One of angle iron that extends from the rear of the bed over the front of the cab, sturdy enough to support a couple of ladders, is ideal. It should be high enough to permit rolling in the mower and other large equipment. If you're buying new, see about a factory-made rack from the dealer. It's cheaper than custom-made. On each side of the bed near the cab you can bolt four-foot lengths of 2 x 4, one on the rack's top rail and the other on the rail along the top of the bed. Each one has 2" holes spaced along them for tool handles. There are people in the business who stick the tools in a small trash can in the back, but it looks pretty messy.

You can also get a lockable tool carrier for hand tools. Throw in a small tool box with a wrench set and screwdrivers. You'll always need to tighten small nuts and bolts or adjust one or another piece of equipment. Include repair and service kits—pre-gapped plugs, belts, O-rings, etc.—for mowers, string-trimmers, and other motorized equipment. Keep small plastic containers in the tool box, with spare nuts and bolts, and empties for those you have to remove for one reason or another. It helps to label them, so add a ballpoint and a small roll of masking tape. Be sure you also have enough room in the truck for bags of fertilizer, soil conditioners, tarps, buckets and trash cans for cuttings, and all the other gear that becomes part of your kit.

Finally, you will need a pair of clear, straight-grained 2 x 10 or 2 x 12 planks to wheel the mower into the truck. Bolt heavy steel L-brackets at the end of each plank to hook into the tailgate hinge.

Commercial vehicle insurance, which you should have on the truck, usually covers the trailer. You'll probably have to insure the trailer's contents separately. Check in advance, because not all carriers provide this coverage, and policies differ among those that do.

Gloves

The first thing you need is a pair of comfortable but tough leather gloves for pruning and handling plants. The spines of some weeds will go right through any but the toughest hide. We recommend goatskin, one of the more puncture resistant leathers. Good goatskin gloves are not cheap. They run about $15 a pair and up. Don't be taken in by cheap imitations, which often are fragile sheepskin. Like sheepskin, goatskin is rich in lanolin and stays soft, but it's twice as durable as pigskin and cowhide. Tests show that after abrasion it's three times as durable as similarly scuffed pigskin and 10 times tougher than scuffed cowhide. Several sources of goatskin work gloves appear in the Appendix.

Get a good fit. Loose-fitting gloves are clumsy and get caught in machinery. Make sure, also, that they fit snugly at the wrist, otherwise dirt and debris will dribble inside them while you work.

Earth Moving

You will need the basic gardening tools, shovel, spading fork, hoes, garden rake, pick, and mattock. Any good gardening book will inform you that a spade is made for digging and a shovel is for working in loose earth only. But you can always dig with a square shovel and sometimes a pick. The square shovel often doubles for spade work, but in a pinch a sharp spade, not shovel, will spot edge lawns.

For earth-moving tools, the rule is look for heft. Feel for weight and balance, and don't get one too large for long jobs. Look at the handles end-on. The best are straight-grained ash or hickory with the end grain running vertically to the bending force. The handles can also be solid-core fiberglass. The best D-handles are part of the wood or fiberglass, not metal add-ons. Inspect the metal parts for one-piece forging. Watch out for cheap welds or open seams that will break. For shovels and forks, the back of the metal shank reveals the quality. Good shanks are forged and socketed, not stamped of mild steel bent around the handle. Look for "drop-forged," "tempered," or "heat-treated" for extra preparation. Good steel rings clearly when you tap it; it's hard to sharpen but stays sharp. Tools with forged shanks are usually heat-treated or tempered high-carbon steel and made to last. Many of these tools are made in England, which has a tradition of quality garden tools. It's hard to buy them used.

Pointed shovels cut faster but don't move as much earth as square-end shovels. The round point is intended to pierce dense soil and sink into dirt, compost, or gravel fairly easily. It is a digging, scooping, cement-mixing tool. Again, the best are one-piece, drop-forged steel. Good shovels have a tread—where the foot pushes the tool down—with a wide, comfortable roll forward to step on.

How much earth you want the shovel to move depends on what pace you can keep up. The U.S. Forest Service developed a pointed fire-line shovel, about seven-eighths regular size. It was tested so fire fighters could use them without fatigue on a 10-hour shift. They keep them razor sharp for cutting brush, digging, and shoveling. Ben Meadows Company sells shovels that conform to U. S. Forest Service standards. They cost $50. Shop around.

Spading forks come with flat or square tines. The square-tined forks are called English spading forks and will dig circles around the flat-tined variety. They won't bend out of shape whenever they hit a respectable rock. The English forks also cost about $50. The four square tines look slender but are all but unbreakable. They are made from one bar of high-carbon steel and finished with either a long socket or straps riveted through the handle. The metal is heated and rolled over blocks to make it thin for sharpness and thick in areas of maximum strength. They deal with buried rocks and they lift plants with less root damage than a shovel or spade. In soft earth, flat-tined forks lift bulbs, roots and tubers more gently than the square-tined variety.

Hoes come bent in the general garden variety and in a straight scuffle hoe. The long handled garden hoe is meant for cultivating or weeding, while the scuffle hoe will cut weeds on the pull and push strokes. The U.S. Forest Service also developed an all purpose fire-line tool called a MacLeod, which is a large hoe on one side and a coarse rake on the other. Nothing beats a MacLeod for chopping tough vegetation, and for moving and leveling a lot of dirt, mulch, or other material. A good one will take and hold a sharp edge. Ben Meadows sells USFS quality MacLeods for $80. You can find cheaper versions in large garden supply stores.

Picks are for piercing and breaking up hardpan, mattocks for cutting and chopping hardpan, roots, and anything else you find underground. Speaking of which, if you have to dig deep, check with the local utility companies to locate buried lines. Picks and mattocks come from the store with wood handles that seem to shrink away from the head as soon as you get them home. You'll have to saw a kerf in the handle's working end and drive in a wooden wedge sold at hardware stores to keep it tight-fitting. Do this when the weather is hot and dry, otherwise both wedge and handle will shrink together.

Hoses

You probably won't need a garden hose often, but when you do you'll want a ¾- or 1-inch hose for placing a lot of water fast. A couple 50-footers and a control nozzle to keep you from running back and forth to the faucet will do for most jobs. A high-quality hose, treated well, will last for years. Here's what makes for quality:

Hoses must be completely flexible but withstand the same pressure as rigid plumbing. None are steel-belted yet, but manufacturers build them like tires out of synthetic resins strengthened with plies of fabric—in this case mesh sheaths wrapped with spiral windings. You want lots of plies, but don't rely on plies alone. Every manufacturer counts differently.

Hose resins are typically polyvinyl chloride—that's PVC or just "vinyl." The best hose vinyls incorporate synthetic rubber for flexibility and strength. Flexibility is a must. Test for it. Hoses are usually sold coiled and twist-tied. Undo a tie and bend 18 or 24 inches of hose-end in a tight U. Cheap hose is stiff and will kink easily. The best hoses bend tightly with no kinks. Look also for good abrasion resistance.

Couplings count, too. The worst are plastic or thin pressed brass. The best are heavier cast brass with flat facets you can put a wrench on. A good coupling's tang inside the hose is longer and more secure. Warranties are unrealistic but at least help identify grades of quality.

Treat hoses gently to make them last. Don't strain the couplings. Don't bend the hoses against the tang, which can cut them. Don't drag them over rough surfaces. Kinks never go away, so lay hoses down in a loose figure-eight. They'll take up more room but are less likely to kink than if coiled sailor-style. Off-season, drain and store hoses indoors away from solvents, oil, and chemicals.

Weeding, Pruning, Shearing

The dandelion weeder - Carry a "dandelion weeder" in your back pocket or on your belt. This is chisel-like tool, bent in a slight S-curve with a fish-tail at the end. If you come across a weed while working, you can jimmy it out without having to drop everything to get the tool. A. M. Leonard sells a stand-up model for big weeding sessions. It's easy on the back, but you can't take it with you while you work at other tasks. You'll want good quality steel for prying in hard soils. You can also use an old screwdriver in a pinch.

Pruners - Hand pruners are for cutting stems up to about ½" across. You will need a very sharp pair of pruners and a sheath to stick them in. Pruners come in the bypass and anvil variety. Good sharp bypass pruners cut cleanly with a scissor action. They get closer to the base of a twig and are less likely to crush it. They are preferable to anvil pruners which generally are cheaper and will crush part of the stem on the flat-topped anvil blade or, if the blades mismatch badly, will leave it hanging by shreds. Carry hand pruners in a sheath on your belt. They're handy to snip an overgrown berry vine or the like that may interfere with mowing.

Pruners come in different sizes. Thirty minutes to an hour or more of pruning is real work, so try out pruners' for weight, fit, and balance before buying. Too big a pruner will tire the hand fast. A couple of practice squeezes in the store won't tell how a few hours' work feels. And although many reputable mail-order sources let you return unfit goods, it's probably better to try out a friend's pruners for a day or two if you can.

The best pruners have replaceable parts. They should be easy to take apart, sharpen, and reassemble. If that's what you buy, make sure you can get replacement parts. Make sure also that the lock is up by the pivot rather than on the handle where it will cause a blister. Locks seem to be a weak point on cheap pruners. They break early. If you carry pruners in a sheath on your belt, that shouldn't be a major problem. The blades of right-handed pruners spread apart in the left hand, so lefties need a southpaw version. The correct tool makes the job easier, with clean cuts, healthier plants, and satisfied customers.

Keep your pruners clean, sharp, and well oiled. Disease can go from plant to plant on dirty pruners. Wipe them off with a *clean* rag after every plant. When pruning diseased plants, disinfect them after each cut. Some suppliers sell a small belt-mounted vial for a disinfectant like bleach or denatured alcohol. Sometimes you have to get out the Swiss army knife and scratch away at the gunk. Wipe off and disinfect the knife, too, if necessary. Keep debris out from between bypass blades so they close tightly. Live plants are wet, and you should oil pruners after each use. Follow the directions to take them apart for sharpening. Then sharpen only the beveled blade edges, whether anvil or bypass.

Loppers, pruning saws - You may spring the blades of bypass pruners if you underestimate a twig's hardness. You probably just need a bigger tool. For heavier branches use loppers, which are pruners with heavier blades and handles about 2 feet long for better leverage and to reach large stems inside the plant. All the pruner rules apply to loppers. Look also for rubber shock absorbers and consider fiberglass handles that can be replaced as needed with other or longer handles. The blade tangs should connect to the handles with heavy screws and nuts, rather than being merely stuffed into the ends. Some loppers have one-piece metal handles and are forged for a lifetime of heavy use. Best quality or not, maintain them like pruners.

A gear and ratchet mechanism on a lopper permits cutting wood up to 2" across. But ratchets add weight and more squeezes per cut. Instead, use a pruning saw for wood thicker than 1½ inches. Larger teeth generally cut quickest with a rougher edge. New Japanese blades called turbo or frictionless blades cut fast with small teeth. For limbs up to 3" a Grecian pruning saw with a curved blade to cut on pull stroke will fit in tight places. The blade of some fold into the handle and fit in a back pocket. A narrow-nosed bow saw with a thin blade that cuts on the push stroke is fine when there is room. A straight pruning saw, like a carpenter's but with different teeth, should not have teeth on both edges; the off side can gash the wrong branch. An electric- or gasoline-powered chain saw is useful but can be dangerous. Loggers' chaps and protective vests (from Bailey's, Ben Meadows, etc.) are a necessity around chain saws. You should also wear high boots with traction soles and steel toes, a padded jacket to protect the upper body, a certified hard hat with face shield or safety glasses, and possibly a dust mask. Treat these tools with a lot of respect.

You throw a high-limb "chain saw" over a limb and hand-pull it back and forth. It's like a bicycle chain with chisel blades. *Forget it.* Instead, use a pole pruner, which has a handle- or rope-activated lopper on top, and often a Grecian saw on its head. Using the pruner head with less than three hands is tricky and tiring unless you stick the pole's butt in the socket of a flag or surf-casting belt, or the front pocket of a carpenter's apron. You might want to remove the saw to get into tight places. (Did you remember to bring wrenches and screwdrivers?) Again wear goggles or face shield and a hard hat for large branches and limbs. And watch out! When tree limbs fall they can move fast. Finally, before you buy, make sure the pole's length-adjusting nut works easily and tightens snugly. A gas powered version costs about $700.

Hedge shears - Hand hedge shears are fine for topiary shrubs. Longer blades and handles extend your reach but add weight. Check out the handles' shock with a series of vigorous cuts before buying. Serrated blade edges are supposed to keep stems from sliding away, but sharp edges will handle the problem. If you have to shear many linear feet of hedges you will want power shears. Hedge clippers with an oscillating set of cutting teeth help put a flat top and sides on a hedge. Don't get an electric trimmer. Gasoline powered versions have a carburetor that works in all directions. They're more versatile than electric clippers but noisy and heavy. They require good ear protection but their efficiency usually justifies the inconvenience. Be careful because, heavy as they are, they can be dangerous when you're tired. They are lubricated with graphite to keep sap from gumming up the blades.

String trimmers and brush cutters - String trimmers can be real time and back savers. They consist of a powered hub from which one to four nylon strings or "whips" extend and slash grass and small brush. The string goes right up against walls, fences, posts, curbs, rocks, and against trees, sometimes gashing the bark of young trees.

Gasoline powered trimmers with 20- to 25-cc 2-stroke engines are your best bet for professional work. Check for automatic string feed. It is also worth getting a trimmer with the brush-cutter option, a circular saw blade, for knocking down heavier brush and branches.

Try this tool before you buy. Check for balance and adjustability. See that the brush cutter, if any, takes different blades and that you can change them easily. When you cut, move the cutting head in the direction of spin to draw material into the whip or blades. When you use the blade, wear goggles, your hard shoes, and heavy clothing, preferably including logger's chaps. A brush removal firm in the San Francisco Bay Area adds umpire's shin guards that cover the feet and ankles.

Ladders

Get a three-legged orchard ladder to prune trees. Three points define a plane, and this ladder will never wobble from it as long as it is on firm ground.

Clean-up

For clean up, you need a leaf blower, a stiff house broom, a stiff push broom, a pitch fork, tarps, and buckets (*e.g.*, plastic buckets that paint or spackling compound comes in). Occasionally, you might need a garden rake. Better garden rake heads have a "bow" design, with two arms like an archery bow centered on the handle, with the tines on the straight "string" part. Steel fan rakes' weak point is where the handle joins the tines. Look for a strong joint. You may also want a leaf blower; more on that later. Unless you're starting out very small and need only a bucket for clippings, you will also need a trash can for the day's garden waste.

Leaf blowers are very useful clean-up tools, whose efficiency more than makes up for their noise. There is no faster way to clean up a jobsite, and no easier way to get leaves off a bed of gravel or mulch or to move them into a heap for disposal. The most powerful are the back-pack blowers. One step below these are the shoulder-strap variety. Alternatively, there is a back-mounted leaf vacuum that combines clean-up with bagging and is a real time saver. The problem with all these machines is they put out a lot of decibels, and you need very good ear protection. Some communities have banned them for their noise; so be a good neighbor and use them sparingly.

Maintenance, Service, and Repairs

Cheap or expensive, keep your tools clean and sharp. Poorly maintained tools slow you down, cost you money, and can lead to accidents. Well maintained, they'll last longer and work better. And you want them to look good when you drive around with them sticking out of the truck.

Clean-up is simple for most tools. Scrape them right away with an old putty knife you keep handy in the truck. Or wash off the dirt, dry the tool with a rag, then wipe with oil or spray with a moisture displacer such as WD-40. A medium to coarse wire wheel on an electric bench grinder or hand drill takes sap off cutting blades and mud from shovels and spades. If you prefer to clean by hand, emery cloth in medium and coarse grades also cleans well. You can also use mineral spirits (paint thinner) on steel wool to remove rust and sap. For shovels and other digging tools there's the bucket-of-oily-sand trick. After scraping off the dirt, oil and polish the tool by plunging it a few times into a bucket of sand soaked in used motor oil. It scours and coats the surface.

To keep wooden handles from absorbing moisture and splitting, wipe them down occasionally with a rag moistened in boiled linseed oil, which seals them where you've worn off the finish.

Sharp shears, pruners, and loppers cut better and damage plants less than dull ones. Take them apart and sharpen them once or twice a year—or more if necessary. For occasional honing without taking the tool apart there's a triangular ceramic stone that works well. A diamond sharpener, with diamond grit glued to a thin plastic handle, also cuts well. Slide the hone away from the cutting edge all along the blade at about a 20° angle. Check for sharpness by cutting paper. Remove the slight burr from sharpening with a few flat passes along the back of the blade. On better pruners you can eventually replace the blades.

Shovels and spades work better with edges sharp enough to chop roots and turf without much effort. A bastard mill file, or coarse grindstone on the bench grinder or drill, is all you need to take out the nicks and produce a sharp edge to ease your labor. Run the grindstone slowly in order not to damage the steel's temper. Otherwise, touch the blade to the wheel briefly each time so it doesn't overheat.

If you come across a good but neglected tool, you can sometimes salvage it by removing the rust mechanically or chemically. Once cleaned, paint the non-working surfaces with a good enamel and oil the rest. You may find replacements for handles and other parts by contacting the manufacturer if it's still in business. Some parts such as handles are standard and are available in hardware and garden supply stores.

Finally, paint the handles of your tools with a brightly colored enamel—any color but green. This not only helps you find those you drop, but helps identify them as yours.

Engine maintenance & repair - With all your power equipment you will need at least one gasoline can, two if you have both two-stroke and four-stroke engines. Spare plugs and other replacements are a necessity in your tool kit.

A short course on small engine maintenance is worth putting on your agenda, too. Repair shop bills at $35 an hour and up can wipe you out. If you want to stay in the business long, you will have to learn to fix your own equipment. In addition to a course in engine repair, you might also take a look at *Walk-Behind Lawn Mower: Service Manual*, the 5th edition, published by Intertec Publishing. You may want a copy of your own. *Chilton's Small Engine Repair Up to 20 HP* is a standard repair manual. It's the most popular guide to small engine repair but not intended for reading end to end. *Walk-Behind* is easier to read, but provides fewer specifications.

Almost every piece of machinery manufactured comes with a shop manual. You should get the manual for all power equipment you buy. If you bought used, write to the manufacturer for the manual. Then sign up for a community college or adult school course in small-engine repair and maintenance. Finally, go out and buy a cheap, broken down mower through your newspaper's classified ads. Rebuild it. Rebuild a couple of them to gain confidence in your ability to troubleshoot, repair, and fine-tune these machines. You can always keep the best one for a back-up and sell the rest to pay for your education.

With Chilton, *Walk-Behind*, the shop manuals, a course, and a few practice tear-down/rebuilds, you can be sure you will have equipment and tools you can always rely on to keep working.

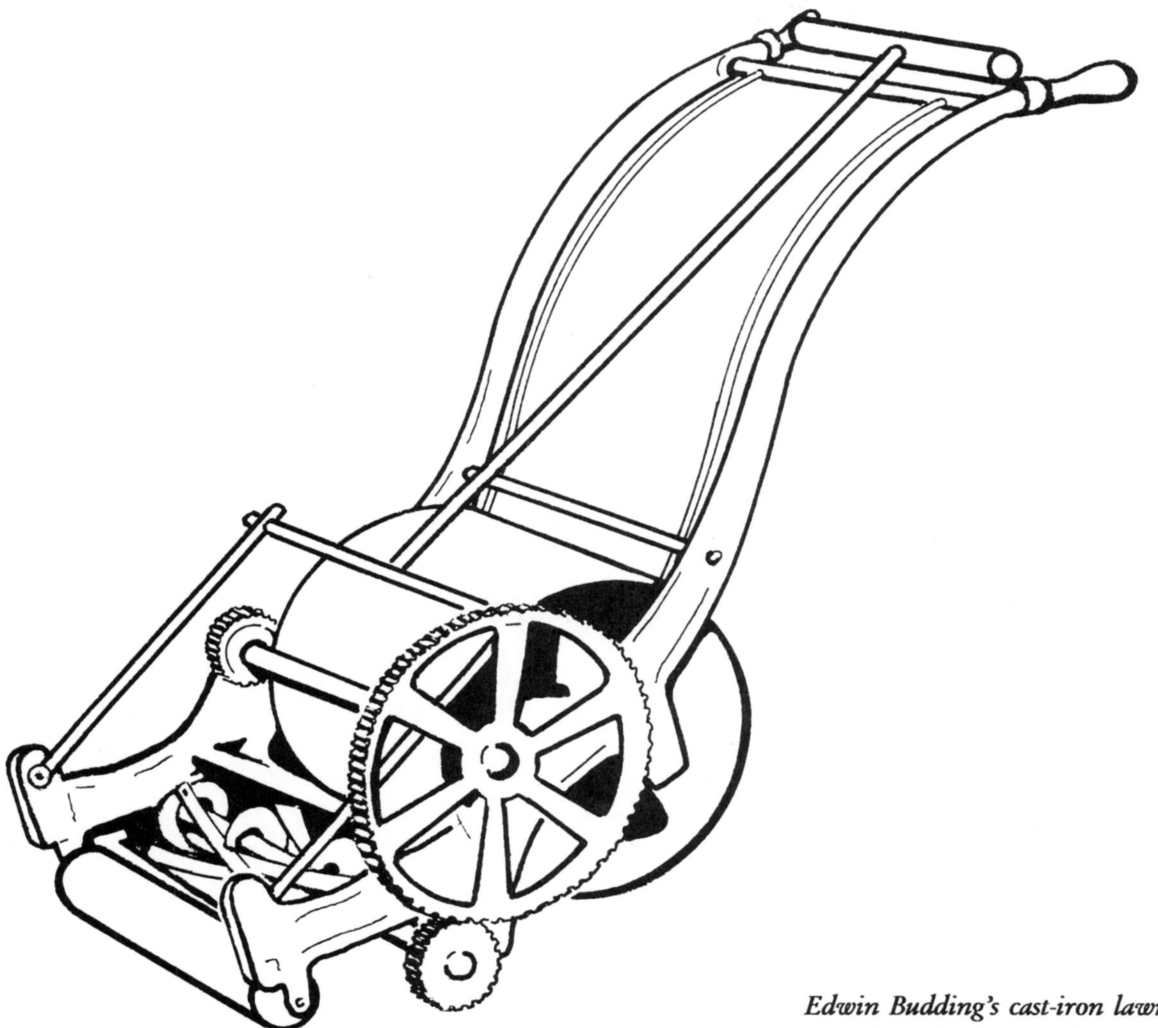

Edwin Budding's cast-iron lawn mower *(circa 1830) at rest between jobs.*

With its heavy back roller, it took two people to work it—one pushing, one pulling. A larger model was drawn by a horse shod in leather shoes that wouldn't hurt the grass. No matter. It was a real advance over scythe-swinging and it's the reason for all those nice lawns we get to work on now.

Varieties of Pests and Controls
The Enemy
Intro to Chemical Warfare
Integrated Pest Management
Equipment for Applying Pesticides
A Parting Shot

Chapter 18

PEST CONTROL – TOWARD INTEGRATED MANAGEMENT

Quick Start: *MANY pesticides, mainly weed and insect killers, are so lethal that the federal government and all the states strictly regulate their distribution and use. Federal law requires every state to certify all professionals in its jurisdiction who use pesticides in their business. Always use extreme caution, including reading and understanding the labeling instructions, every time before you buy, use, store, or dispose of a pesticide. Also, get a sense of the methods of modern pest control by reading the brief discussion in this chapter. Then educate yourself by reading one of the lengthy books on the subject. This chapter and the Appendix note a few.*

THE PREFERRED WAYS to combat garden pests keep changing, not only because some pests mutate and defeat our controls but because we keep trying to find effective controls that are safer to use. The numerous government pamphlets and scholarly books on the subject are constantly revised to reflect the ongoing shifts in approach. It is a complex subject. This chapter, therefore, will only introduce some principles of pest control and tell you where to learn more about it.

Varieties of Pests and Controls

First, pests come in three varieties: animal, vegetable, and pathogens. Animal pests—mostly insects, nematodes, mites, slugs, snails, and rodents—feed on the plant. Vegetable pests, known as weeds, compete with the plant. Pathogens—which include bacteria, viruses, and fungi —sicken the plant.

Second, pest control can never be absolute. All we can aim for is reasonable limits at an acceptable cost. What is reasonable depends on whether we are protecting a prize house plant or 640 acres of feed corn.

Finally, there are four ways to control pests: exclusion, suppression, protection, and resistance.

Exclusion (or prevention) means keeping pests out of the plant's home ground. This is done by planting pest-free stock, the seeds or bulbs of which may have been treated with a pest killer, and by keeping out infected or infested stock by quarantine.

Suppression involves finding and killing the pests. Older textbooks referred to this method as *eradication*. The term has been abandoned as inaccurate at best and unrealistic at worst. Suppression is easy enough when digging or pulling weeds. It's much harder when trying to wipe out insects or pathogens. The best non-chemical suppression choice is to destroy pests' homes by removing host plants, rotating crops, and hauling away infected refuse. Chemical treatment is the easiest but most expensive form of suppression. We will discuss it very briefly below. The aim of suppression should be to reduce pests' numbers so that their natural enemies can contain them.

Protection sets up a shield between the plants and the pests. This includes keeping the soil's temperature, moisture, and *p*H unfriendly to pests. Very often a proper environment for healthy plants is enough to keep infection and infestation under control. Finally, chemicals sometimes can be applied before the pests appear.

Resistance involves modifying a plant genetically to make it tougher and less sensitive to what ailed it. Since the plant's attackers can mutate very quickly, however, every advance in plant resistance works only until the pests catch up.

The Enemy

Vegetable pests - Weeding and cultivation (hoeing, digging) are obvious mechanical ways to suppress weeds. Quarantines and abatement orders offer protection, as do proper watering and clipping practices. Pesticides applied to weeds are called herbicides. They can be *pre-emergent* to stifle weeds before they sprout, or *post-emergent* to kill them once they do. They can be nonselective and kill everything green in their path or tailored to kill only some kinds of plants. For example, broadleaf herbicides properly applied to a lawn should not injure the grass (although you'd better read the label to see *which* grass it won't hurt). Review Chapter 15 on lawn diseases for a brief discussion of using such chemicals.

Many herbicides leave a residue in the soil that will kill plants after application. Other residues may lock up tightly in the soil so that you need not delay planting while the residue leaches out of the soil. Glyphosates (*e.g.*, Roundup®, Kleenup®, and Knock-Out®) attack a gene that exists only in plants and become inactive in the soil. Casoron®, used to kill weeds around woody plants, not only leaves a residue, but can also wash into neighboring yards. Read the labels for residual effects.

Animal pests lead more complicated lives. Their habits and life cycles need study before bringing in the controls. Their major representatives follow.

Insects belong to a large family called arthropods (they have jointed feet), which also includes spiders, mites, lobsters, and so on. Insects have no backbone, but a shell in three segments: head, thorax, and abdomen. Insects' mouths, compound eyes, and antennae are on their heads, with taste organs behind the jaws. They have three pairs of legs on the thorax, and they digest in their abdomens. Most have sensory hairs on their bodies.

They change radically throughout their lifetimes. Some grow from eggs into *larvae* or caterpillars, which eat plants until they reach their *pupa* or chrysalis stage. Then they sleep in a cocoon until emerging as an adult butterfly or other flyer that eats little or nothing while it flits about, mates, and lays eggs to start the whole cycle again. Others pass through a succession of *nymph* stages, shedding shells until they become adults.

You need to research your arthropod to fight it. Applying a control at the wrong stage of its life cycle is useless. Check the Appendix for illustrated guides to insects, their lives and habits. If you can't find the insect in a guide, call your state or county agricultural extension. Then try to target it alone for control.

Types of Insect Attack - Sucking pests sometimes suck sap so quickly it goes right through them and runs onto the plant as a sugary sap that attracts the spores of black mildew. Black mildew does not harm the plant but blocks sunlight and reduces photosynthesis.

Chewing insects' consumption is visible, but they may not be. Some are small and hidden in plant crevices.

Insects also inflict secondary damage by transmitting plant viruses and bacterial infection. Aphids may carry about 50 different viruses. Other pests inject poisons into plants.

Not all insects are pests. Scavenger insects like scarab beetles and crane fly larvae eat garden waste. Certain wasp larvae dine on tomato hornworms. Predators like yellowjackets and wasps eat many insects, as do lady beetles and praying mantises.

Insecticides, even properly applied, usually don't discriminate. Except for specific controls that may kill only, say, mites, most kill the beneficial insect predators along with their prey. Insects are like the other animal groups. As a strategy against extinction, prey multiply faster than predators. After you spray bugs, the prey population bounces back, but the predators may never increase enough to get matters under control if you spray again before they catch up. For that reason, among others, you should use a broad-spectrum insecticide only when the garden is under serious insect attack. Don't let spraying insecticides become a routine that upsets the garden's predator-prey balance. Theoretically, you can buy insect predators mail-order, but bought replacement predators like lady beetles and praying mantises seldom stick around long enough to help. Healthy, genetically resistant plants withstand pests better.

"The Insect Predator Garden"

Although purchased insect predators usually won't settle into a strange landscape, most gardens are full of them already—if they haven't been poisoned along with pests. Introducing plants that attract them may increase or establish a native population, but it takes trial and error. A flower may attract a beneficial insect in one garden but not another. Those with abundant pollen usually work best. Plants with small shallow flowers, like those in the carrot and daisy family, provide readily available pollen.

Ants tend and protect many species of aphids. They attack most aphid predators but not the larvae of mealybug destroyers, whose white woolly covering is like the aphid's. Mealybug destroyers will naturalize in gardens that have members of the daisy and carrot families.

Beetles (Coleoptera), of which lady bugs are the most popular, are fond of plant nectar and nectar-eating pests. Their larvae eat pests' eggs, aphids, and soft-bodied insects. Sunflowers and vetches produce external nectar that attracts them. Members of the daisy family, will encourage west-coast lady bugs (Hippodamia) to stay.

Most gardens have lacewings (Neuroptera). The larvae when small eat insect eggs, mites and thrips, graduating to aphids, mealybugs, whiteflies and small caterpillars. Plants that attract lacewings, wasps, tachnids, syrphid flies, and pirate bugs, are caraway, coriander, bishop's weed, blazing star, coreopsis, cosmos, golden marguerite, goldenrod, sunflowers, tansy, yarrow, scabiosa, sweet alyssum, candytuft, baby-blue-eyes.

Fly larvae (maggots) are important garden predators. Syrphid flies (Syrphidae) buzz around flowers for nectar and aphids. Adults resemble bees and wasps.

Nematodes are microscopic non-segmented worms, pointed at both ends. Some are beneficial and attack insects, weeds, and other nematodes. Others are plant and animal parasites. Most nematode damage to plants is on the roots, which nematodes feed on or lodge in. Their attacks stunt plant growth and production.

Nematodes can be controlled by application of chemical controls and occasionally by other nematodes that prey on them. Always clean your boots thoroughly if you have worked in an area infested with nematodes, as most of them inhabit the roots and soil around them.

Slugs and snails - If you use slug and snail pellets or powder of 2% metaldehyde, it will also attract the family dog. Dogs have been known to tear open the container and gobble it like candy. Two pounds is enough to send a large dog into severe, often fatal, convulsions; even if it survives, its owners will probably incur a veterinarian bill upwards of several hundred dollars. So spread metaldehyde bait thinly over the soil if you use it and remove or store the remainder safely. Other slug and snail measures include: diatomaceous earth, moisture-absorbing grit they won't crawl across; copper bands around stalks that give them a mild electric shock; pit traps, which are sunken pie plates or bowls of beer that they drown in. If the dog laps up the beer, the worst it will get is a hangover.

Moles and gophers - Some moles feed on earthworms and grubs, others eat plants, too. Even if they don't eat plants, their tunnels can aerate the soil thoroughly enough to kill a mature tree. Gophers eat roots and bulbs. To kill either pest you have to locate a main tunnel. The mounds of earth you see are feeding exits that they plug up with earth. Probe for the tunnel between the mounds with a metal rod or sharp stick. Dig down to it and set any of a variety of either traps or baits. Cyanide bombs have a gunpowder fuse that you light before dropping one in the tunnel and covering your excavation. Be sure all the other exits are firmly plugged. Be sure not to inhale the fumes. The cyanide kills a few earthworms, too, but it is a very sure way to eliminate moles and rodents.

Fungi, bacteria, viruses

Fungi - Fungus infections occur among weak plants in environments hospitable to the fungus. It is more effective to improve the environment than to turn to a fungicide. Fungicides are also non-discriminating and kill beneficial soil fungi that help break down dead matter for plant use. You should coordinate fungicide use, when needed, with corrective measures like improving the soil and other growing conditions to protect the plant and discourage further harmful fungus outbreaks.

Young seedlings can be killed by damping-off fungi that are in the soil. Buy seed treated with a protectant. You can fumigate the soil before planting to kill the fungi along with insects and weeds, but again you knock out the good things with the bad.

Powdery mildew is a dusty white fungus that grows on plants' upper leaf surfaces and can kill them. Dusting or spraying with sulfur fights it, and some plant varieties are more resistant than others. Read the label for when to repeat sulfur applications. Repeat applications interrupt the fungus's reproductive cycles. It is best to attack the fungi when they first appear, usually the first warm day after a lot of damp ones. Look for a grayish or white powder on the leaves. Sometimes you can protect leaves by spraying fungicides before the fungus spores blow onto them.

Viruses and bacteria - Common virus or bacterial diseases include irregular or rounded spots, rust-colored raised blisters, brown margins, and other leaf discolorations. Some viruses severely or slightly stunt the plant. Viral infections are incurable. They winter over on the dead residue of infected plants and attack new growth in the spring. Since many viruses live between seasons in neighboring weeds, weeding helps to control them. Remove infected plants from the garden and burn or otherwise destroy them. Sterilize your equipment.

Viral root rots and wilts, which cause a plant's roots and branches to die gradually, exist in the soil. Root rots are hard to control except by moving the plants to a different part of the garden. The only other fix is to replace the soil. Call your agricultural extension service for where to dispose of the old soil.

Bacterial infections are curable but just barely. They come mostly from seeds. The best cure is exclusion by purchasing only inoculated varieties.

Intro to Chemical Warfare

If you look at a garden where a lot of toxic chemicals have been used, you probably won't see anything wrong. One reason is that the harmful effects to good insects, earthworms, and micro-organisms may not show up for years. For example, thatch may build up gradually in an overdosed lawn for lack of worms and micro-organisms to digest the clippings. Also we've been taught to reject the slightly chewed-on look of a natural environment. So it's easy to get hooked on chemicals. Meanwhile, all that animal life in the soil that makes plants healthy, is under steady attack by the gardener. Every time pests go for the plant, more chemicals follow. If you're hired to maintain a garden caught up in that cycle, try to introduce the coordinated methods of exclusion, suppression and protection to break the habit. If that advice seems extreme, read on.

As amended in 1972, the Federal Insecticide, Fungicide, and Rodenticide Act (FIRCA) requires professionals who apply "restricted use" pesticides to be certified. It imposes civil and criminal penalties for violating the Act. It also gives each state control over pesticide use as long as state regulations meet or exceed federal standards.

Many state laws do exceed them. In California, for example, the only person who does *not* need a license to apply any pesticide is the homeowner using them at home or very nearby. Everyone else has to pass a qualifying exam and pay for a certificate. If you decide to use pesticides in the business, contact your state department of agriculture for its requirements.

Garden chemicals in history - Think of chemical pest control in three historic phases: Before, During, and After the "miracle chemicals." What we are most familiar with are those magic compounds that began with DDT. Their impact seemed truly miraculous until we noticed that they got into the food chain and killed off fish and birds.

Pesticides are not plant medicines. Even the most innocuous are *poisons.* They don't cure sick plants; they kill, sicken, or repel the pests. The really potent ones can also sicken and kill you, unless you treat them with the respect they deserve.

The first insecticides and fungicides were inorganics like sulfur, arsenic, mercury, and copper. They injured the plant as often as not and were poisonous to people as well. Early botanical organics were rotenone ("ROTE-known"), which comes from a South American bean, and pyrethrum from the flowers of a chrysanthemum.

The Swiss invented DDT, the first chlorinated hydrocarbon just before World War II. Organophosphates were developed in the 1950s from phosphoric acid. These break down faster than chlorinated hydrocarbons. Carbamates, developed in the late 1950s from carbamic acid, break down even faster. Newly developed synthetic pyrethrums called pyrethroids are more effective and long-lived than organic pyrethrums. Most insecticides in use now are organophosphates and carbamates, and there are a lot of them.

Chemical pesticides today - The number of pesticide products and active ingredients constantly changes as new ones come on the market and others are withdrawn. An Environmental Protection Agency (EPA) official estimated that at one point in the 1990s the market comprised some 21,000 products and 849 active ingredients. Federal law requires that all products sold as pesticides be registered with the EPA and carry labels that specify the proper dosage, the net contents, the active ingredients, the relative toxicity to mammals, other hazards to

Parts of a Pesticide Label

1. **Brand Name** or trademark shows plainly on the product label's front and panel. It is the name used in advertising.
2. **Common Name** stands in for the complex scientific description and is the same regardless of brand name.
3. **Ingredients Statement** must show the percent of active and inactive ingredients, by chemical or common and chemical name. Regulations soon will require also listing inert ingredients.
4. **Type of Formulation** tells whether it is a liquid, wettable powder, dust, emulsifiable concentration, or the like. It will also tell how to use the formulation.
5. **Child Hazard Warning** on every pesticide container' front label must state "KEEP OUT OF REACH OF CHILDREN."
6. **Net Contents**, in ounces, liters, pounds or other units, must show how much product is in the container.
7. **Directions for Use** must tell how to use the product (properly and legally) for the best results. This includes:
   a. Pests the product is registered to control
   b. To what the product can be applied
   c. In what form to apply it
   d. How to apply it
   e. How much to apply
   f. Where to apply it
   g. When to apply it
   h. How often to apply it
   i. How soon after applying it's safe to use the treated item
8. **Warning or Caution Statements** must tell about hazards (corrosive, flammable, toxic, etc.) and how to avoid them. Pesticide warnings fall into four toxicity Categories, I - IV. Category I, "Danger Poison," means a few drops to a teaspoon will kill an average adult. Category II, "Warning," means a teaspoon to an ounce will kill an average adult. Category III, "Caution," means over an ounce will do it. Category IV, not toxic, carries no warning. If the product is highly poisonous, it must tell physicians the proper treatment. Highly poisonous or not, the label must say what kinds of exposure call for medical attention. The label must recommend first aid, but often it's not up to date. When you call the local poison center for help, have the label ready to read to medical personnel.

   Warning/Caution statements also explain **how** the product may threaten people and animals. It will recommend—but in very general terms—how to minimize risk with protective clothing, face masks, etc.

   The label may also address environmental precautions to protect wildlife, water and air.
9. **Misuse Statement** reminds you that it's a violation of federal law to misuse the product.
10. **Registration and Establish ment Numbers** for the federal Environmental Protection Agency must be on the front label as "EPA Registration No. _____" and the establishment number, a code for the manufacturer usually follows the registration number.
11. **Name and Address of Manufacturer** of the product must be on the label to tell who made or sold the product and where to get a Materials Safety Data Sheet.

Figure 18.1. Description of pesticide label contents. (Sample label on facing page.)

people and the environment, the manufacturer's name and address, and the product's EPA registration number. Each product must also have labeling that provides detailed information about it. Most "labels" are on the product container. We've seen labeling that covers 25 single-spaced typewritten pages. Figure 18.1 discusses the contents of pesticide labels; an illustration above accompanies it.

The so-called inert ingredients in pesticides can be harmless, like wheat flour. They can also be another pesticide or a potentially hazardous chemical, such as an industrial solvent. They include dyes, wetting agents and adhesives. Often they are more toxic than the active ingredients. Some are flammable.

The EPA will soon require manufacturers to list inert ingredients on pesticide labels. It now requires a full description of a pesticide's ingredients in a "material safety data sheet" or MSDS. The MSDS lists health and other hazards like flammability and explosiveness, and recommends protective equipment for safe handling, storage, and clean up.

1. **Slayz 'Em**

2. **Thanatopzion Insect Spray**

3. Active Ingredients by wt.

Thanatopzion*	52%
Petroleum based solvent	31%
Inert ingredients	17%

*5,7-hydrochloroxymoron trochee precipitate

4. Makes up to 16 gallons.

Emulsified spray kills insects, including apple maggots, codling moths, fernweevils, flies, and aphids.

5. KEEP OUT OF REACH OF CHILDREN

6. Net contents 12 fl. oz. Store in cool, dry place. Use according to label directions. Keep in original container.

7. Directions: 1½ to 2 tbsp/gal of water. Spray where insects collect. Keep away from food, utensils, and drinking water. Repeat as necessary. Do not apply to beans or peas within 1 day of harvest or to lettuce, cabbage, broccoli within 5 days of harvest. Use on root vegetables up to day of harvest.

8. Caution: Harmful if swallowed. Do not breath fumes or spray. Avoid skin and eye contact; wash all body parts thoroughly after use. Keep children and animals away from newly sprayed areas. Call physician if poisoning occurs. Physicians: Call (987) 000-000. Eggwhites for antidote. Use only as directed on this label.

Flammable. Keep away from open flame or extreme heat. Don't reuse container.

9. Notice: Buyer assumes responsibility for harm if used other than as directed.

10. Product 8888888 EPA Reg. No. 77777 Est. 55-2-5555

11. Not A Real Chemical Co., 23 Main St., Intense, MI 98231

(This is very simplified, and real labels aren't numbered like this.)

If you have employees, OSHA requires you to instruct them about the proper use of each pesticide based on the MSDS. Chapter 7 on employees also discusses this requirement as it applies to all chemicals, including pesticides; it suggests where to get MSDS copies. You must also inventory chemicals by their hazard rating and report inventory that exceeds specified limits.

Insecticides - We discussed herbicides in the chapter on lawn diseases. Insecticides are oral or contact poisons, or both. Insects must eat the oral poison. They absorb contact poisons sprayed or dusted on them. Plants absorb "systemic" oral poisons, and the insects die from eating the plant juices. All are neurotoxins. They kill by attacking the nervous system. Pyrethroids paralyze insects and work almost instantaneously. Many of those that interfere with nerve impulses are being investigated for suspected risks to humans and birds. The studies are still unfinished.

How long an insecticide takes to break down is called its "persistence." That's not usually on the label, but labels may tell how long to wait before eating vegetables from a treated garden. Sunlight, moisture, and soil microorganisms break down most pesticides in a few weeks. Residues of DDT have persisted for over 20 years in home carpets and curtains. So be sure windows and doors are closed before spraying. Synthetic insecticides haven't been completely tested for long-term toxicity. Nobody knows whether repeated exposure to some of them will cause illness many years later.

Using pesticides safely - Always read the product labels before you buy an insecticide, or any pesticide, every time you use it, when you store it, and before you dispose of the container. *Understand* what the labels say. If you can't understand what a label says—and that's not unusual—ask someone who should, like your extension agent, the nearest EPA office, or the store where you bought the pesticide.

People absorb pesticide molecules as easily as pests do. They enter most easily through the lungs. The eye is the next easiest entry, followed by areas on the skin, especially at the scrotum, armpit, and scalp.

When you spray these chemicals on a regular basis, they can build up in your body. You must put on protective gear before using pesticides. Such gear includes unlined industrial grade rubber gloves with long cuffs, a tightly woven cotton long-sleeve shirt and pants or overalls (including disposable Tyvek ones—try the suppliers in the Appendix), a waterproof hat or hood, rubber boots, a disposable paper mask for dusts, a respirator for sprays, and goggles or a clear face shield. This is a lot of bother, so try to group your pesticide jobs into a few days if the pests permit.

Test respirators with "banana oil" (isoamyl acetate, a pungent liquid sold as lacquer thinner or nail polish remover). Put on a snug-fitting respirator. Open the banana oil container, pour some on a cotton cloth, and wave it from side to side in front of your face. Then nod and shake your head vigorously and talk loudly. If you still can't smell banana oil, the mask passes the test. If you smell it, readjust the mask and try again after the air clears. If it still flunks, get one that fits. Once you get a good respirator, maintain it carefully and re-test it all the time.

> Keep careful RECORDS of WHO used HOW MUCH of WHAT pesticide when for what PURPOSE at what JOBSITE. Post the record on the pesticide closet or locker next to the big sign with the telephone numbers for nearby doctors, hospitals, and the poison control center. Your telephone directory probably has the poison control center's number where it lists 911 services. Store each of these records in a safe place when filled up. Keep them for life. There is a telephone number on the pesticide label for emergencies. You can also telephone the National Pesticide Hotline at 1-800-858-7378, seven days a week from 6:30 a.m. to 4:30 p.m., Pacific Time.

After applying pesticides take a long, hot, soapy shower. Wash the vulnerable areas of your skin the most. Proper wash-up also requires scrubbing rubber boots, gloves, hat, goggles, and respirator with soap and warm water, and storing them out of the way, preferably in plastic bags. Use rubber gloves to handle all of this gear. Before washing your clothes (still using the rubber gloves) rinse them in a tin washtub full of soapy water. Don't combine clothes from separate pesticide applications; wash them right away in small batches. After their pre-soak run them through the washing machine at the hottest setting for the full cycle, using the largest recommended amount of a strong laundry detergent. If you can still smell pesticides on the clothes after washing, keep washing them until you can't. Otherwise dispose of them—carefully. Afterwards, run the washer empty through another cycle to clean its insides. Hang the clothes outside to dry; don't chance contaminating the family dryer. Store the washed garments away from other clothing and the chemicals.

Rinse out your spray equipment well with three or four flushings of water. On the last rinse pump up the pressure and rinse out the hose and nozzle. After washing pressure sprayers turn them upside down to keep out dust and let them drain. Wedge something under the mouth to tilt it or put it on a rack to dry completely. Read the label for how to dispose of the pesticide container.

Integrated Pest Management

If all this sounds like you have signed up to work at Chernobyl or Three Mile Island, you may want to investigate more benign merchandise and gentler methods.

Current good practice favors *Integrated Pest Management* (IPM) which involves establishing a program of controls that benefits plants and their neighbors over the long term. IPM's purpose is not to try to kill all pests in the world. It won't work. It is very unlikely that a single insect has been put on the extinct or endangered list by a pesticide, even DDT.

Here are the five steps of IPM:

1. See that problems have been prepared for in advance, ideally before planting, with good soil preparation, pest resistant plants, and proper water and fertilizing.
2. Familiarize yourself with a plant's common pests and the symptoms they cause.
3. Learn to recognize when pest levels are getting too high.
4. Use more than one control method for best results. The preferred components are exclusion (prevention), regular pest surveys, setting thresholds for taking action, and combining the most compatible, least harmful controls.
5. Keep records of the problems and treatments, and build up a pest control history. (Become a local expert.)

The purpose of IPM is to create an environment that pests don't like. It's a live-and-let-live deal; pests may come but they are not welcome. The question is, how much pest damage will you (or your customers) tolerate?

Exactly when damage becomes intolerable depends on personal feelings about blemished plants and how much time you need in order to act effectively. If it takes several days to lower pest numbers, you need enough lead time to control them before the plants suffer. Plants are more vulnerable to pests at some times than others; so lead times will vary during the growing season. Also a weakened plant will need more protection than one with plenty of water and nutrients, and little weed competition.

The only way to learn when to apply controls is by keeping records of the treatment you chose and what results you got. Anyone in pest control should keep a special notebook, anyway.

Also get a 10-power magnifying glass, and small plastic vials and bags for samples. Trying to control the wrong pests is a waste of time, money, and effort. A lot of insects look alike; it's easy to kill the good bugs. Sometimes the villain has fled. Or the cause of the damage may be obscure, like a root pathogen. Sometimes the damage is from over--watering, over- or under-fertilizing, pollutants, wind, heat, cold, or the plants' genetics. Much of the time, you will be plain stumped and have to ask an expert. Do it.

You don't have to reinvent the wheel and lever. The experts have been there before you. One good, practical illustrated guide to pest management is Mary Louise Flint's *Pests of the Garden and Small Farm*, which the University of California's agricultural extension service (ANR) has published. *Pests of Landscape Trees & Shrubs: An Integrated Pest Management Guide*, ANR's leading bestseller, has 300 color photos and 50 pages of problem-solving tables. George G. Ware's *Complete Guide to Pest Control With and Without Chemicals* is encyclopedic. Also check with your own state's service for local guides to integrated pest management, otherwise Flint's will be a good start. See the Appendix and search the Internet for state extension sites.

When pests do show up, people who use IPM combine available methods and materials. They weigh the risks and effectiveness of each, in order to choose the best combination. They use each element correctly and in the proper sequence. Then they bring the pest level down to where the natural controls take over.

Here are a few possibilities. Biological controls include introducing and assisting the pests' natural enemies, such as spiders, beetles, toads, frogs, lizards, birds, and bats for insects. Basic IPM principles would rule out applying an insecticide that injured these species. Other combinations could include mechanical and cultural controls (pulling weeds, horticultural oils for insects, trapping rodents), exclusion by government quarantine, or suppression by weed abatement. A combined approach might use certain pheromones to trap, say, coddling moths in order to count them and estimate how much to spray of chemical insecticides, insecticidal soaps, or horticultural oils. The prior census could greatly reduce the amount of spray required.

In addition to the chemical sprays we usually think of as pesticides, there are alternative insect poisons that in normal doses won't harm warm-blooded animals. Pesticidal soaps with sodium or potassium in them dissolve insects' shells; horticultural or dormant oils stuff up their breathing apparatuses, smother their eggs, and interrupt their metabolisms. A dusting or weak solution of boric acid is harmless to mammals and birds (it's in borax, a laundry product) but fatal to insects. New products are just coming on the market now, such as microbials or fungi that infect the pests with diseases, nematodes that attack the pests, and pheromones that confuse pests' biological responses. Some of these are broad-spectrum killers but are nontoxic to humans. Many reduce the number of pests to be controlled, and others merely permit counting the pests. They are used most effectively as part of a coordinated plan.

Although good practice now reduces their use, spraying standard chemical pesticides may still be a part of your business. If you want to ply the trade and learn how not to poison yourself, consider reading *Safe and Effective Use of Pesticides* and *Residential, Industrial and Institutional Pest Control*. They are part of a four-volume set published by ANR Communication Services as the *Pesticide Application Compendium* for qualifying as a certified applicator in California. The compendium is well designed, clearly written, illustrated, and authoritative.

Equipment for Applying Pesticides

Chemicals for gardens come as granules, dusts, or solutions or wettable powders, which are dusts suspended in liquid. Whether to use liquid spray, dust, or dry granular pesticides depends on price, availability, the particular task, and customer preferences. Most pesticides are applied as liquid sprays.

Solutions and wettable powders can be sprayed by compression tanks, backpack sprayers, hose-end sprayers, or slide sprayers. The nozzles of each should be adjustable to control the zone of spray. The spray is either flat from a "flat-fan" nozzle, which has a slot on its tip and is preferred for herbicides, or round from a tip with a pin-hole. You can adjust the size of the spray from a stream to a fog by twisting the nozzle left or right. Powered backpack sprayers run on small 2-cycle gas engines, they reduce muscle power to discharge the liquid but are heavy. Wick applicators soak up herbicide from a container onto a sponge or cloth wick for daubing on broadleaf weeds. They're good for spot application without drift from sprays.

Hand-operated granular applicators—centrifugal, drop, or hopper spreaders—work for fertilizers, seed, or pesticides. Granular pesticides are safer to handle and usually contain a lower concentration of active ingredients. They reduce personal risk and the chance of over-application. They are less effective and harder to find than liquids, but they cause fewer customer concerns about the dangers of chemical pesticides.

Dusts are applied dry, with dusters of varying size. We discuss them briefly later.

Compression tank sprayers look like old fashioned fire extinguishers. They need a stable base, so that when you unscrew the pump they are steady while you pour concentrate and water in the wide funnel shaped mouth at the top of the tank. Be careful of spills and splashes. A 1- to 3-gallon sprayer has a hose, a wand, a control valve, and, ideally, a release valve to empty air from the tank. It uses the principle that air can be compressed but liquid can't. You screw the pump back in the tank's mouth, pump up the pressure as hard as you can. Then—with the pump handle locked, and the tank in one hand and the wand in the other—you press the control valve to let compressed air force the liquid out the nozzle. When the pressure drops you pump it up again. They also offer adjustable nozzles and nozzle shapes for a variety of sprays, from a mist to a fan or a thin jet that reaches the top of 25- to 30-foot trees. You can spray big plants or wide areas. The wands let you spray without stooping or reaching inside a shrub to coat bottom of leaves.

Since spray tanks need room for air, the sizes usually understate how much liquid they'll hold. Although 1-gallon sprayers hold a gallon, 3-gallon sprayers usually hold 2½ gallons of liquid, and 2-gallon sprayers usually hold 1½ gallons.

Pressure sprayer tanks are polyethylene plastic, stainless steel or galvanized steel. Galvanized steel tanks are usually coated inside with an epoxy finish. Stainless steel is nearly indestructible. Plastic tanks, while less durable than steel, are lighter and, when translucent, let you see the liquid inside.

Hoses vary, too. Some use a stiff and cheap vinyl-like plastic. The best are rubber or vinyl reinforced with nylon braiding for flexibility and strength. A short hose can make you hold the tank in an awk ward position for a better reach. If you can't find or make a longer replacement hose, choose a sprayer that already has a long one.

The best sprayer wands and nozzles are brass, but plastic, while less durable, is more flexible and will probably bend, not break, if you step on it. Wand length influences how accurately you can direct the spray. Length varies from 9 to 22 inches, depending on the model. One brand's telescopes from 21 to 37 inches. Some brands offer specialized nozzles in addition to adjustable ones. A fan nozzle is a common variation, and one maker offers a fan nozzle with a spray shield behind the tip to keep chemicals from nearby foliage—useful when you spray herbicides.

The worst thing about sprayers is lugging them around. A gallon of water weighs 8.3 pounds, so 2½ gallons in a sprayer weighs over 20 pounds. Three-gallon sprayers have a nylon shoulder strap that gives your arm a rest but soon cuts into your shoulder. Try to get knapsack shoulder-strap pads from an outdoor or camping goods store. Use a smaller sprayer if the size of your jobs permits.

When you get new spray equipment fill it with water to practice and learn how it performs. You can do this when you fill it with a measured quantity of water to time how long it takes to cover a measured area of turf, shrubbery, or tree crown. You'll need the information to calculate how much to charge for spraying, which we discuss below. Flush sprayers with water before use—even brand new ones and even if you flushed an old one when last cleaned. This makes sure *all passages are open* before it's filled with some kind of poison. Probably the best all-around sprayer is a two- or three-gallon compression tank. For a lot of jobs you may not even have to fill it all the way. Once you pump up the pressure, you just point and shoot. Be

Good Pesticide Practice

- Use only products registered with the EPA.
- Follow the directions on the *labeling* precisely. Doing otherwise is not only hazardous, but violates federal law.
- Use the *lowest* recommended concentration. Don't increase it for any reason, and don't mix pesticides for a "combined" spray.
- Apply pesticides on a calm day, never before it rains, and be careful on hot days, over about 85 degrees, when they can vaporize.
- Mix only what you can use up. Use a couple of small doses if you have to. Don't discard the remainder; use it up where it won't do any harm.
- Don't eat, smoke, or chew gum while mixing or spraying.
- Don't spill any. If you do, pick up spills with cat litter and dispose of the litter at your local poison control center or as the EPA directs.
- Use a tight, small spray pattern on the target plants only; don't nuke the neighborhood. If you have a big job scheduled, check whether any neighbors are allergic or sensitive to what you will be spraying.
- Spray early or late in the day to spare bees.
- Don't spray insecticides around beehives or pollinating bees, or use any pesticide where it can get into streams and lakes.
- Use one sprayer or set of sprayers for herbicides and another for insecticides, and never use one for the other.
- Mark sprayers clearly in very plain, simple English and whatever else you speak around the shop. Use pictures if you think they'll help.
- Use up pesticides fast because they can corrode containers.
- Dispose of them and their containers only at toxic waste sites and as the label directs.
- Lock up your pesticides in a closet or locker that has a big warning sign on it.

sure to get one with a pressure release valve in case it empties before the pressure is gone or you need to unclog the nozzle during a job.

Releasing pressure from some models at the end of a job can be troublesome. You have to hold the tank upside down and open the valve to let the air out. Some sprayers put pressure release valves on top. A few of these include pressure gauges and relief valves to prevent over-pressurization. Although you're unlikely to pump in enough air to burst the tank, a sprayer left in the sun might build up too much pressure without a relief valve to de-pressurize it. Valves on top have two problems. They can release chemical vapors into your face if you're careless, and they don't clear the hose as upending the tank does; so draining the hose should be a last clean-up step.

A thorough cleaning after each use is the key to long sprayer life. Even traces of garden chemicals can corrode both metal and plastic. Rubber fittings are especially vulnerable. Parts like the nozzles are usually made of very corrosion-resistant materials, but even they will corrode, clog, and malfunction if you let them go. Wettable powders abrade the equipment. Most manufacturers tell where to order spare parts as they wear out and corrode, and many stores stock replacement gaskets and O-rings for some brands. Even with regular and thorough cleaning, however, never use one sprayer for both herbicides and insecticides. Use one for each.

Backpack sprayers - The largest sprayers are backpack pump sprayers that hold about five gallons. A good backpack pumper with five gallons of liquid in it will weigh over 40 pounds. You hold the hose and wand with one hand and work the side pump with the other. Protect against spilling chemicals down your back with a special vest; the Appendix lists suppliers that sell protective clothing. Less cumbersome is a 25-pound shoulder slung compression sprayer; it is lighter but hard on the packing shoulder. The pump sprayer makes up for its added weight by needing fewer refills; and you don't have to top it up all the time.

Slide sprayers work on a suction principle. You drop the screened intake end into a bucket of solution or wettable powder and, at the other end of about a six-foot hose, you point and pump. The nozzle is also adjustable and when narrowed to a single stream can reach about 25 feet, compared to 40 feet for a backpack pumper and 15 to 30 feet for smaller compression sprayers. Slide sprayers can be tiring when you adjust the nozzle for a fine spray. The biggest drawback, however, is the chance of kicking over the bucket of liquid they draw from while you're working.

Hose-end sprayers - You have to mix the concentrate-to-liquid ratio precisely for the above sprayers. The hose-end sprayer, while limited in many ways, is self-calibrating and will release a set amount of concentrate into the water stream from the hose. You can adjust the calibration on some hose-end sprayers.

Calibrating spray equipment is necessary to determine how much to use for a given area and how much to charge. The calculation applies to spraying fertilizer or any other liquid. We've placed it here because legal and environmental considerations make it critical to apply pesticide precisely and accurately. The calculations are lengthy but not complicated.

To calculate cost, you need to measure how long it takes to spray a standard sized area. So, put as large a measured amount of liquid as you can into the sprayer. Say it's 2 gallons. Start the clock and spray in a straight line until you empty the tank. Keep the spray density and area as uniform as you can. Measure your distance and your time, including time to pump up again. When the tank is dry, write down your time. Next, measure the distance and width of the spray. Repeat three times for each sprayer and spray tip, and get an average time and area. Once you have average time and area covered for a measured volume from one sprayer/tip combination, you can calculate how long it takes to spray a standard unit like 1,000 SF.

Say that 2 gallons covered a strip 108 by 3 feet, or 324 SF, in 4 min 20 sec. You know—since 324 is less than a third of 1,000—that it will take about three times longer to spray 1,000 SF. To find exactly how much longer, you must *divide* your time by the the 324 SF fraction of 1,000 SF you sprayed:*

Time to spray 1,000 SF = 260 sec ÷ 324/1,000
= 260 sec. ÷ .324
= 802 sec.
= 13 min. 22 sec.

Now you know how long it takes this sprayer-tip combination to cover 1,000 SF. Measure each tip for each sprayer and throw out worn or unreliable tips. You might also have to test different spray settings for each tip. (Note also that spraying shrubbery will take more time and won't give you as consistent a result.)

You do the same thing to calculate how much liquid pesticide, fertilizer, or whatever to spray per 1,000 SF. If 2 gallons covers 324 SF, then 2 gal. ÷ .324 = 6.17 gallons for 1,000 SF. Again you divide for a bigger number. That 0.17 of a 128-oz. gallon is about 22 ounces, and that's a pint (16 oz.) plus ¾ of a cup (6 oz.). In mathematics, "of" is usually a synonym for "times."

That's all there is to it. We've tried to make it easy to figure and remember, but there's no sense doing it every time. Once you have

* Think about it. If you sprayed half a unit in 4 minutes, you know you'd have to double to 8 minutes to spray the whole. Without thinking you just divided by ½. Remember how in fractions to divide you turn the fraction upside down and multiply? That's what you did when you doubled 4 minutes and it's what you do here, but it's not obvious because you aren't working with simple numbers like ½ and 2. As a check, you know you should need more time not less.

your numbers for each sprayer and tip, write them down where you can't lose them, such as right on the equipment and in a record book.

Now you can do the next step, which is figuring exactly how much pesticide (or what-have-you) to apply to 1,000 SF. To apply 4 ounces of active pesticide ingredient per 1,000 SF, mix the 4 ounces—very carefully, using all the precautions mentioned—into all 6 gallons 22 ounces of water. Fill the sprayer with about a quarter of the total mix four times. Don't forget to calculate times to fill, re-fill, and pump-up.

What if you have to spray, say, 375 SF? You need a fraction of the full 4 ounces, that is, 375/1,000ths of 4 ounces, or 4 x .375, or 1.48 ounces. Call it just shy of 1.5 ounces. And, if 6.17 gallons cover 1,000 SF, then 6.17 x .375 (375/1,000) or 2.3 gallons cover 375 SF. You'll need accurate measuring tools and probably a calculator, pencil, and paper. Keep measuring containers for insecticides, herbicides, and fertilizers separate, and clean them after each use! Be sure also not to confuse fluid ounces (volume) with dry ounces (weight).

> The EPA must systematically review pesticide safety under the 1996 Food Quality Protection Act. What is "safe" is not carved in stone. In early 2000, for example, the EPA upgraded the risk of using an insecticide sold as Dursban (known also as chlorpyrifos), thus halting its use by consumers. It's an organophosphate; the more potent of these are nerve gases used as chemical weapons. At the time the EPA upgraded the risk, farmers used 11 million pounds of it per year, and 3 million pounds went to the home and garden market.

Always be sure that what you add to the tank is based on the right application rate. Product labels usually list pesticide application rates by how much product to put on a given area. Federal and state agencies' rates are in amount of *active ingredient* per area. Pesticides rarely have 100 percent of active ingredient. If you lose the label, you'd better have a record of the percentage of active ingredient so you can convert from the manufacturer's recommendation to the county extension agent's active-ingredient recommendation. Then you divide the product's volume by the percentage of active ingredient to know how much *product* to apply—just as with how much fertilizer you need for applying the right amount of nitrogen.

Granular applicators—hand operated centrifugal, drop, or hopper spreaders—work for fertilizers, seed, or pesticides. Granular pesticides are safer to handle and usually contain a lower concentration of active ingredients. They reduce personal risk and the chance of over-application. They are less effective and common than liquids but raise fewer customer concerns about the dangers of chemical pesticides.

Relative humidity affects how well granular pesticides spread and the inert carrier determines their concentration, so you have to recalibrate the spreader for each different product. Many spreaders come with a calibration pan stuck under the working parts. If there's no calibration pan, run the spreader over a pre-measured smooth surface, like a shop floor or driveway. Then sweep up and weigh the material that went on it. Divide the surface area into 1,000 and multiply the weight by the quotient to get how much to use per 1,000 SF. If the amount delivered varies from the calibration setting, make adjustments based on your measure. For centrifugal spreaders use a wide plastic sheet or several of them to collect the granules. The calibrations will all end up being very approximate.

Dusters come in a pump variety of different sizes, or a crank style for big jobs. Unless you plan to work on an acre or two at a time, a pumper should work fine. As with the sprayers, get one that will handle your bigger jobs. For spot treatments, you can get bulb dusters for one-handed use. You can use dusters less than full. Try out a new one with a harmless dust for practice and to time jobs. Always use a dust mask when filling or emptying dusters. Clean by tapping them. Don't blow. You'll get a face full of who knows what? Lubricate the working parts with graphite. The dusts stick to oil.

A Parting Shot

All the safety precautions stated in this chapter may seem excessive, especially if you spray only a plant or two, but over the course of your work you may be continually exposed to chemicals. These precautions are part of the basic safety procedures meant to give you that healthier, happier, and longer working life. Use them. Also, don't think your customers won't notice your businesslike attitude and careful use of garden chemicals. A few years ago a chain landscape maintenance company that charges a monthly fee to douse yards with pesticides dropped many chemicals in favor of pesticidal soaps, because of customer demand.

Try to make it a practice also to solve every pest problem (animal, vegetable, or pathogen) without chemicals. You may even find a niche to fill in your area for organic pest control.

Part IV

Estimating and Bidding

Why You Estimate Each Job
What the Market Will Bear
Estimates, the Short . . .
. . . And the Long of Them
Site Inspection
Analysis of the Work

Chapter 19

WHY YOU ESTIMATE – KNOW WHAT YOU CAN AFFORD

Quick Start: *EVEN if you skim these next three quick-start capsules, come back and read the chapters when you can. They explain why careful estimating should be the foundation of your business.*

If you live where lots are about the same size or you do fairly routine work, you can probably rely on tables or the going rate to help set your prices.

Estimating for more complex jobs requires a close inspection of the site with the owner, asking questions, drawing a good site plan to measure the size of the garden zones, analyzing the work, estimating costs, then making the bid.

Estimating by one method or another is a habit you should get into. It lets you adjust your prices to stay competitive and prepares you for bigger jobs.

With any estimate, try to visualize the steps of each job and look for potential problems. Work you overlook is work that you, not the customer, will pay for.

A LOT OF PEOPLE in this business wing it when it comes to estimating. With a little experience even you will be able to eyeball a yard and make a pretty good bid, especially for simple jobs. Starting out, it is better to do some analysis of your first small jobs so that you know what expenses each one is covering and so you are prepared to move up if you wish. Even when you reach the point where you can look at a front and back yard, and bid a price that will give you a good profit, keep in mind that analyzing the job will provide you with figures that you can tabulate and adjust so that you *know* what your costs are, no matter how simple or complicated the job.

This chapter introduces a short and long method for estimating. At first, they may seem long and very long. The time will come, however, when you can zip right through your estimates. Zip if you want, but do them to be sure you are making the money you think you are.

Why You Estimate Each Job

Even if you stick to mowing small lawns, which can pay very well if you organize your routes tightly, the heart of a successful business is estimating.

Bidding is harder when starting out because you have to consider "time to break-even," which can be two months or two years. Until then, even though you're in the red, each job has to pay for itself.

To survive for the long haul, you must know all the business's expenses and meet them. Without that as a foundation, your business won't make it. Remember about record-keeping in Chapter 6? That's where estimating comes in. **Estimating is the process of figuring what each job *costs* you to do**. Now read that sentence two more times, slowly and with feeling.

Costs - Bidding jobs at any time involves considering whether the job fits your business and maintains your competitive advantage. That's the first "cost" consideration: Whether you should do the job at all. You shouldn't if it won't cover costs. In tough times you may have to find another advantage. That could be working a new neighborhood, improving the quality or appeal of your services, developing a new specialty, or shaving costs to the bone.

Be careful. No matter how hard times are, cutting costs does not mean omitting essentials like the cost of wear and tear on equipment you will need to replace, or compromising the quality you are trying to build. As new advantages go, cutting necessary costs is a last resort and not recommended. Cost considerations aside, you may also want to turn down a job that doesn't fit your plans for the business. This may be hard to justify when you're starting out, but keep it in mind so that you don't end up doing a lot of work you dislike and didn't really want in the first place.

Labor - After costs, add in what your labor is worth. Project what it will be worth in six months, a year, two years. Don't underpay yourself.

Profit - Next set a profit range with a high and low limit. It should not start at zero. Profit compensates you for what you estimate to be the risks of being in business. As a practical matter, you should not go below the low profit limit—not if you want to stay in business—although it's sometimes okay to exceed the high end.

What the Market Will Bear

Before you do any bidding, you will have to get a feeling for the going rate. See what the competition is charging. Read the ads and talk to other people in the business. Find out where they work and assess the job quality, then make your estimate on the basis of your observations.

At the low end you will be competing with kids and "vagabond grass cutters" who will underbid the market. The kids will grow up; the vagabonds go broke or try something else. Both offer limited service at best. To compete, you will have to sell on the basis of reliability, permanence, and better quality. Some people don't care about that, so forget them. Aim for a market that prefers quality to lowest cost, the one that knows it will get what it pays for.

For even the simplest job, good estimating and successful bidding require you to plan carefully without cutting corners. You must account for *all* the time you will spend on the job, and for what you will pay and charge for the materials.

From beginning to end this process involves four steps. They are (1) site inspection, (2) analysis, (3) estimating, and (4) bidding. Much of the detail provided in these chapters anticipates use of the long approach to estimating, but good site inspection and analysis are essential even with the short method. You must know the property you are working on, regardless of how you estimate.

Estimates, the Short . . .

The short estimate is a trial-and-error method that involves working backwards from what you charge, not hourly, but for each job. There is a minimum charge that you can't go below without losing money, no matter how small the job is. That will set your base rate; you can adjust upward from it for any important differences in a job.

Income minus everything - Consider each job an income producer. The price you charge per job is so much income from which you have to deduct its share of your costs of doing business, including (1) expenses, (2) salary, and (3) profit. Remember the Profit and Loss statement in Chapter 6? It should list all monthly totals, including fixed expenses and depreciation. To get *expenses per job*, divide the monthly expenses ("costs" in the P & L statement) by as many jobs as you plan to do each month. Forget salary and profit for now.

Subtract the expenses per job from what you charge. The leftover is salary and profit. Multiply this leftover-per-job times the projected number of jobs per month in order to get your monthly salary and profit. Subtracting your planned salary leaves profit.

If expenses eat up the price you charge, leaving little for salary and profit, try to increase the charge if you can, or see what expenses you can reduce.

Jobs sometimes cluster in different classes of size or complexity. You can do the above calculations for each class. Keep your pricing structure simple, however, with as few steps as possible, and keep an eye on the market. Don't worry about how many of each class you do in a month, as long as each one pays its way.

. . . And the Long of Them

The long method of bidding outlined below introduces a lot of detailed calculations that are suitable for a competitive bidding situation. It lets you analyze your costs precisely and breaks the job down into its smallest steps in order to squeeze out the last drop of profit. Unless you get involved in complex commercial bidding, or want to double check your short estimates, you may prefer to skim the next chapters after reading below about site inspection and analysis. Some inspection steps, like site plans and photographs are not necessary for simple jobs, although the procedure provides a framework for any inspection. Common sense will steer you away from needless toil here.

Site Inspection

A successful bid—one that provides what the customer wants and covers costs, salary, and profit—begins with a careful inspection of the job site in order to gather all the necessary facts on which to base your analysis and estimate.

Inspect with the customer - Unless you inspect when making a sales call, a potential customer will have responded to your marketing efforts. Set up an appointment to meet and view the property together. That lets the customer specify what services are needed while you gather facts from the inspection and from the customer. You must know exactly what the customer wants. Will the contract include maintaining a tree? If so, will your work be limited to pruning and fertilizing? Mention whether you will subcontract to bring in a specialist when necessary. Make a thorough inspection and, if appropriate, draw a detailed site plan. The follow up walk-through inspection also provides an opportunity to educate the customer, to show that you will provide a quality job for which the customer will be happy to pay.

Often it's better to give the property a quick once-over and arrange to come back alone later to spend time measuring and inspecting. Then you and the customer can go over your inspection after you've had time to take everything in and consider it. When you do the walk-through with the customer you can tie up loose ends and agree on exactly how to do things.

Watch for the details - Even a lawn on a standard suburban lot requires close attention to details. Look for things like planting beds or mulched areas between the lawn and all structures and trees that allow you to mow without having to use a string trimmer. Visualize how to mow the turf with the fewest turns and with alternate patterns to reduce making ruts. Calculate whether there are long perimeters to edge and see if there is room to maneuver the mower in narrow places. That all takes extra time. For a short-method analysis remember that you are looking for features that will require adjustment from your standard job.

Inspect each garden area as a separate zone. These zones include lawns, ground covers, grouped shrubs, mulched areas, annual beds, and individual trees and shrubs. Note anything that can complicate the job, like slopes, ditches, rocks, the ground surface, design elements like statuary and trellises, and utility structures. Check also for swing sets in lawns, which are difficult to mow around; toys you may have to spend time picking up on each visit; hard to reach areas that may require lifting the mower, negotiating steps, or using a ramp; and small areas with lots of trees, shrubs or obstacles that are hard to negotiate. Write down in general terms what labor and materials each zone needs. Make notes of the plants and their condition in each zone. Look for problems and suggest improvements.

Whether site inspection takes two minutes or half an hour, it has to include all you need to analyze your costs—or you may do some of the work for free.

Recommend and get a soil test if you think the site needs it. For your own protection, you want to be sure you're not taking on problems you haven't allowed for. When you ask customers what they want you to do, try to let them know what you'll have to do to get it done. The landscape will reflect on *your* reputation.

Take your time - You have to consider every potential problem on the job, like having to get your equipment up steps or along a narrow path. It helps here to try to visualize each step of the work. Some of the work is routine and it won't take much thought. If it involves anything unusual, this is the time to catch it. You will be able to analyze the steps better when you are back in the office, but that requires good first-hand observation.

Use abbreviations to note what equipment you will need for each zone. Even for just a lawn you will need a mower, string trimmer, and clean-up tools. Once you work through the steps and tools needed for each job, think about the equipment you need to clean up. Usually this is pretty obvious, but sometimes you may need something special, like a larger container for debris or one that you can haul into an overgrown area. You need to remember to bring those special items with you on the job, and using them may add extra time.

Estimate as you go - With a little experience you will begin to make a rough estimate as you inspect. With the short method you will complete the estimate on site. The point is to try to think of *everything that will add to cost.* That's easy on basic jobs using the short method but it gets more difficult as you move up to more complex jobs. If you miss something at this stage, you may have to work part of the time for nothing or tell the customer you made a mistake and try to raise your charges. It's better to make a good inspection.

Site plan - While you are inspecting, asking questions, making suggestions, and taking notes, draw a site plan if the job needs it. This should include the dimensions of the yard and all structures on it, as well as the size of the various zones, and the location of beds, trees, and large shrubs. You will need a clipboard, a sharp pencil, plain or graph paper, and, unless you have a perfect pace, a 100-foot cloth tape measure. A large nail or spike works to pin down one end of the tape measure. Get accurate figures for each zone, whether square feet, linear feet, or individual plants. Sometimes, if you're lucky, owners of custom houses have site plans you can work from. Make a copy for your own use and give the customer back the original.

If you inspect a large garden, it may be hard to squeeze enough detail on an 8½" x 11"sheet of paper. You might have to identify major plants and features with numbers where necessary and list them on another sheet. Sometimes you will run into a plant you can't identify, especially when starting out. Take cheap or used envelopes with you to hold small cuttings. Label them with the number on the site plan, then learn all you can about the plant.

Don't miss the big picture. Make a record of how the site looks before you start. It can be a photograph or in writing. You'll want something, if only for yourself, to show how you've improved things.

Other aids - A checklist of tasks, even a simple one, helps organize your inspection and gives you a place to write notes and identify features that you number on the site plan. Photographs will help you remember details that a site plan may not bring out, so a digital, Polaroid or even a simple point-and-shoot camera might be a useful option for big or complex jobs. Sometimes you can borrow and copy an existing site plan, but that is the rare exception rather than the rule. Moreover, plans are drawn before construction starts and may only be about 75% accurate at best. You'll end up having to draft at least a rough plot plan for complicated jobs.

Analysis of the Work

Long-method analysis of the work for each zone involves (1) deciding what the whole task involves, breaking it down into its smallest steps, and accounting for unusual features; (2) estimating how much of each material you need for every task in each zone; and (3) scheduling the tasks and the materials you will apply. Then you multiply tasks over the contract term and divide materials into separate applications.

This is the time to review anything else that would affect the job in addition to what you observed on your inspection. Analysis may sound like just a breather between the hard work of site inspection and the detail of cost estimating, but it is the critical time when you evaluate your on-site judgments and try to anticipate the unknowns.

Tasks - During the site inspection you will have considered the tasks to do on the job in a preliminary way. Review your notes and go through each step of each task to be sure you have accounted for all the work, both routine and unusual. You must charge for setting up and breaking down the job, as well as clean-up, but you should also determine whether there are special circumstances to factor in like inconvenient parking, steep slopes, stairs, difficulty bringing in heavy equipment or bagged materials. In rare instances, you—or anyone—may have to charge for the effort of getting to the site. Finally, remember that you're calculating for present equipment. New equipment may throw off your calculations.

Materials - Regardless of which method you use, make a list of all the materials that the job will require and match them to each zone to be sure you don't overlook any. The next chapter goes into more detail on this.

The process - That's the groundwork. You may have noticed that analysis and estimating tended to merge and interact. That's as it should be. All these steps are part of a continuous process.

Remember that this is when you schedule extra tasks like fertilizing, etc., for the master calendar. If you mow on an irregular schedule, that goes on the calendar, too.

Monitor costs and income as you go. Costs may rise as you become more efficient, and there may be no difference overall. You'll want to know that. When the quality of your work improves, you may charge new customers a little more, and try to increase them slightly for old customers. You shouldn't lower prices unless it's to stay competitive (while covering costs and keeping up quality). If you're making more money because you're better than you were, you ought to keep it.

Basic Estimating
Time
Hourly Rate
Materials
Mark-up for Materials
Scheduling Tasks & Materials
Estimating the Cost
Submitting the Bid

Chapter 20

How to Estimate – Figure What It Costs You

Quick Start:

THE long method of estimating is based on the time it takes to do standard tasks, then multiplying the time for each by an hourly rate. Note that you charge hourly with the long method, not per job. Many costing services use 1,000-square-foot and 100-linear-foot standard tasks. If you use those standards, too, you can check your times against those services. It's easy to develop your own standard times by using the formulas in this chapter.

Your hourly rate should cover (1) your costs of doing business, (2) what you pay yourself, and (3) a percentage for profit. For costs per hour, add up all your projected costs for the year and divide by the hours you plan to work in a year. Pay yourself a reasonable hourly wage and add a profit margin for taking the risks of enterprise.

ONCE YOU ANALYZE what kind of tasks and materials the job needs, you must then calculate how much of that labor and those materials to apply. That's all estimating is. This chapter discusses how to calculate. Much of what we discussed earlier about profit and loss and scheduling jobs goes into estimating.

Basic Estimating

Labor costs for each job are the product of your time on the job and the rate you charge. You can estimate your time from commercially prepared tables and those you make yourself. The examples below are for illustration only.

Time - Labor charges will be based on how long you estimate it will take you to work on the areas you measured in your site inspection and evaluated in your analysis. Your estimate of time might be based servicing a standard 1,000-SF level plot of lawn or ground cover, or 50 or 100 linear feet of hedge. Trees and often shrubs are counted individually.

Standard measures - There are industry tables of charges per 1,000-square-foot standard area. They vary from publisher to publisher but are useful as guides. The best estimate will be based upon your own experience. Probably you will not be able to time yourself on level lawns that are exactly 1,000 feet square. Instead, time yourself on a number of lawns, divide the actual SF by 1,000, and then divide your time by the quotient. That will give you the time to mow and edge 1,000 SF. An inexpensive digital stop watch will help.

Time

Getting a standard - Let's work through a few easy hypotheticals to get a feel for how to estimate average time:

1. Divide to get the fraction of 1,000 SF for the yard mowed. We can call it our *SF Quotient.*

750 SF ÷ 1,000 SF = 0.75
1,000 SF ÷ 1,000 SF = 1.00
1,500 SF ÷ 1,000 SF = 1.50
2,000 SF ÷ 1,000 SF = 2.00
800 SF ÷ 1,000 SF = 0.80

And so forth. Real lots will not be round numbers like this, but these should give the idea.

2. Divide the *actual time* it took to mow each lot by the fraction that each lot was of 1,000 SF, its SF Quotient.

Actual time	÷	SF Quotient	=	Standard Time
750 SF: 5.45 min.	÷	0.75	=	7.27 min.
1,000 SF: 7.10 min.	÷	1.00	=	7.10 min.
1,500 SF: 10.50 min.	÷	1.50	=	7.00 min.
2,000 SF: 14.00 min.	÷	2.00	=	7.00 min.
800 SF: 5.50 min.	÷	0.80	=	7.10 min.

3. Average time to mow 1,000 SF is estimated to be 7 minutes.

Now you have your average time for your level of experience and using your mower. If you have to mow a 1,200 square foot lawn, you express the lawn as a fraction of 1,000 SF. the standard measure. That fraction is 1.20. If you multiply your average time of 7.00 minutes by 1.20, it gives you 8.40 minutes. Got it?

4. You are charging by the hour, so you have to convert 8.40 minutes into hours. Divide 8.40 minutes (or 60ths of an hour) by 60 to get .14 hour. Don't worry if it is a tiny fraction. It's still the same amount of time and you will charge it over and over for the whole contract term. You will also add in set-up, clean-up, breakdown, and related tasks like edging. You'll be on the site awhile. And for, say, 20 mowings alone, the total time is 2.80 hours. If you include all the tasks multiplied by all the elements of your rate, you probably won't get many surprises.

Variations to take account of are slopes, long rectangles, or other irregularities (including swing sets, closely planted trees and shrubs, etc.) that may affect your time. You need these figures, but try not to take them too seriously. Play with them like statistics in a ball game. If it takes you longer than estimated to do a job, try to find where you are losing time and adjust your methods or the standard. If it takes less time but you got the job anyway, congratulations—but be careful not to price yourself out of the market.

Using the standard - Many neighborhoods these days are parts of subdivisions, with little more than a few square feet difference between one lot's size and another's, and you could use the short estimate method for them. You can also use the long method in these neighborhoods to calculate average prices for the average lawns or for the unique site. Your prices will get standardized, but it is worth recalculating now and then to be sure your standard is still accurate.

You will also find that the going rate, based on local custom, jumps up in a number of steps for, say, small, medium, and large lots, and that the price of mowing does not rise smoothly along with size, but moves up in steps that are also standardized. This is a result of "guesstimate" pricing. It is all right if prices reflect the average lot, and the "custom of the trade" does not cost you money. An advantage of working out your own estimate for each lot is that you can tell whether the going rate rewards or penalizes you.

Other standards - Some costing manuals estimate times for edging lawns on a standard of 100 linear feet. Whether you want to calculate edging separately, or simply estimate mowing and edging as one service to a 1,000-square-foot unit, depends on how much the lawns in your area vary. If you deal with standard subdivision lots, edging a rectangular lawn may not vary much from edging a square one. On the other hand, if you service irregular suburban yards, with beds, paths, and other boundaries, you might want to break out edging as a task to bill separately.

These time formulas also apply to fertilizing lawns or pruning ground cover areas, and shearing hedges. Get a standard time by dividing the actual dimensions by the standard, 1,000 SF or 100 linear feet. Divide your time by the quotient for the standard time. Multiply the standard time by the actual area or length as a fraction of 1,000 SF or 100 linear feet.

Pruning shrubs and trees takes more thought, and you will want to develop a set of *average* tables based on the size of the plant and the amount of work that each requires. Although there are tables for pruning times, it may be impossible to apply a formula to pruning a tree or shrub unless you plan to crop it like a poodle dog. This procedure is inappropriate for most shrubs and all trees.

Once you learn the principles of pruning you can do a good job fairly quickly, unless the shrub or tree needs major work. Remember that pruning that requires a ladder is in a different class from ground level work. Also consider hauling expenses the job generates.

Finishing touches - Be sure to add in the time to set up, clean up, and break down the job. You are being paid to be there and do the work, and that includes unpacking and packing up the tools. Since you can't charge for travel time, except generally as part of overhead, try to keep it to a minimum by grouping your jobs together. One final consideration is that there is more travel time per day for many small lots than for a few larger ones. You can charge more for small lots on a square-foot basis to compensate for lost travel time, because the cost of mowing a smaller lot can be raised to cover the extra time without adding too much money to the job.

Hourly Rate

Your hourly rate will include all costs of doing business, including overhead costs, your salary, and a profit. You will note when you get to the Cost Estimate Sheet that it multiplies the time to do a task by the Hourly Rate. That Hourly Rate includes three parts and may be broken down as follows:

Labor:	$16.25	65.0%
Overhead:	6.25	25.0%
Profit:	2.50	10.0%
Hourly Rate:	$25.00	100.0%

Overhead represents all your costs of doing business: any rent, utilities, telephone, office supplies, advertising, tools, and equipment, vehicle costs—everything it takes to be in business. To estimate overhead, add up all your expected costs for the year. Estimate your total hours per year by multiplying the planned hours in your work week by the number of weeks you plan to work each year. Divide your annual costs by your total hours per year to find how much you must make each hour to cover costs. That's where you will appreciate keeping a low overhead.

Labor, or what you pay yourself, is up to you but it also depends on the going rate. You may have to start off at a low rate but, as you gain skill and the business prospers, you can evaluate it and give yourself a raise.

Profit, remember, is what you pay yourself for taking the risk of running your business. You'll be a better judge of that as you settle into the work.

Even if you don't know exactly what your overhead, salary, and profit will be, make your best estimate based on the going rate, and establish your hourly rate accordingly. Later on you can adjust it as needed. If you foresee a struggle coping with these numbers, consider directing that energy to learning how to use a computer. Programs like *QuickBooks* will automatically determine overhead as well as the percentage of gross income that each expense consumes. We recommend getting a computer as soon as your business activity permits it.

Materials

You will use the measurements from your site inspection to calculate how much fertilizer, mulch, or spray, as requested, to apply to each zone in the garden.

Fertilizer - Chapter 11 discusses figuring how much fertilizer to apply by determining the weight of nitrogen per bag, then how many pounds of mix you need for one pound of nitrogen. Remember, use a unit like a pound divided by the percent of nitrogen to get the number of pounds of mix.

Cubic measures - Mulches and the like are often sold by the cubic yard or cubic foot but applications are specified by the depth in inches. Fortunately, there are tables, often on the bags themselves, that state how many SF the material will cover when spread so many inches deep. It's easy to figure for yourself.

All you have to know about a cubic yard is that there are 27 cubic feet in it. It will cover 27 SF one foot deep, 54 SF half a foot (6") deep, 108 SF a quarter of a foot (3") deep, and so on. It will cover 150 to 160 SF 2" deep. Materials sold by the cubic foot are even easier to deal with. This is no place for hand calculators. You can get close enough by doubling coverage as above and not worry whether you pour it 2" or 1½" deep.

Mark-up for Materials

Figuring mark-up - You should be able to purchase materials in bulk at a discount. Or you will be allowed a discount as a business purchaser. When businesses charge their customers for materials they add an amount to cover all the costs of providing them, including transport and storage. That is called a mark-up. There are almost as many ways to project a reasonable mark-up as there are kinds of businesses. For example, if overhead is 25.0 percent and profit is 10.0 percent (35% total), you may decide that your cost of materials should be 65 percent of what you charge the customer. If you divide your cost of a 50¢ item by 65 percent (dividing by 0.65 gives you the bigger number that you want) you would charge 76.9¢—call it 75¢—for the item.

Until you settle on how to calculate a mark-up that covers your costs and profit, aim for one that doesn't penalize you for the cost of buying and storing the materials, then bringing them to the site. On the other hand, do not mark up higher than the customer would pay retail. Later, if you have time, and like to play with figures, you may decide on some other way to calculate mark-up.

Sales tax - State laws on sales tax vary, but the idea is that the end user pays the tax. Business people who purchase goods for resale to end users in the ordinary course of business get a resale license. They pay no tax but must charge it to their customers then pay it to the state taxing agency. It means more paperwork. If you supply only a few materials, you probably won't want to bother about resale licenses and charging your customers sales tax. You will probably pay the tax yourself and pass along the cost, regardless of whether you mark up the materials. If you begin to supply materials on a regular basis, you should contact your state tax agency about how to handle sales tax.

Scheduling Tasks and Materials

For all but a one-time job, the cost of labor and materials are best spread out over the contract term in equal payments. If the contract ran through the year, you would "annualize" the costs for labor and materials by totalling them and dividing by 12. If your contract ran from, say, March through October, eight payment periods, you would total and divide by eight.

In the eight-month example, if you mowed and edged the lawn 34 times, you would multiply the cost of your labor 34 times and divide by eight. If you fertilized three times, you would multiply your labor three times and divide by eight. You would divide the total fertilizer for the year by eight. If you fertilized trees, pruned, and hauled away the leaves just once, you might also want to divide each cost by eight. As a practical matter, you would add up all the projected tasks over the contract term and divide the total bid price by eight. The Cost Estimate Forms (Figures 21.3 through 21.5) in the next chapter illustrate this procedure.

If unscheduled work arises, you'll have to bill separately for it. There shouldn't be much trouble collecting from a steady customer, but be careful not to get caught in a collection trap. Use your judgment. In the worst case, you could stop working so you don't lose money. If you use a written contract, be sure to put a warning clause in it about your right to stop for nonpayment. And—now that we're getting legal—if you have a written agreement, see that it says extra work must have its own signed agreement in writing. If you get more complicated than this, see a lawyer, take a course in business law, or read a legal business guide, such as the one listed in the Appendix.

Estimating the Cost

Figures 21.1 through 21.5, the Requirements Sheet and the Cost Estimate Forms together illustrate how you arrive at the total cost estimate upon which to bid for the job. The stages of making your estimate are set out step by step on the estimate form. There is one area for estimating labor costs and another for estimating materials costs. The requirements sheet is set up so that you can take off the site data directly to the left column of the estimate forms and make calculations across the page to reach your subtotals.

There are spaces for set-up and break-down times. You would also add time for clean-up and other incidental tasks there.

Submitting the Bid

The rule of making bids is to estimate and charge by the hour but bid by the job. This prevents the unpleasantness of having a customer who clocks you on the job. Figures 21.6 and 21.7 illustrate the cover letter and bid that would be made from the site analysis and estimate sheet.

The bid should be on one page for easy reading. If it won't fit on one page, summarize it and spell out the details in attachments. It's better to write out every detail on an attachment than to be vague and have to work them out once the job starts. It's also a way to confirm exactly what the customer wants. You will sign the bid and make a copy that the customer can accept by also signing and returning to you. Once signed it forms a binding contract. Sample contract terms appear on the reverse of the form. You should get a lawyer to review whatever you use for a contract. If you deliver the proposal to the customer personally, it can be signed on the spot. A personal visit, as always, is best because you can explain any details that the customer may have forgotten since you inspected the property. If the customer wants to think the proposal over, leave a stamped return envelope, say thanks and to contact you by telephone if there are more questions.

If for some reason you cannot deliver the bid personally, mail it with everything, at least a cover letter, that will persuade the customer to accept. Think of the proposal as advertising and try to create as appealing a package as possible.

If the customer accepts your mailed bid, telephone to say thanks, say when you plan to be on the job, and confirm that it is a satisfactory time. If you do not get the job, send a follow up letter thanking the customer for the opportunity to bid, with a reminder that your bids are based on high quality service, and say that you look forward to the opportunity to bid in the future.

Many of the steps outlined here may seem excessive. For small jobs they are. Tailor your efforts to the job but don't ignore the process or principles. The owner won't mind when you take your time to make a careful estimate. A small job won't take more than a few minutes to estimate. Even when you get a contract to mow the smallest lawn in town, you are building a reputation and learning good habits. When the big residential and commercial jobs are within your skills and reach, you will have a superior service to offer. It starts with that first knock on the door.

Red top. (USDA)

The Property
The Forms
The Bid and Cover Letter
Competitiveness
And So to Work . . .

Chapter 21

THE ESTIMATE AND BID – THEORY INTO PRACTICE

Quick Start: *THIS chapter provides an example of the estimating and bidding process. It involves more than mowing, edging, and maintaining a lawn, but they are included. A quick review of the facts and analysis will show how to use the forms provided.*

THE EASIEST WAY to illustrate the estimating process is to go through it step-by-step. For simplicity's sake we've assumed a sole proprietor without employees. If you had to schedule for employees, you'd factor in skill level to adjust both charges and time to do the job.

The Property

This exercise is illustrative. Our example supposes a large wooded lot in a hilly section of town. It has a large front lawn, which slopes uphill at about 15°, with a driveway south of it and four birch trees set among shrubs and bedding plants on the north. Two more birch trees are south of the driveway. The back yard slopes more steeply. There is no back lawn; instead, English ivy covers most sloping areas, and there are decks and terraces. Some areas are in partial shade. A set of steps goes uphill in back and is bordered with prostrate roses.

The lawn - Measuring the lawn is simple but takes a few steps. It would be a rectangle without the grove of birch trees. The trees and plants make a roughly semi-circular intrusion into the rectangle. It requires measuring the rectangle's area and *subtracting* the semi-circle of trees, plants, and shrubbery.

Sometimes the area you need to service is irregular. Don't worry about it. Break it down into regular pieces and add them up to figure the total area. Having a plot plan makes sure you don't leave any pieces out. There are a few basic geometric formulas in the Appendix. If the pieces you deal with aren't perfect geometric figures, don't worry. They will usually be close enough.

Total square feet works out to 1,513, more or less. Allowing for the error of a rough survey, we can call it 1,500 square feet.

The lawn perimeter to edge involves the two straight lines along the street and driveway measuring about 96 linear feet.

Regular mowing would be every week with edging every other week, and a heavy fertilization with conditioning in the fall. Remember some jobs may no longer have a regular weekly mowing schedule. The lawn appears to be suffering from compaction and a little too much thatch, so the homeowners agree to aeration coordinated with fertilization, amendment, re-seeding, and dressing with a good topsoil. We will aerate four times a year to lighten the soil and reduce the thatch, and will recommend continuing this quarterly program.

The homeowners also want some patches of white clover removed from the lawn, which we would do with a few hand-applied doses of a broadleaf weed killer.

Ground cover - The ivy ground cover, just under 1,000 square feet of it, needs no assistance from the homeowners or anyone. It does need heavy pruning at least once a year. If it were Algerian Ivy, it would need pruning twice, anyway, during the growing season. Pruning requires wading into the plant to take out excess runners and strip it from trees, shrubs, and structures it has started climbing. Measurements are paced off pretty roughly, and costs take account of climbing uphill into it and hauling out the clippings.

Shrubs - There are 14 shrubs in front and 24 in back that need to be pruned. The homeowners agree that pruning should be minimal, mainly thinning where needed. This keeps pruning time short for each shrub.

Trees - There are six trees in front and 12 in back. Two in front are south of the driveway. They are all basically healthy and won't need much care. The four birch trees at the north end of the front yard, about 15 or 20 years old, look as if they have gone for some time without adequate fertilizer, including micronutrients. They are mature enough to tolerate an injection treatment without weakening the trunks; so we agree to use a concentrated solution under slight pressure. We choose injection over foliar spray because the treatment will last a few years. It is also faster and simpler to do. A liquid injection, which leaves the smallest wounds, will reduce the chance of introducing disease. We time and meter the treatment so that the trees' transpiration rate will assist the injections without causing leaf burn or loss.

The other two trees south of the driveway apparently get fertilizer from next door.

If the trees were in the turf rather than among shrubs and bedding plants, lawn fertilizer—typically applied very generously—might keep them going with no sign of deficiency. We agree to set up a maintenance fertilization schedule for the trees, which the homeowners would start after the treatment wore off.

Bedding plants - There are about 250 SF of annuals planted under the birch trees and next to part of the house. One edge of the birch grove is bordered with shrubs. The homeowners say they usually put in bedding plants under the birches as soon as the bulbs die back in spring. We agree on weeding and fertilizing the annuals during the growing season.

The Forms

Maintenance Requirements - At this point you might scan the sample Landscape Maintenance Requirements form. (Figures 21.1 and 21.2.) It's a take-off form that lists all the measurements for the garden just mentioned. The form provides places to enter Location, Size/Number, Number of Times, and Materials. To keep things simple, note under Materials the frequency and amount of any materials that have to be applied. We will come back later to other materials calculations on the Requirements sheet.

The entries on the Maintenance Requirements form correspond to those on the Maintenance Estimators (Figures 21.3 to 21.5), except where space limitations under "Lawn" required varying the Estimators slightly.

Zones - The zones—that is garden areas or features—to measure or count correspond to the arrangement on the Maintenance Estimator sheets. "Lawn Care" is separated into two groups on both forms, separating the common tasks from the less frequent ones.

Notes - The last part of this form is for writing reminders and things that help to analyze the job.

Landscape Maintenance Estimators - The times in the example are for illustration only. A number of factors influence standard times. With experience you vary the standard for things like slope, obstructions, lots of turns, and so on. For now, just follow the process.

Labor - As with all forms, this one is for the average job and may not fit all. Overall, they worked for this one, and they let you take the figures off the Maintenance Requirements sheet as you go.

Lawn - The 1,500-SF lawn is a 1.5-unit job, that is, 1,500 SF divided by 1,000 SF. To arrive at a time for the job, you just multiply the mowing time in minutes for a standard 1,000-SF lawn by 1.5.

The space for "edging" breaks the succession of SF units, but logically it goes right under mowing. It could go to the bottom of the form.

Seven and a half (7.5) minutes per 1,000 SF worked out to 11.25 minutes for 1,500 square feet. Divide 11.25 by 60 minutes and you get the time as a fraction of an hour. Multiplying the fractional hours per mowing by Times per Season gives the total mowing hours over the contract term.

If you service standard lots, you might want to estimate for "mowing *and* edging" in the first space on the Labor form, as based on a standard time you have estimated for the combined tasks.

Other zones. Charges for other zones involve similar unit calculations, based on either square or linear feet. You can simply count trees and shrubs.

Calculations for linear-foot units are like those for square feet. Divide the 96 feet of lawn perimeter by 100 feet for 0.96, and multiply that by an estimated 5 minutes per 100 feet for power edging. We could have rounded up to 100 here, but leave it as-is to demonstrate the math.

Bedding plants - Estimating work on bedding plants can be tricky. Some costing manuals base bedding plant jobs on a 1,000-SF unit. It works in this case. It may not work when the plants are strung out in a line or otherwise hard to service, as in planter boxes or a remote part of the garden.

Sometimes you must break a task down into its smallest steps, estimate the time for each step, then put them together and see if the total looks right. Once you think you have a good estimate, try to run it by someone else with some experience in that activity.

Set-up/Breakdown - For every operation we're using five minutes on average for set-up and breakdown time. In real life it will vary for different people and different equipment. Five minutes doesn't seem like much, but it allows for the economies of setting up several tasks at once. It was an average. Set-up/breakdown time also includes clean-up, which can be nil if you are only mowing into a grass catcher, but longer if it means sweeping or blowing along an edged walk after mulch-mowing. It can be even longer if you allow for giving those finishing touches that can make a difference.

If you think set-up and breakdown times are unimportant, note that they came to over almost five hours for the contract term. And that is for one job over eight months. Don't think you shouldn't charge for this time. It is part of the many tasks the customer would otherwise have to do, and you would be cheating yourself if you left it out.

To arrive at a total set-up/breakdown time for the contract, add all the Times per Season numbers marked with asterisks and multiply the sum of these numbers by the average time in minutes. Divide that product by 60 minutes for the hourly time, and enter it in the Total Hours column. In this case it meant setting up and breaking down equipment 58 times; times 5 minutes it is 290 minutes. Divided by 60 minutes it is 4.831 hours. Converting minutes to fractions of an hour gives the same answer. If you need to set up and break down equipment for a job without an asterisk, jot one into the "Number of Times" column.

Generally, no one charges for the effort of getting to a job or going from one to another, but your hourly charge has to cover a lot of time on the road. It should be pretty much already factored into the going rate. That's an assumption that may not be true everywhere. In any case, controlling travel time will put you ahead of the game.

Other - Sometimes the tasks in "Other" on the supplement page fill up that part of the form fast. A supplementary labor estimator provides more room for the extras that many jobs require.

Summing up - Before you add up for TOTAL HOURS on the first page of the Labor estimator, add the total hours from supplement page 1a and enter it in the space on page 1. Then total everything in the "Total Hours" column of the labor estimator.

Materials - To estimate materials, take the Unit calculations from the Labor sheet (Figures 21.3 and 21.4) and the materials times number of applications under Materials from the Requirements sheet (Figures 21.1 and 21.2). It is best to use the Requirements Sheet to multiply the number of applications times the amount of materials per application. (If you broke out pounds of mix to add a pound of N, as described in the Appendix, writing pounds of mix for one pound of N on all the bags eases matters.)

All # per Unit - Calculating amounts on the Requirements sheet helps keep things straight.

For example, if you fertilize by pounds of nitrogen, to apply 2 pounds to the lawn twice, first determine how many pounds of mix are needed per 1,000-SF unit. The number of pounds of mix per pound of nitrogen (N) on the fertilizer bag shows you need 6.25 lbs. of mix. So, for 2 pounds applied 2 times, you only multiply 2 x 2 x 6.25 (pounds of mix) = 25 lbs. To shortcut the process, you could estimate the need for 4 pounds over the season and multiply 6.25 pounds of the fertilizer mixture times 4. Usually, however, taking the process step-by-step keeps your figures straight. It can also help keep track of how much to apply each time. (Finally, of course, you can skip all of this if you apply what's recommended on the bag.)

Next enter the estimate of 25 pounds on the Requirements Sheet on the materials sheet, under "All # per Unit." (The "#" symbol represents pounds, cubic feet, cubic yards, and so on.) This means the total pounds of mixture per 1,000-SF unit.

Total # - The "Units" x "All # per Unit" gives you "Total #" needed over the contract term. In this case it is 25 pounds x 1.5 or 37.5 pounds. The Unit figure came from the Labor Estimator.

Total cost - Multiplying "Total #" times the "Cost per #" gives the "Total Cost." Bad news: You need to do more figuring for Cost Per #, or per pound in this instance. Good news: it's easy. If 20 pounds cost you $7.50, divide $7.50 by 20 and you get $0.375 per pound. It is an extra step, but it's not that bad. Then, 37.5 pounds x $0.375 per pound = $13.88 as the Total Cost.

Mark-up - You can then adjust your cost with a Mark-Up to give the Price charged on the job. Be sure to keep your marked up price at or below retail. Here is some more math, but you can skip it if you don't want an exact mark-up. Say you are figuring cost at 65% of the price to be charged. You could divide the cost by 0.65. See the discussion in the previous chapter under Mark-up. To multiply, as set up in the Materials Sheet, divide 1 by 0.65. That gives you 1.54, by which you multiply your cost. It's easy to do with a calculator, but you don't have to. The example uses a 10% mark-up.

Equipment Rentals / Subcontracts - There were no equipment rentals for this job, but we enter the cost of subcontracting four lawn aerations here. It's like renting equipment, except you get the operator, too. We added our standard markup to the cost of $62.50 per treatment, giving the customer a cost of $275 for four lawn aerations. You probably wouldn't mark up rental costs.

The Grand Total - At this point you can add up Materials, Rentals, Labor and any Sales Tax for a Grand Total. The Grand Total here was $970.92, including $275 to subcontract out four lawn aerations. Add sales tax if required. Refer to the previous chapter about who does and doesn't have to charge it. Some states levy a sales tax on labor and materials, so you would add it to everything, regardless of how many materials you supply. The contract covered eight months, and the homeowners agree to make eight payments of $120 per month, which is the bid after rounding.

All the forms illustrated here appear full-size in the back of this book. You may use any of them as-is or alter as needed. If you want to make life much easier, you can put all these formulas on an electronic spreadsheet, such as Corel Quattro Pro or Microsoft Excel. If you're not handy with computers, perhaps a member of your family (like a 14-year-old) can whip one up. The chief advantage of putting it on a computer is that you can make all the changes you want as you go without wearing out an eraser.

The Bid and Cover Letter

The cover letter - The bid should be accompanied by a cover letter (Figure 21.6) that summarizes very briefly what the maintenance will be and inviting the homeowners to comment if there are questions. Try to be sure that you are submitting the terms agreed on, so that there won't be any questions. You can always telephone a potential customer to settle any doubt you have. It's expecting a lot to get all the details right when you inspect. Like all the examples in this book, you may use this cover letter as-is or change it to suit your needs.

The bid based on the estimate can be submitted as a proposed written agreement for the homeowners to sign and return with the first month's payment. (Figure 21.7.) Not everyone bills in advance, but it's a good idea. We leave it up to you and your customers.

The proposal, which would become a contract when signed, has a space on the front page for describing the work to be done. If that space is too small, write a brief summary concluding with something like, "as more fully described in Attachment A, which we make a part of this agreement." Then make a place on Attachment A for both parties to initial it. It's important to cover all the details as exactly as possible.

Competitiveness

What if your estimate is higher than the competition? Since you know what makes up your charges, you can figure where the competition is low. If you have to cut to stay competitive, you will know what you are cutting and whether it will work. Knowing what your competitors don't know gives you an advantage, and getting an advantage is the point of estimating.

And So To Work . . .

We hope by now you've learned a little about the landscape maintenance business and are eager to get started. If you're as lucky as we've been, you and your customers will soon share a goal of shaping the space around you. It's a common enterprise that can be very rewarding to all concerned. Wherever you set up, you'll have the chance to make a difference in how your little patch of this earth looks. You may have to coax your customers a bit to get them on your team, but gradually the places you service will begin to improve and just shine. In the end, you'll be an educator—someone who instills a bit of knowledge and leaves things better than they were. That's how I see it and I think you will, too.

LANDSCAPE MAINTENANCE REQUIREMENTS

Customer ID: JONES, 45 ARGONAUT, LELAND, CA
Telephone: 000-0000
Work Proposed: ALL LAWN MAINTENANCE & AERATE; PRUNE IVY, SHRUBS, TREES; WEED/FEED BEDDING PLANTS; FERTILIZE 4 TREES

Task	Location	Size/No.	No. of Times	Materials
Lawn Care:				
Mow	FRONT ↓	1,500 SF	34	–
Edge		96 LF	17	–
Fertilize		1,500 SF	2 (2×6.25#)	25#/1000
Amend		1,500 SF	1	20#/1000
Re-seed		1,500 SF	1	2#/1000
Topdress		1,500 SF	1	1 CU. YD.
Ground Cover:				
Prune	BACK TERRACES	1,000 SF	1	–
Fertilize				
Amend				
Other				
Hedges:				
Shear				
Fertilize				
Other				
Shrubs:				
Prune	FRT/BK	38	1	
Fertilize				
Other				
Trees:				
Prune	FRT/BK	18	1	
Fertilize	FRONT	4	1	4 UNITS
Other				

Figure 21.1. Requirements or take-off sheet, page one.

LANDSCAPE MAINTENANCE REQUIREMENTS - Page 2

Task	Location	Size/Number	No. of Times	Materials
Additional Lawn care:				
Dethatch				
Aerate	FRONT	SUB. OUT	4	
Spray:				
Herbicide	FRONT	SPOT	2(x1 PT.)	1 QT.
Insecticide				
Other				
Bedding Plants:				
Plant				
Feed	FRONT	250 SF	1	8.75#/1000
Mulch				
Spray				
Weed	FRONT	250 SF	1	–
Other				
All other:				

Notes:

OWNERS TO IRRIGATE AND WILL FERTILIZE; MULCH, WEED, & SPRAY REST OF PLANTS.

KEY TO BACK YARD UNDER 3D BRICK FROM DOWNSPOUT.

Figure 21.2. Requirements sheet, page two.

LANDSCAPE MAINTENANCE ESTIMATOR

Customer: JONES   Page 1: (LABOR)   Date: ______

LAWN	Units x	Min. per Unit =	Est. Time (Min.)	Hours (Min./60) x	Times per Season =	Total Hours
1,500 SF ÷ 1,000 SF =	1.5					
Mow	1.5	7.5	11.25	.1875	34 *	6.375
Edge 96 ÷ 100 LF	.96	5	4.80	.0800	17 *	1.360
Fertilize	1.5	6	9.00	.1500	1 *	.1500
Amendments	1.5	6	9.00	.1500	1 *	.1500
Re-seed	1.5	6	9.00	.1500	* 1	.1500
GROUND-COVER 1000 SF ÷ 1,000 SF =	1.0					
Prune	1.0	72	72	1.200		1.200
Fertilize						
Amendments						
HEDGES ______ LF ÷ 100 LF =						
Shear					*	
Fertilize						
SHRUBS No. =	38					
Prune	38	6.5	247	4.117	1	4.117
Fertilize						
TREES No. =	18					
Prune	18	11	198	3.300	1	3.300
Fertilize	4	12	48	.800	1	.800
*** Set-up/Brkdn**	(Av. S/B Min. X Times per Season.)		5	.0833	58	4.831
SUPPLEMENT	Enter any Subtotal of hours from supplement sheet (page 1a).					1.542
					TOTAL HOURS:	23.975
					X $25.- /HR = TOTAL LABOR:	$599.38

Figure 21.3. Estimate sheet. Labor.

LANDSCAPE MAINTENANCE ESTIMATOR

Customer: JONES Page 1a: (LABOR SUPPLEMENT)

LAWN 1.5 SF ÷ 1,000 SF =	Units x	Min. per Unit =	Est. Time (Min.)	Hours (Min./60) x	Times per Season =	Total Hours
	1.5					
Dethatch					*	
Aerate	———	———	SUB	OUT	——— *	———
Spray	SPOT	18	18	.300	2 *	.600
Topdress	1.5	15	22.5	.375	1 *	.375
Other						
BEDDING PLANTS 250 SF ÷ 1,000 SF =	.25					
Plant					*	
Feed	.25	6	1.5	.025	1 *	.025
Mulch						
Spray					*	
Weed	.25	30	7.5	.125	1	.125
Other						
OTHER Unit Calc.:						
*** Set-up/Brkdn**	(Av. S/B Min. X Times per Season.)		5	.0833	5	.417
					TOTAL HOURS:	1.542

Figure 21.4. Estimate sheet. Labor supplement.

LANDSCAPE MAINTENANCE ESTIMATOR

Customer JONES　　　Page 2: (MATERIALS & TOTALS)

	Units (From p.1) X	All # per Unit =	Total # X	Cost per # =	Total Cost X	Markup =	Price
LAWN Fertilizer	1.5	25 LB	37.5 LB	$ 0.375	$ 14.06	1.1	$ 15.47
Lime/Gypsum	1.5	20 LB	30 LB	$ 0.275	$ 8.25	1.1	$ 9.08
Seed/Sprigs	1.5	2 LB	3 LB	$ 5.00	$ 15.00	1.1	$ 16.50
Topdressing	1.5	—	1 CU YD	$ 17.50	$ 17.50	1.1	$ 19.25
Other SPRAY	1.5	—	1 QT	$ 5.00	$ 5.00	1.1	$ 5.50
SHRUBS, HEDGES Fertilizer				$	$		$
Mulch				$	$		$
GRNDCVR Fertilizer				$	$		$
Lime/Gypsum				$	$		$
TREES Fertilizer	4	1 EA	4	$ 6.81	$ 27.24	1.1	$ 29.96
BDG PLTS Fertilizer	0.25	8.75 LB	2.19 LB	$ 0.326	$ 0.713	1.1	$ 0.78
OTHER				$	$		$
				$	$		$
				$	$		$
						Total Materials Cost:	$ 96.54

EQUIPMENT RENTALS / SUBCONTRACTS

LAWN AERATION : $ 62.50 X 4 per Season X 1.1 (Markup) = $ 275.00

________ : $______ X ____ per Season X ____ (Markup) = $

________ : $______ X ____ per Season X ____ (Mark p) = $

Total Labor: $ 599.38

Sales Tax: $

Grand Total: $ 970.92

÷ by 8 Periods = Payments of $ 121.36

\# = pounds, cubic feet, cubic yards, and other basic measures.

No markup on equipment rentals.

Figure 21.5. Estimate sheet. Materials and totals.

CLASSIC
LAWN CARE
and Gardening

P. O. BOX 1234 YERBA BUENA CA 90000 (101) 123-4567

February 23, 2000

Mr. and Mrs. Thomas Jones
45 Argonaut Road
Leland, California 90000

Dear Mr. & Mrs. Jones:

Here is my proposal for maintaining the landscaping around your home on Argonaut Road.

Maintenance will run from March through October 2000 and will involve weekly lawn mowing with bi-weekly edging; four lawn aeration treatments; pruning of shrubs, trees, and groundcover once; fertilization and soil conditioning; and fertilizing the four birch trees in your front lawn.

My proposal includes all labor and materials to accomplish these tasks, and it provides for payment in equal monthly install-ments over the maintenance period. Please read the proposal over and, if you find it acceptable, sign and return it to me with the first month's payment.

Contact me right away if you have any questions about the proposal or if you want to discuss any changes. It is my aim to provide you with the best lawn and landscape care available, and I welcome your comments and suggestions.

Yours truly,

Sandy MacDuff

enclosures

Figure 21.6. Cover letter.

CLASSIC
LAWN CARE
and Gardening

P. O. BOX 1234 YERBA BUENA CA 90000 (101) 123-4567

PROPOSAL FOR LANDSCAPE MAINTENANCE

This proposal by CLASSIC LAWN CARE AND GARDENING (Gardener), P.O. Box 1234, Yerba Buena, California, to M/M Thomas Jones (Owner), 45 Argonaut Road Leland, California, is made on 2/28, 20 00 , at Yerba Buena, California, and, if accepted below by Owner, is an agreement between them for the following.

Gardener will provide materials and perform the following services for Owner for a term of 8 months, beginning on approximately 2/28, 20 00, and ending on approximately 10/31 , 20 00 :

LAWN: Mow weekly and edge bi-weekly. Aerate four times in season. Fertilize twice in season. Amend with gypsum. Re-seed & topdress. Treat white clover in lawn chemically.

OTHER: Prune all shrubs and trees, and ivy in back. Fertilize four birch trees in front lawn.

In consideration of these services, Owner will pay Gardener a total of $ 960.00 , in 8 installments of $ 120.00 , on the first day of each month of the contract term. Owner will pay Gardener a late charge of 1½% per month (18% per annum) for any payment not received by the tenth day of the month. Owner agrees to pay any costs of collection, including attorney fees.

Figure 21.7. Sample bid.

Gardener will perform these services as an independent contractor and in a manner it considers reasonable; it will supply all the necessary tools and equipment; and it may employ assistants and subcontract for such services as it considers beneficial. Gardener will carry liability insurance acceptable to Owner; it will provide workers' compensation for its employees; and it will defend, indemnify, and hold Owner harmless against any claims arising from performance of these services. Gardener will not be responsible for delays caused by acts of God or other events beyond its control.

Gardener will not assign this agreement without Owner's written consent.

Gardener may stop work if Owner does not pay.

Gardener or Owner may give the other 30 days' written notice to terminate this agreement, either by delivery in person or by mailing to the other at the other's above address.

This is the entire agreement between Gardener and Owner, and any prior agreements, understandings, or terms are revoked by this agreement. The above price is based on the services described above. Owner agrees to negotiate a reasonable price adjustment with Gardener for any changes in those services. Any change to the agreement must be in writing and signed by both parties.

If a lawsuit or other proceeding arises from a dispute over any term of this agreement (or any written change) or its performance, the losing party will pay the winning party all the costs it causes the winning party to incur, including reasonable attorney fees. This agreement will be governed by the law of the state where it was made. If a court holds that any of its terms is invalid or unenforceable, the rest of the agreement will continue in full force and effect.

[SANDY MacDUFF]
Sandy MacDuff
CLASSIC LAWN CARE & GARDENING

Accepted by:

[THOMAS JONES]

For ______________________________.

Figure 21.8. Sample bid, continued.

Timothy grass. (USDA)

Appendix

Calculating Nitrogen in Fertilizer

Nitrogen: How much fertilizer mix to apply per 1,000 SF?

1 lb Mix ÷ percent of N = Lbs Mix per 1,000 SF.

Here's how to figure how much fertilizer mix to use for each pound of nitrogen (N) per 1,000 SF. A 20-10-10 mix has 20 percent N by weight. For how much *mix* per 1,000 SF you need for each pound of *N*, divide a pound of the mix by your 20% (0.20) of N, that is, 1 ÷ 0.20 = 5, or 5 lbs of mix for 1 lb of N.

Then, mark the fertilizer bags, e.g., "5#" to show that 5 pounds apply 1 pound of N per 1,000 SF.

How much per lot size?

If you have a 1,200-SF lawn, it's 1.2 times 1,000 SF. (You divide the lawn's size by 1,000.) Multiply 1.2 by the "5 lbs" marked on the bag (1.2 x 5) to get 6 lbs of mix for the 1,200 SF lot. To apply 2 lbs of slow-release N per 1,000 SF per year, multiply the 6 lbs by 2. That's 12 lbs of mix for the whole contract year. For practice, work this out with the USDA amount of N for your local varieties of turfgrass. Step by step it's not too bad. Remember to reduce the amount of fertilizer by about half if you mulch-mow.

How Long to Hold Records

Permanent retention: Annual and audited financial reports, articles of incorporation, corporate minute books, stock and bond transaction records, stockholder records, deeds and titles, general ledger and year-end journal entries, account ledgers stock ledgers, register of loan notes given and taken, pension records, property records including sales and purchases, appraisals, plans and specifications, all tax returns, trademark records, union labor contracts,

20 years after termination: corporate contracts

10 years: Check registers; terminated franchise agreements; workers' compensation reports, cash and other journals, tax records, worksheets, and paper; personal property and sales/use tax returns.

7 years: settled accident reports; bank statements; sales slips; paid and canceled checks (AD); employee applications;contracts,evaluation,disability/unemployment claims, earnings records, pay checks, files, and correspondence, (AT); payroll and social security records; vendor contracts; credit and collection correspondence; depreciation schedules (AD); fixed asset records (AD); invoices; inventory records (AD); leases (AT); accounts payable, receivable and customer ledgers; building and machinery maintenance and repair records; canceled noted; depreciation records (AD); sales and purchase invoices; uncollectable accounts records; W-2 forms.

6 years: sales commission reports; equipment leases; fire damage reports.

5 years: bills of lading; shipping tickets; freight drafts, bills and claims; accounting correspondence; cost accounting records; department and employee expense reports.

3 years: bank deposit slips and reconciliations; budgets; general correspondence; delivery receipts; equipment repair records; interim financial reports; petty cash records; expired insurance policies; terminated surety bonds; terminated garnishments; employee travel records.

AT: after termination; AD: after disposal of underlying property.

Job Description - Gardener/Laborer

Summary Statement :

Semi-skilled manual labor tasks related to gardening, often unsupervised.

Qualities/Skills:

Understand and follow oral and written directions, manuals, labels, maps, plans, and work orders.

Speak clearly with supervisor, co-workers, and the public.

Write work orders, safety records, supply lists, and others.

Relate well to customers and potential customers.

Team member able to get along well with others.

Tasks, Responsibilities:

Maintain lawns, plantings, shrubs, and trees.

Knowledge and skill to prune, thin, fertilize, water.

Follow all safety rules and regulations

Clean up over-grown landscapes

[Plant vegetation such as lawns, annuals, perennials, shrubs, and trees.]

Know basic plant physiology, form and structure.

Identify typical landscape plants

Use equipment such as riding and push mowers, string trimmers, blowers, edgers, chainsaws, hedge trimmers, tractors, chippers, power washers, and hand tools.

Maintain and make minor repairs on the above with specific operating and maintenance manuals, and appropriate tools. Clean and grease, maintain proper fluid levels, change plugs, replace belts and parts, and do other minor repairs.

Operate vehicles while pulling and backing trailers.

Move equipment, supplies, and materials safely.

Minor plumbing and electrical repair of irrigation systems.

Physical Requirements:

Able to see, hear, speak, stoop, kneel, move over uneven ground, climb, lift and carry up to 100 lbs., labor outside for 8-hour days in dust and pollen, and hot, cold, and rainy weather.

Other requirements:

Working weekends, on-call, overtime, and, properly trained, using chemical pesticides and herbicides.

Company Policy Manual

Our Goal: high quality service, maximum efficiency, best possible value.

[Company] revolves around teamwork to provide the best possible service to the customer. [Company] is the sum total of everyone here working together—from the sales people procuring the jobs, the office staff scheduling the work, the maintenance mechanic keeping our equipment in top form, to the gardeners who provide the customer exceptional service—this team will continue to make [Company] the best it can be.

[Company] strives to satisfy each customer by providing the excellent service customers expect and are entitled to. A customer's recognition of excellence in our service results in hiring us again in the future and referring us to friends, family, and neighbors.

Performing our service efficiently will produce the profit that pays all of our wages. If an employee cannot turn a profit for the company, the company won't be able to pay the employee, and the employee will be out of a job.

ATTENDANCE

[Company] expects all employees to report to work on time every day. Absenteeism and lateness will impair [Company's] reputation for premium service, and it places an unfair burden on other employees. Therefore we have instituted the following attendance policy to deal with attendance fairly and equitably.

Attendance point system:

For each instance of excused absence, one in which the employee calls in or contacts his/her supervisor, you will get one attendance point. An illness of one or two days in a row counts for one point. An employee who fails to call in to report an absence gets six attendance points. For each instance of lateness, you will get one attendance point.

IMPORTANT: Excessive attendance problems, including excused absences, are grounds for discipline up to and including termination, regardless of how many attendance points you have. The following schedule is a general guideline for supervisors to use to determine whether an employee's absences are excessive.

In any six-month period of work:

Fourth Point	Verbal warning
Fifth Point	Written warning
Sixth Point	Suspension
Seventh Point	Termination

If you are going to be late or absent, it's your responsibility to contact your supervisor each day as far in advance of your starting time as possible. Asking a friend, relative, or other employee to contact your supervisor is not acceptable.

BREAKS AND LUNCHES

All employees of [Company] are entitled to a 10-minute break per four hours of work. Employees whose total daily work time is less than three and a half hours are not entitled to a break. No one will take breaks at the beginning or end of a work shift to adjust the shift's start or ending.

All employees shall be entitled to an unpaid 30-minute lunch period when working five or more hours in a day.

OVERTIME PAY

Overtime is paid at the rate of one-and-a-half times the hourly rate for any time worked [*e.g.*, in excess of eight hours per day.] *Check on laws' current status.*

DRESS CODE

All employees must wear sturdy, soled shoes that fully encase the foot, and full length pants. Clothes with holes or that are otherwise worn out are not acceptable. Open-toed and open-heeled shoes are prohibited on the job. All employees will wear the uniform shirts provided.

DISCIPLINARY ACTION

The purpose of discipline is to correct unacceptable behavior on the job. The intent of disciplinary action is to insure through a progressive process, that employees know specific company rules, policies or performance expectations, and gets the opportunity to comply with them.

How much an employee does not comply will determine whether the employee receives a verbal reprimand, a written reprimand, suspension or termination. A verbal warning usually precedes a written warning. If the employee does not improve within the time period given in the verbal warning, a written warning will follow. Copies will go to the employee and the Personnel Department. If the employee still fails to improve, the consequence will be suspension or termination.

An outline of unacceptable conduct, "Causes for Termination," appears below in this handbook.

SAFETY

Any operation's efficiency can be measured directly by how well it controls loss. Accidents resulting in personal injury or damage to property and equipment represent needless suffering and waste. Anyone who forsakes safety just to "get the job done" is not using proper judgment. Every person at [Company] has the responsibility to maintain the safety conditions and equipment at all times. Our company policy of safety is:

1. The safety of the employee, the public, and the operation is paramount. Every employee will make every attempt to reduce the possibility of accidents.
2. Safety shall take precedence over expediency or shortcuts at all times.
3. [Company] will comply with all safety laws and regulations.
4. Every employee is expected to demonstrate an attitude that reflects this policy and to maintain safe work habits.
5. Every employee must immediately report to the supervisor any unsafe or hazardous equipment, conditions, or acts, so that the supervisor may take steps to correct the situation.

SEAT BELT POLICY

Seat belts save lives and reduce the severity of injuries, as well as giving drivers the greatest control of a vehicle in an accident. [Company] requires all drivers and passengers to wear seat belts correctly at all times in company vehicles. Failure to do so will result in disciplinary action.

DRIVING POLICY

[Company] requires every driver to operate company vehicles in a courteous, defensive manner, and to observe all motor vehicle laws and posted speed limits. This policy is in the interest of safety and of presenting a positive image to the public.

All drivers must have a valid [your state] driver's license and a clean driving record. If any employee's driver's license become invalid, the employee must report it to his/her supervisor. Failure to do so will result in termination.

SUBSTANCE ABUSE POLICY

[Company] is concerned about the dangers of drugs and alcohol in the work environment. Drugs and alcohol in any work environment adversely affect an employee's performance, efficiency, safety, and health. They are worse if the employee must use power tools. In addition to endangering the employee and diminishing productivity, drug and alcohol use endanger coworkers and the public. Therefore, the use, possession, distribution, dispensation, purchase or sale of drugs or alcohol while on or in company property or while on company time, including breaks and lunch, is absolutely forbidden. Any breach of this policy is grounds for immediate termination.

CAUSES FOR TERMINATION

[Company] has established specific rules to protect our employees, property, and customers. The following are examples of conduct that breaks those rules and will not be tolerated. Such conduct may result in discipline up to and including immediate discharge and possible criminal prosecution.

We prohibit the following:

1. Pilferage or theft (of all kinds, including but not limited to, the theft of time).
2. Intentional damage to company or employee property.
3. Unauthorized use of company credit cards or checks.
4. Falsification of employment information.
5. Refusal to follow supervisors' instructions.
6. Carrying passengers who are not [Company] employees in company vehicles without prior authorization.
7. Excessive traffic tickets or accidents, or any accident involving gross negligence.
8. Change of driving record or use of invalid driver's license without notifying supervisor.
9. Failure to report accidents, damage, or hazardous materials spills immediately, or falsification of those reports.
10. Excessive or unexcused absences or lateness, as your supervisor determines.
11. Using, possessing, purchasing, selling, transferring, dispensing, or being under the influence of drugs or alcohol (including prescription drugs if such drugs impair your ability to perform your work duties safely) while on the job or on company property.
12. Sleeping on the job.
13. Unauthorized use of company vehicles or equipment.
14. Fraudulent reporting of hours worked.
15. Fighting or any other act that may interfere with the safe or efficient operation of the company's business or other employees' safety.
16. Conduct that is disruptive or destructive to customers, fellow employees or [Company].
17. Possession of firearms on company property
18. Violation of any company policy, etc.

EQUAL OPPORTUNITY EMPLOYER

[Company] is an equal opportunity employer. It is our policy not to discriminate against any employee or applicant for employment based on race, color, religion, age, sex, sexual orientation, national origin, handicap, medical condition, or other consideration made un-lawful by applicable federal, state or local laws.

[Company] employs those applicants it deems to possess the necessary skills, education, and experience required for the position applied for.

EMPLOYEE EVALUATION, PAY RAISES, AND BONUSES

[Company] will evaluate each employee every three months, when [Company] and the employee will discuss his/her performance. An employee who has achieved and maintained all performance levels required will receive a $.25 per hour raise. After eight pay raises, the employee will have reached the top of the pay scale for that position.

Employees who achieve a perfect attendance record over a six-month period will receive a bonus. Employees who maintain an injury-free/accident-free performance over a one-year period will receive a bonus.

Further Reading

GARDENING BOOKS

Popular Works

Popular gardening books published by *Sunset Magazine* in the West, or Ortho, Time-Life, and so on, are good, cheap, well illustrated and understandable. A sound start for your business library could be, for example, *All About Lawns*, by Ortho Books. It's the publishing division of Chevron Oil's chemical division but does not push company products. Books published by magazines such as *Horticulture*, *Fine Gardening* (Taunton Press) and *Organic Gardening* (Rodale Press) are also good. If you can't get a "serious" book, one from the above publishers or their like will give you a basic knowledge. For more detail, you can look at some of the books below. Your public library, college, or extension service might have or help locate them.

GENERAL WORKS

Brickell, Christopher, and Judith Zuk, eds. *American Horticultural Society A to Z Encyclopedia of Garden Plants* (New York, 1997, DK Publishing, 1,092 pages, $79.95). A definitive work with over 15,000 entries and 6,000 photos, begun in the U.K., but with about 40% of entries for North America. Index is fair: Latin binomials but few common names or synonyms.

________, Elvin McDonald, and Trevor J. Cole, eds. *American Horticultural Society Encyclopedia of Gardening* (New York, 1993, DK Publishing, 700+ pages, $59.95). A benchmark gardening encyclopedia.

Ingels, Jack E. *Ornamental Horticulture: Principles and Practices* (Albany, NY, 1994, Delmar Publishers, 554 pages).

Sunset Western Garden Book, 6th ed. (Menlo Park, CA, 1995, Sunset Books; 624 pages, $34.95). Best used with another reference, but valuable for gardening west of the Rockies.

Tenebaum, Frances, Rita Buchanan, and Roger Holmes, eds. *Taylor's Master Guide to Gardening* (Boston, 1994, Houghton Mifflin, $60.00, 612 pages). A standard for North American gardeners.

Western Garden Problem Solver (Menlo Park, CA, 1998, Sunset Books, $24.95). Easy-to-read practical solutions for Westerners.

GRASS, TURFGRASS, LAWNS

Alderson, James, and W. Curtis Sharp. *Grass Varieties in the United States* (Washington, DC, 1995, U.S. Department of Agriculture, 304 pages, $45.00). A working guide to more than turfgrass. Named and experimental grasses for use in North America. Physical descriptions. Maps and Plant Hardiness Zones. Method of breeding, who selected or increased specific varieties, the releasing agency, and sources of breeder seed.

Danneberger, T. Karl, Ph.D., and Cindy Code. *Turfgrass Ecology and Management* (Cleveland, OH, 1993 Lawn and Landscape Maintenance [G.I.E., Inc.], $39.00). A well regarded intermediate/advanced ecological reference.

Beard, James B. *Turfgrass: Science and Culture* (Englewood Cliffs, NJ, 1973, Prentice-Hall, Inc., $117.15). A standard intermediate text.

Daniels, Stevie, and Steve Daniels. *The Wild Lawn Handbook: Alternatives to the Traditional Front Lawn* (New York, 1995, IDG Books Worldwide, 223 pages, $22.00). Flowers in the lawn and more.

Marinelli, Janet and Margaret Roach (eds.). *The Natural Lawn & Alternatives* (Brooklyn, NY 1993, Brooklyn Botanical Garden, 80 pages). More flowers in the lawn.

Pedrotti, Robin M. *Lawn Aeration: Turn Hard Soil into Cold Cash* (San Diego, 1992, CA Prego Press, $35.00, 200 pages). A good grasp of his subject.

Turgeon, A.J. *Turfgrass Management*, 5th ed. (Englewood Cliffs, NJ, 1998, Prentice-Hall, $86.00, 432 pages).

Vengris, Jonas, ed., and William A. Torello, ed. *Lawns: Basic Factors, Construction and Maintenance of fine Turf Areas* (Fresno, CA, 1982, Thompson Publications, $15.50, 195 pages). An economical intermediate text.

Interior Landscaping

Furuta, Tokuji. *Interior Landscaping.* (Reston, VA, 1983, Reston Publishing Co., $57.00). Aspects of interior landscape design and management.

Manaker, George H. *Interior Plantscapes.* (Englewood Cliffs, NJ, 1987, Prentice-Hall, $92.00, 352 pages, textbook binding). Intro to interior landscaping.

Mower & Engine Maintenance

Freeman, Kerry A., ed. *Chilton's Small Engine Repair Up to 20 HP* (New Brunswick, NJ, 1994, W.G. Nichols Pub., $22.95).

Walk-Behind Lawn Mower: Service Manual, 5th ed. (Chicago, 1997, Intertec Publishing, $26.95).

Pests & Pest Control

Flint, Mary Louise, *Pests of the Garden and Small Farm: A Grower's Guide to Using Less Pesticide* (Oakland, CA, 1999, Regents of the University of California, Division of Agriculture and Natural Resources, 2nd ed., 288 pages).

Olkowski, William, Sheila Daar, and Helga Olkowski, *Common-Sense Pest Control* (Newtown, CT, 1991, Taunton Press, $39.95, 716 pages).

Pests of Landscape Trees & Shrubs: An Integrated Pest Management Guide (Oakland, CA, 1994, the University of California, Division of Agriculture and Natural Resources, 2nd ed., 288 pages).

Vargas, John M., Jr. *Management of Turfgrass Diseases* (Los Angeles, 1994, Lewis Publishers, $89.95). An industry standard.

Vittum, Patricia J., Michael G. Villani, Haruo Tashiro. *Turfgrass Insects of the United States and Canada* (Ithaca, NY, 1999, Cornell Univ. Press, 496 pages, $60.00). New edition of a standard reference.

Ware, George G. *Complete Guide to Pest Control With and Without Chemicals* (Fresno, CA, 3d ed., 1996, Thompson Publications, $29.95). No color illustrations; good for common pests but hard to identify passing strangers. On the other hand, tables identify each pest by the damage it causes. Excellent tables of controls for plant and animal pests. Coverage so exhaustive that organization seems to overlap. Good discussion of pesticide handling, storage, hazards, and laws. Worth owning.

Pruning

Brickell, Christopher (ed.), and David Joyce. *American Horticultural Society Pruning & Training* (New York, 1996, DK Publishing, 336 pages, $34.95). Brickell knows everything about pruning. His original text, now available only in the UK, was the leading reference. This is expanded (and more expensive), with more illustrations. The original is available at www.amazon.uk, for about £7.5 and shipping.

Reich, Lee. *The Pruning Book* (Newtown, CT, 1999, Taunton Press, hb $27.95, ppr $19.95, 240 pages). Basic principles and good practice clearly illustrated. Not as detailed as Brickell in many ways, but together both have all the pruning knowledge you'll need.

TREES

Harris, Richard W., James R. Clark, Nelda P. Matheny. *Arboriculture: Integrated Management of Trees, Shrubs and Vines in the Landscape* (Englewood Cliffs, NJ, 1998, Prentice Hall, $103.55, 687 pages, textbook). Trees and other woody plants.

Hartman, John R., T.P. Pirone, Pascal P. Pirone, M.A. Sall. *Tree Maintenance* (New York, 6th ed., 2000, Oxford University Press, $49.95, 514 pages). *The* book on tree care.

FINALLY, don't overlook your own state extension service. California's produces an Agriculture and Natural Resources (ANR) catalog through the University of California at Davis (http://anrcatalog.ucdavis. edu), with titles such as *The Natural Enemies Handbook: The Illustrated Guide to Biological Pest Control*, a cheap *Illustrated Guide to Pesticide Safety*, its bestselling *Safe and Effective Use of Pesticides* and *Residential, Industrial, and Institutional Pest Control*. The street address for ANR is 6701 San Pablo Avenue, Oakland, CA 94608-1239; tel. (800) 994-8849; fax (510) 643-5470.

BUSINESS BOOKS

Bangs, David H., Jr. *Business Planning Guide*, 7th rev. ed. (Dover, NH, 1997, Upstart Publishing Co., $19.95, 208 pages). Excellent.

Clifford, Denis, and Ralph Warner. *The Partnership Book*, 5th ed. (Berkeley CA, 1997, Nolo Press, $34.95).

Kamoroff, Bernard, C.P.A. *Small Time Operator*, 5th ed. (Laytonville, CA, 1997, Bell Springs Publishing Co., $18.95).

Levinson, Jay Conrad. *Guerrilla Marketing: Secrets for Making Big Profits from Your Small Business* (Boston, 1994, Houghton Mifflin)

Marsh, D. *Guide to Developing a Landscape Maintenance Business* and *Maintenance Addendum* (McLean, VA 1985, American Nurseryman/Associated Landscape Contractors of America, $150 & $90). At 150 Elden St., Suite 270, Herndon, VA 20170; (800) 395-2522; fax (703) 736-9668

Professional Grounds Management Society. *Grounds Maintenance Estimating Guidelines* (Cockeysville, MD, 1995?, PGMS, $35.00 + $3.20 S/H). Charts to help do estimates, including projects' "hidden costs."

Steingold, Fred S. *The Employer's Legal Guide*, 3rd ed. (Berkeley, CA, 1999, Nolo Press, $31.95).

______ *Legal Guide for Starting & Running a Small Business, Vol. 1*, 5th ed. Vol. 2 contains forms. (Berkeley, CA, 1999, Nolo Press, $24.95). "One of the top six business books." *Inc. Magazine.* We second the nomination and highly recommend it.

Thomas, William. *Contract Lawn and Landscape Estimating*, Custodial Maintenance Library (Oakland, CA, 1988, Marsh-Wentworth Pub., $55.00).

U.S. Department of Treasury, Internal Revenue Service. *Taxpayers Starting a Business* (Bulletin 583, Washington, DC, U.S. Government Printing Office, telephone 1-800-829-3676, or go to your local IRS office.) Free.

________, *Tax Guide for Small Business* (Bulletin 334, Washington, DC, U.S. Government Printing Office). Free.

Supplies, Associations, Internet Sites . . .

SEEDS

Blight Native Seeds, Ltd. (Jim and Kevin Blight), Box 244, Oakville, Manitoba, Canada R0H 0Y0; (204) 267-2686; fax (204) 267-2699.

Bozeman Bio-Tech, Inc., P.O. Box 3146, Bozeman, MT 59772; 800-289-6656 Insects, seed packets, more. Free catalog.

Clyde Robin Seed Co., P.O. Box 2366 Castro Valley, CA 94546; 510-785-0425. Wildflower seed packets. Free catalog.

Cornflower Farms, P.O. Box 896, Elk Grove, A 95759; 916-689-1015. Plant stock; perennials, shrubs, trees. Free Catalog

Gardens Alive! 5100 Schenley Place, Lawrenceburg, IN 47025. Lawn grass mixes: turf fescues, slow-growing drought-resistant and endophytic.

Hanna's Seeds. Box 849, 5039-49 Street, Lacombe, Alberta, Canada T0C 1S0, Catalogue free. Bentgrasses and clovers; native grasses and mixes, lawn grasses and mixes; custom grasses.

Harmony Farm Supply. P.O. Box 460, Graton, CA 95444. Catalog $2.00, refundable with order. *Trifolium gargiferum, T. repens;* native grasses; lawn grasses, grass mixes, endophytic varieties. Large inventory of fescues, including native California Blue Fescue.

Hobbs & Hopkins, Ltd. 1712 SE Ankeny, Portland, OR 97214. Catalogue free. Ecology Fleur de Lawn mixes; custom lawn grass and flower mixes; extensive inventory of lawn grasses including many of the new disease-resistant and endophytic varieties.

Jacklin Seed Co., Susan H. Samudio, W. 5300 Riverbend Ave., Post Falls, ID 83854.

Nichols Garden Nursery. 1190 North Pacific Highway, Albany OR 92321-4598. Catalogue free. *Achillea milifolium, Bellis perennis, Chamaemelum nobile*; ecology lawn mixes.

Peaceful Valley Farm Supply, P.O. Box 2209, Grass Valley, CA 95945; 916-272-4769. Beneficial insects, seed packets, cover crops. Free Catalog.

Sharp Brothers Seed Company, P.O. Box 140, Healy KS, 67850. Seed list $1.00. Wide variety of pasture, lawn, and native grasses, including buffalograss.

Stock Seed Farms, 28008 Mill Road, Murdock, NE 68407-2350; (800) 759-1520; fax (402) 867-2442, e-mail, stockseed@navix.net. Wildflowers and prairie grasses, including a floodplain mixture to re-establish damaged floodplains, and a cool-season "shady" mixture for deep to partial shade which also tolerates drought, disease, and close mowing.

On the Internet: Grass information "without the hype" at seedland.com and globalseeds.com. They seem to be the same company with several addresses, but the selection is enormous.This barely scratches the surface. If you search the Internet, you can let your imagination roam.

SUPPLIERS

A.M. Leonard, Inc., P.O. Box 816, Piqua, OH 45356-0816; (800) 543-8955; amleo.com. An excellent source of professional quality tools and supplies at competitive prices.

American Arborist Supplies, Inc., 882 S. Matlack St., West Chester, PA 19382; 800-441-8381. Free catalog.

Bailey's, Inc., 44650 North Highway 101, Laytonville, CA 95454. Logger's supplies, including chain-saw equipment and loggers' chaps.

Ben Meadows Company, P.O. Box 80549, Atlanta, GA 30366; (800) 241-6401. Calling itself a supplier of Equipment for Natural Resource Managers, Meadows sells U.S. Forest Service quality shovels, Pulaskis, and MacLeods; respirators; soil guides and testers; and much more. There are a few gardening tools it does not carry, but the range of its stock is impressive.

Forestry Suppliers, Inc., P.O. Box 8397, Jackson, MS 39284-8397; (800) 647-5368, fax (800) 543-4302. Tools, supplies, books for arboriculture, horticulture, grounds maintenance. Free catalog.

Northern, P.O. Box 1499, Burnsville, MN 55337-0499; (800) 533-5545. Good prices, often discounted, on heavy duty machinery and equipment, including replacement I/C engines: Briggs & Stratton iron-cylinder-sleeved 5-HPs, Honda 5.5 HP OHV's, small engine parts, etc. You can also shop Northern for bench grinders, heavy-duty garden sprayers, trailer parts, winches, and the like.

Orchard Equipment & Supply Co., Route 116, Conway, MA 01341; (800) 634-5557 (MA: 413-369-4335); fax 413-369-4431. Prices and selection comparable to A.M. Leonard, but emphasizing agricultural and heavy duty equipment. See Suppliers, above.

Stillbrook Horticultural Supplies, (800) 414-4468 sells English digging fork and spade, as does Smith & Hawken, (800) 776-3336. Compare prices before buying.

Walter E. Clark & Son, 550 Grassy Hill Road, P.O. Box 756, Orange, CT 06477-0756; (203) 795-1235 or 795-0174. Fax (203) 799-8683. Supplies tree wound dressings, grafting wax, pruning compounds, tree wraps, and vinyl tree guards at good prices, sometimes discounted.

PROTECTIVE CLOTHING

Farm and ranch supply stores sell high-quality outdoor work clothing, as do contractor-supply and industrial-equipment stores. Here are mail order outfitters for respirators, face-masks, chemical-resistant clothing, chaps; hand, knee, leg, shin, and foot protection; hearing protectors, anti-vibration gloves, back-support belts.

Conney Safety Products, P.O. Box 44190, Madison, WI 53744; (800) 356-9100. Hard hats, ear and eye protection, guards, respirators.

Crackshot Products, Inc., 9152 East Oklahoma St., Tulsa, OK 74115; (800) 667-1753. Chaps with protective inserts.

Gempler's, P.O. Box 270, Mt. Horeb, WI 53572; (800) 382-8473. Chemical-resistant clothes, work shoes and gloves.

Green Mountain Outfitters, P.O. Box 4193, Winston-Salem, NC 27115; (800) 929-1948. Chemical-resistant clothes, safety vests.

A.M. Leonard for respirators, hearing protectors, anti-vibration gloves, back-support belts.

Sears Workwear catalog, 141 Longwater Drive, Morwell, MA 02061; (800) 305-1001. Heavy-duty work gear.

W.E. Chapps, Inc., P.O., Box 29154, Pt. Orange, FL 32129; (904) 761-2427. Chemical-resistant clothes; arm and leg guards.

GOATSKIN GLOVES

Fortress Products. Toll free number 1 (877) 286-4268.

Supply Pro, 5630 Harvey Wilson Drive, Houston, TX 77020; (713) 672-9080; fax (713) 679-7659; www.supply-pro.com.

Vermont Garden Shed, RR2 Box 180 East Street, Wallingford, VT 05773; (800) 288-7433; webmaster@vermontgardenshed.com; http://vermontgardenshed.com.

Also check Ben Meadows and A.M. Leonard catalogs.

INTERNET SITES AND ADDRESSES FOR LANDSCAPE ASSOCIATIONS

Plant information on-line at http://plantinfo.unm.edu. University of Minnesota. Requires an annual subscription to use its encyclopedic data about plants—$39.95 for individuals, $59.95 for businesses.

Associated Landscape Contractors of America (ALCA), 150 Elden St., Suite 270, Herndon, VA 20170; (800) 395-2522; fax (703) 736-9668; web page, http://www.alca.org. A good source of books on horticulture, pest control, trees, management and marketing. Books are sold discounted to members, but annual dues are $375 for sole proprietors.

American Nursery and Landscape Association (ANLA) is at www.anla.org. The postal address is 1250 I Street, NW, Suite 500, Washington, DC 20005; (202) 789-2900, fax (202) 789 1893.

One site well worth examining is University of Missouri extension service at http://muextension. missouri.edu. Click on the "horticulture & gardening" icon. You'll find brief reports on lawn care topics. The range is extensive and not limited to Missouri ("Caring for flooded lawns").

Possibly the best on-line illustrated plant encyclopedia is the extension service site at Oregon State University's www.orst.edu/dept/Idplants.

Another good site is www. ohio-state.edu/ ~ ohioline; its "/hyg-fact" extension takes you into very useful home yard and garden fact sheets.

More generally, http://www.plantamerica.com lists many but not all nurseries and nursery associations for all 50 continental United States.

A good site for locating wholesale and retail nurseries nationwide is at http:/gardennet.com. For the directory, add the following extension without a break: .../informationDirectory/fruit.idc.

ASSOCIATIONS

Professional Lawn Care Association of America (PLCAA) is at www.plcaa.org. 1000 Johnson Ferry Road, NE, Suite C-135; Marietta, GA 30068-2112; (800) 458-3466; fax (770) 578-6071. Videos, books, audios. Member discounts; individual membership $285/yr. Links to helpful sites, including EPA, OSHA, Virginia Tech, The Lawn Institute, Lawn & Landscape Magazine, Toro Company.

NaturaLawn of America (www.naturalawn.com), a franchise. (301) 694-5440/natural@nl-america.com. Environmentally friendly lawn care business; address: NaturaLawn of America, Inc. 5 West Church Street, Frederick MD 21701; (301) 694-5440; fax 694-0320.

American Association of Nurserymen, 1250 I Street, N.W., Suite 500, Washington, DC 20005; (202) 789-2900. Representative of horticultural professionals since 1875. Activities include legislative and regulatory action, continuing education, public information. Since 1967 divisional associations have included the **National Landscape Association**, which for 50 years has served landscape design, planning, and maintenance firms. Catalog of publications and information services. Publishes *AAN Today* bi-monthly, as well as newsletter, *Update*.

Professional Grounds Management Society, 120 Cockeysville Road, Suite 104, Hunt Valley, MD 21030; (800) 609-7467; fax (410) 584-9756. Established in 19ll by grounds managers of all specialties for educational and economic advancement. Annual conference, monthly newsletter, technical aid releases, information clearing house, legislative and regulatory action, certification program, *PGMS Grounds Management Forum* published bi-monthly. Good library of books and videos.

Job Math

MEASURING TEXT BOOK AREAS

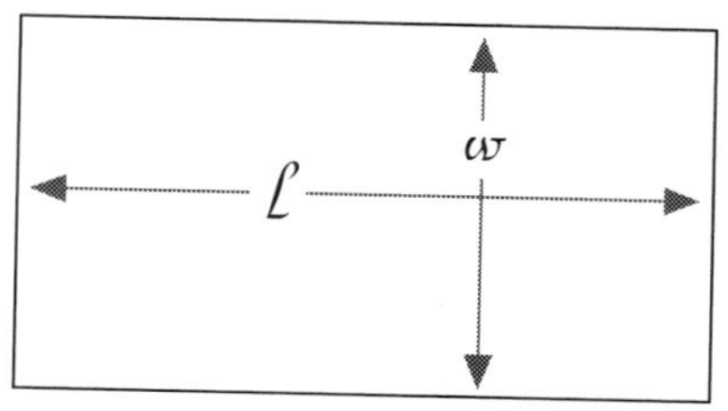

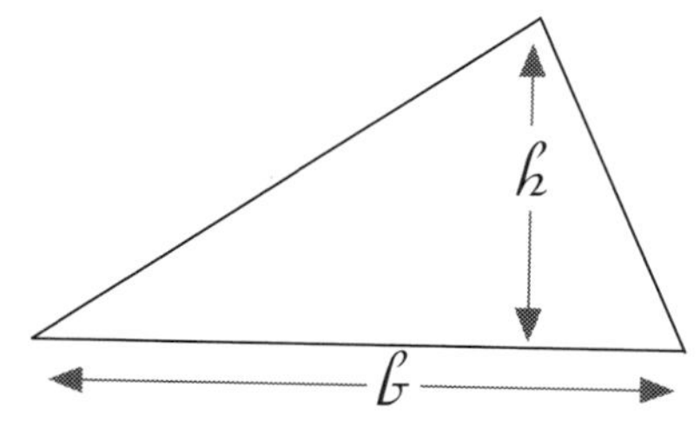

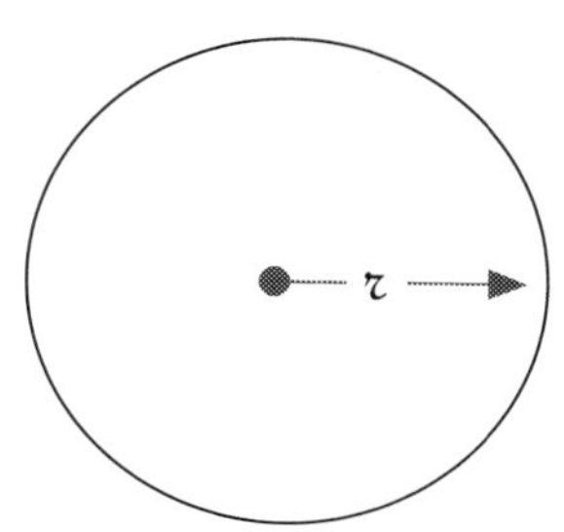

$A = l \times w$

$A = ½\, h \times b$

$A = 3.14 \times r^2$

MEASURING IRREGULAR AREAS ON THE JOB

Combine areas of regular or nearly regular shapes

Total $= A + B + C$

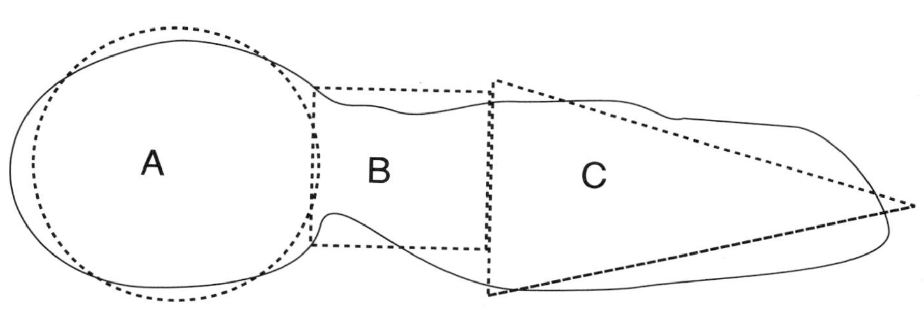

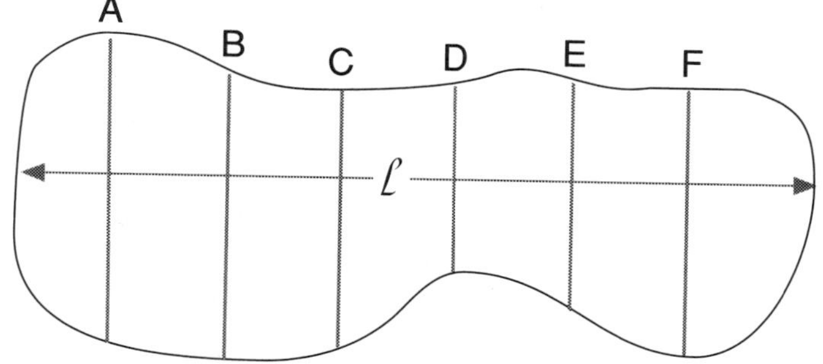

Length times average width

$$A = \frac{A + B + C + D + E + F}{6} \times l$$

Square the average radius

$$A = 3.14 \times \left(\frac{A+B+C+D+E+F+G+H+I}{9}\right)^2$$

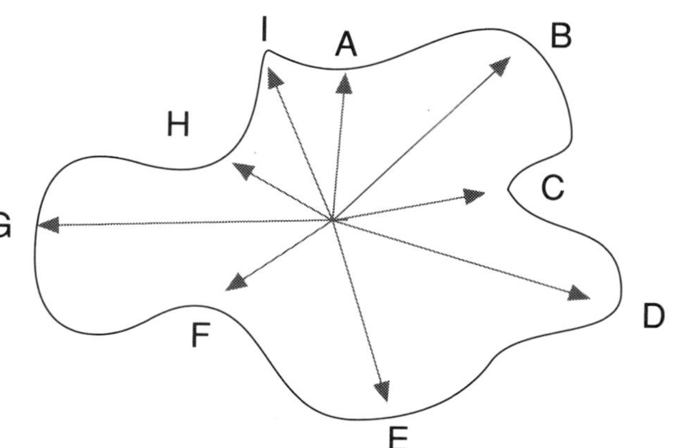

Index

LANDSCAPE MAINTENANCE REQUIREMENTS

Customer ID: ______________________________

Telephone: ______________

Work Proposed: ______________________________

____

Task | Location | Size/No. | No. of Times | Materials

Lawn Care:

Mow ______________________________

Edge ______________________________

Fertilize ______________________________

Amend ______________________________

Re-seed ______________________________

Topdress ______________________________

Ground Cover:

Prune ______________________________

Fertilize ______________________________

Amend ______________________________

Other ______________________________

Hedges:

Shear ______________________________

Fertilize ______________________________

Other ______________________________

Shrubs:

Prune ______________________________

Fertilize ______________________________

Other ______________________________

Trees:

Prune ______________________________

Fertilize ______________________________

Other ______________________________

LANDSCAPE MAINTENANCE REQUIREMENTS - Page 2

Task Location Size/Number No. of Times Materials

Additional Lawn care:

Dethatch ____

Aerate ____

Spray:

Herbicide ____

Insecticide ____

Other ____

Bedding Plants:

Plant ____

Feed ____

Mulch ____

Spray ____

Weed ____

Other ____

All other:

__________ ____

__________ ____

__________ ____

__________ ____

__________ ____

__________ ____

Notes:

____

____

____

____

____

LANDSCAPE MAINTENANCE ESTIMATOR

Customer:______________________ Page 1: (LABOR) Date: ______________________

LAWN ________ SF ÷ 1,000 SF =	Units X	Min. per Unit =	Est. Time (Min.)	Hours (Min./60) X	Times per Season =	Total Hours
Mow					*	
Edge ______ ÷ 100 LF					*	
Fertilize					*	
Amendments					*	
Re-seed					*	
GROUND-COVER ________ SF ÷ 1,000 SF =						
Prune						
Fertilize					*	
Amendments					*	
HEDGES ________ LF ÷ 100 LF =						
Shear					*	
Fertilize					*	
SHRUBS No. =						
Prune						
Fertilize					*	
TREES No. =						
Prune					*	
Fertilize					*	
Set-up/Brkdn	(Av. S/B Min. X Times per Season.)					
SUPPLEMENT	Enter any Subtotal of hours from supplement sheet (page 1a).					
					TOTAL HOURS:	
				X $______/HR =	TOTAL LABOR:	$

LANDSCAPE MAINTENANCE ESTIMATOR

Customer:________________________ Page 1a: (LABOR SUPPLEMENT)

LAWN _______ SF ÷ 1,000 SF =	Units X	Min. per Unit =	Est. Time (Min.)	Hours (Min./60) X	Times per Season =	Total Hours
Dethatch					*	
Aerate					*	
Spray					*	
Topdress					*	
Other						
BEDDING PLANTS _______ SF ÷ 1,000 SF =						
Plant					*	
Feed					*	
Mulch						
Spray					*	
Weed						
Other						
OTHER Unit Calc.:						
*** Set-up/Brkdn**	(Av. S/B Min. X Times per Season.)					
					TOTAL HOURS:	

LANDSCAPE MAINTENANCE ESTIMATOR

Customer ____________________

Page 2: (MATERIALS & TOTALS)

	Units (From p.1)	X All # per Unit	= Total #	X Cost per #	= Total Cost	X Markup	= Price
LAWN Fertilizer				$	$		$
Lime/Gypsum				$	$		$
Seed/Sprigs				$	$		$
Topdressing				$	$		$
Other				$	$		$
SHRUBS, HEDGES Fertilizer				$	$		$
Mulch				$	$		$
GRNDCVR Fertilizer				$	$		$
Lime/Gypsum				$	$		$
TREES Fertilizer				$	$		$
BDG PLTS Fertilizer				$	$		$
OTHER				$	$		$
				$	$		$
				$	$		$
						Total Materials Cost:	**$**

EQUIPMENT RENTALS / SUBCONTRACTS

______________________: $__________ X ______ per Season X _____ (Markup) = $

______________________: $__________ X ______ per Season X _____ (Markup) = $

______________________: $__________ X ______ per Season X _____ (Markup) = $

Total Labor: $

Sales Tax: $

Grand Total: $

÷ by ______ Periods = Payments of $

= pounds, cubic feet, cubic yards, and other basic measures.

No markup on equipment rentals.

Copy this page to order from

ACTON CIRCLE

Lawn Care & Gardening: A Down-to-Earth Guide to the Business, **Second Edition, by Mickey Willis.** Everything about soils, fertilizers, grasses, plants, pests, tools, techniques, and the good business practices that make a landscape care business pay. 258 pages, 8½x11" index, bibliog., full-size reproducible forms, $22.95.

The Baker's Trade: A Recipe for Creating the Successful Small Bakery, **by Zachary Y. Schat.** Everything you need to know to start and operate a successful small retail or wholesale bakery. 275 pages, 8½x 11", index, bibliog., $24.95.

Bookkeeping and Tax Preparation: Start and Build a Prosperous Bookkeeping, Tax, and Financial Services Business, **by Gordon P. Lewis.** The techniques and information you need to build your flair for figures into a highly profitable, well-rounded business. 179 pages, 7x10", index, bibliog., forms, $18.95.

The Poison Ivy, Oak & Sumac Book: A Short Natural History and Cautionary Account, **by Thomas E. Anderson.** For the first time, color photographs of each North American species of this noxious family of plants in different seasons. Full of little-known historical, medical, and botanical facts. 138 pages, 6x9", illus., index, anno. bibliog., $14.95.

Send your check or money order to

Acton Circle Publishing Co.
P.O. Box 1564
Ukiah, CA 95482

Enclosed is $________ for ______ copy(ies) of
____ $__________

and $________ for _______ copy(ies) of
____ $__________

Shipping/Handling ($1.75 1st book; $1.00 others)* $__________
CA residents add 7.25% sales tax $__________

Total $__________

Name____
Street_____________________________ Apt. ______________
City________________________________State_____ZIP____________
* Allow 3 to 4 weeks for shipping or use Postal First Class $3.50 per book.
You may return any book for a full refund, no questions asked.

Copy this page to order